Death's Dominion

Studies in Ancient Religion and Culture

Series Editor:

Philip L. Tite, University of Washington

Studies in Ancient Religion and Culture (SARC) is concerned with religious and cultural aspects of the ancient world, with a special emphasis on studies that utilize social scientific methods of analysis. By "ancient world," the series is not limited to Greco-Roman and ancient Near Eastern cultures, though that is the primary regional focus. The underlying presupposition is that the study of religion in antiquity needs to be located within cultural and social analysis, situating religious traditions within the broader cultural and geopolitical dynamics within which those traditions are located.

This series also encourages cross-disciplinary research in the study of the ancient world. Due to the historical development of various academic disciplines, there has arisen a set of largely isolated and competing fields of study of the ancient world. Often this fragmentation in academia results in outdated or caricatured scholarly products when one discipline does use research from another discipline. A key goal of this series is to help facilitate greater cross- and inter-disciplinary work, bringing together those who study ancient history (especially social history), archaeology (of various methods and geographic focuses, as well as theorists in archaeology), ancient philosophy, biblical studies, early patristics/church history, Second Temple and formative Judaism, and Greek and Roman classics, as well as philologists.

Given the focus on the social and cultural context within which religion functions, the series also publishes studies which explore the various social locations in which real people in antiquity practiced or interacted with their religious traditions. Examples include the domestic cult, food production and consumption, temple worship, funerary practices/monuments, development of social networks, military cult, and ancient medicine.

Finally, the series encourages a broader application of theoretical and methodological tools to the study of the ancient world. While the main perspective is social-scientific (understood broadly), specific analyses from the reservoir of critical theory, narrative theories, economic theory, bio-archaeology, gender analysis, anthropology of religion, and cognitive theory are welcome.

Death's Dominion

Power, Identity, and Memory at the
Fourth-Century Martyr Shrine

Nathaniel J. Morehouse

SHEFFIELD UK   BRISTOL CT

Published by Equinox Publishing Ltd.

UK: Office 415, The Workstation, 15 Paternoster Row, Sheffield, South Yorkshire S1 2BX

USA: ISD, 70 Enterprise Drive, Bristol, CT 06010

www.equinoxpub.com

First published 2016

© Nathaniel J. Morehouse 2016

All rights reserved. No part of this publication may be reproduced or transmitted in any form or by any means, electronic or mechanical, including photocopying, recording or any information storage or retrieval system, without prior permission in writing from the publishers.

British Library Cataloguing-in-Publication Data

A catalogue record for this book is available from the British Library.

ISBN-13   978 1 78179 081 6   (hardback)
           978 1 78179 082 3   (paperback)

Library of Congress Cataloging-in-Publication Data

Morehouse, Nathaniel J.

Death's dominion: power, identity, and memory at the fourth-century martyr shrine / Nathaniel J. Morehouse.

pages cm. -- (Studies in ancient religion and culture)

Includes bibliographical references and index.

ISBN 978-1-78179-081-6 (hb) -- ISBN 978-1-78179-082-3 (pb)

1. Shrines. 2. Martyrs--Cult. 3. Pilgrims and pilgrimages. 4. Christianity and other religions. 5. Cults. I. Title.

BL580.M655 2015

272'.1--dc23

2015010611

Typeset by ISB Typesetting, Sheffield

Printed and bound by Lightning Source Inc. (La Vergne, TN), Lightning Source UK Ltd. (Milton Keynes), Lightning Source AU Pty. (Scoresby, Victoria)

Contents

Acknowledgements	vii
Introduction: Discursive Acts and the Formation of Memory at the Graves of the Saints	1
1. To Begin: The Life of the Dead is Set in the Memory of the Living	19
Romans and the Afterlife: An Afterlife of Memory	21
Monuments	23
Monuments to the Important Dead	29
Who Cares for the Dead?	30
The Family	31
Voluntary Associations	31
Christian Differentiation, Isolation, Self-Expression	34
The Origins of Christian Burial	36
Christianity as a Voluntary Association	36
The *Koimeterion* Debate	39
Burial of the Poor	43
The Burial of the Important Christian Dead	45
Conclusion	48
2. To Build Up: The Erection of Shrine and Reputation	53
Constantine	57
Damasus	67
Conclusion	79
3. To Control: The Places and Practices Associated With the Remains of the Saints	82
Ambrose of Milan	85
Augustine of Hippo	100

	Paulinus of Nola	109
	Sulpicius Severus	116
	Apa Shenoute	117
	Conclusion	123
4.	To Reject: Not Everyone Loves a Corpse	126
	Julian "The Apostate"	127
	Other Non-Christian Opponents	133
	Christian Opposition to the Martyr Cult	135
	Athanasius of Alexandria	135
	Vigilantius	141
	Conclusion	143
5.	To Accept: Unification Through Travel	146
	Pilgrimage as Unifier	152
	Early Pilgrim Narratives, the Bordeaux Pilgrim, and Paula	156
	Egeria	159
	Healing Pilgrimage	162
	Prudentius	164
	Conclusion	170
Conclusion		172
Bibliography		179
Index		191

Acknowledgements

I imagine anyone who has ever worked on a book-length project, or even anyone who has ever read an "acknowledgements" section of a book, already knows that a staggering number of people help even the most accomplished authors. Clearly this work is no exception. As this book is a revised version of my doctoral thesis, the number of people who should be thanked is even longer.

Sadly a complete list of those who helped me throughout the creation of this work would be so long that even the most dedicated reader of acknowledgements would quickly grow wearied. Briefly then I offer my gratitude to my advisors: Dixon Slingerland, who opened the door to Religious Studies as a discipline to me and for which I will forever be grateful, and William Arnal, who advised my MA work and has been a consistent source of sane advice and reassurance.

During my doctoral work I had a number of advisors, which at the time I felt was a serious detriment. Yet with each advisor I learned valuable lessons and for that I would like to thank Allen Kirk and Lawrence Broadhurst, in addition to Heidi Marx-Wolf who ultimately saw me through my thesis. Dr Marx-Wolf read and re-read chapter drafts, providing guidance at a time when she could easily have turned her attention to more important matters. In addition to the extremely helpful comments from Dr Marx-Wolf, this work has benefited from the attention and suggestions that came from my committee. Dawne McCance (who also briefly served as my advisor), Roisin Cossar, as well as my external committee member Willi Braun all gave very useful feedback and helped make this work considerably better than it would have been if I had been left to my own devices. Any errors in this work are entirely my responsibility.

David Brakke lent his assistance to the endeavor when he charitably heard my appeal for his help with translations of Shenoute's *Since it Behoves Christians* from the Coptic original. I am humbled by his generosity.

Philip Tite, the series editor for Studies in Ancient Religion and Culture, has been patient and gracious as he guided me through the publication process.

I would also like to thank my friends and family who have supported me during this long, and occasionally turbulent, process. The support of my parents David and Claire Morehouse has allowed me to study and work on material which I am sure was nowhere in their mind when they sent me off to college. Nicole Goulet's and Robbert Penner's encouragement and sympathetic ears have been most appreciated.

Finally, Amanda Cobes, I cannot ever thank you enough. Thank you for moving to Winnipeg for my academic hubris, and for supporting me fiscally and emotionally after our return. You have reassured me when I needed it, and given me the time and motivation to write when I might have wanted to do anything else. It is in no way an understatement to say that I would not have been able to do this without you.

Introduction:

Discursive Acts and the Formation of Memory at the Graves of the Saints

> The formation and contestation of identity are fundamentally about *power*, the power to represent.[1]

> Death is the sanction of everything that the storyteller can tell. He has borrowed his authority from death.[2]

Through their demarcation of the deceased's final resting place, gravestones allow the dead a chance to live in the memory of the observer. Mark C. Taylor taps into this relationship with tombstones in his work *Grave Matters*.[3] Here Taylor presents the reader with a series of stunning black-and-white photographs of the graves of his important dead, the graves of the philosophers and artists that he considers to have been part of his "tribe," his intellectual family. This book provides Taylor with an *ad sanctos* burial of sorts, alongside his personal saints; the last photograph is of the location where he expects to be buried. These are the graves of Taylor's ghosts, those who live on in his memory and whose specters haunt the words of his books. To turn the pages of these photographs is to become a sort of pilgrim, to be in the "presence" of the graves, to see how his dead are commemorated, to continue to remember them. These images bring the dead to mind, where they live for a moment if only through the acknowledgement of their death. The book offers a glimpse into how Taylor views himself through those he selected to include and who he omitted. He, like a number of figures discussed in this work, is able to choose which saints to commemorate and which to ignore.

Taylor's work in many respects is nothing new; it draws upon the traditions of inhumation and the cry for remembrance (especially for those

---

1. Richard Miles, "Introduction: Constructing Identities in Late Antiquity," in *Constructing Identities in Late Antiquity* (ed. Richard Miles: New York: Routledge, 1999), 6.
2. Walter Benjamin, "The Storyteller: Reflections on the Works of Nikolai Leskov," [1936] in *Illuminations: Essays and Reflections* (by Walter Benjamin, ed. Hannah Arendt and trans. Harry Zohn: New York: Schocken, 1968), 94.
3. Mark C. Taylor, *Grave Matters* (London: Realtion, 2002).

who can afford it) that predate the Christian traditions which are the foundations for Taylor's work, and will be the centerpiece of my own. Taylor attempts to control the message of his important dead, to situate himself alongside them, and to act as a mediator for them through the presentation of their graves to his audience. At the same time he has to have been aware of the subversive acts that each individual reader brings, of necessity, to this attempt; his viewers interpret the graves in their own way. Ultimately, the meaning of the text is one that cannot be dictated by its author, but that comes from the organic struggle for the ability to influence the lives of others: the power to represent, the power to affect. This is the same endeavor in which many fourth-century and early fifth-century Christian leaders involved themselves: they too sought to control the message, the actions, and the meaning associated with the graves and remains of their important dead.

Graves are the earliest physical sites of Christian identity. The expansion of the martyr cult grew from the veneration of the remains of the martyrs as it had been practiced by local Christian populations, which in turn was an extension of the veneration that Christians and non-Christians paid to the important dead within their own family. In the fourth century, specific agents directed the way in which the martyr cult would ultimately develop. They did this through their own individual attempts to control the sites of Christian cultural memory at the martyrs' graves, desiring to craft the physical monuments to the dead in such a way that established their own control over the message that each monument projected to the observer. The spaces and practices associated with the important dead thus became battlegrounds for political and theological control.

Ultimately, one cannot place the genesis of the martyr cult at the feet of any one individual.[4] Rather, it developed through the struggle for hegemony which played itself out between the imperial seat, the bishops, and the people who visited the martyr shrines to venerate the dead. It was only through the rise of the practice of pilgrimage to martyr shrines that there developed a degree of uniformity in the veneration of the martyrs and their relics which would lead to the practices and artifacts that are commonly found tucked in dark corners of today's art museums, and

---

4. Cf. Marianne Saghy, who credits Constantine with the genesis of said cult in Rome. Marianne Saghy, "*Scinditur in Partes Populus*: Pope Damasus and the Martyrs of Rome," *Early Medieval Europe* 9 (2000): 275. See also R. A. Markus, *The End of Ancient Christianity* (Cambridge: Cambridge University Press, 1990), 98ff. Markus is not as explicit with the absence of the martyr cult prior to Constantine, but does posit a fourth-century origin for it.

other modern-day collections. Through an investigation of the ways in which various important actors sought to control the remains of the dead, and to some extent were continually challenged, we can understand the role that those remains would ultimately play in the development of Christianity.

Monuments, specifically burial monuments, provide us with our earliest non-literary evidence for early Christianity. As such, they are tremendously important for our understanding of the development and self-awareness of Christianity, as projected by those in control of those locations. Valerie Hope observes that funerary monuments reflect the "rhetoric of language of the society which produced them."[5] As sites of cultural memory and social identity, Christian graves both create and reflect ideas about the community that created them. They reflect the feelings of the community at the time of the death of the individual. At the same time they create meaning for the future, presenting an image of continuity between imagined future observers with an idealized past serving to remind the community what it deems to be important. One must remember, however, that:

> Every representation is by its very nature partial and incomplete. A representation of "reality" must leave something out, even as it puts something in. A culture's discourse represents not the "real" world, but rather a world mediated through the social categories, relations and institutions operating in the specific culture.
>
> Another way of saying this is that every representation reflects some cultural interest and therefore discourses in a society never just float free. They are informed by, and help to constitute, the societies particular preoccupation and intentions.[6]

Christian burials present images from sacred literature, reinterpreting them in light of Christianity's current situation. They allow Christians to represent themselves to themselves. Burials serve as a reminder of Christianity's past and point a direction for its future.

While it is true that burial monuments may reflect an idealized image rather than the "historical facts" of a society, this does not mean that they do not provide a window into the lives of those who created those monuments. The way a society re-creates its own history can tell us as much, if not more, about the way that society views itself than the "historical facts"

---

5. Valerie Hope, "Inscription and Sculpture: the Construction of Identity in the Military Tombstones of Roman Mainz," in *The Epigraphy of Death: Studies in the History and Society of Greece and Rome* (ed. Graham J. Oliver: Liverpool: Liverpool University Press, 2000), 155–86.

6. Judith Perkins, *The Suffering Self: Pain and Narrative Representation in the Early Christian Era* (London: Routledge, 1995), 3.

on which it bases that re-creation.[7] Burials show how a group within society wants to be remembered, and as such reveal what that group regards as important. The sites for this projection of meaning in early Christian circles are the graves of the important dead, especially those of the martyrs.

With the Edict of Milan in 313 and the post-Nicene creation of Christian "Orthodoxy" in 325, the threat of martyrdom at the hands of non-Christians was replaced by the threat of persecution within the community of Christians. However, although post-Constantinian Christians died for their beliefs to as great an extent as their predecessors had,[8] and there was clearly enduring and substantial conflict over the Arian "heresy" (among others), the disputes in which they died were as often to do with power as they were over theology. Issues surrounding power and control were clear in the peri-Nicene Church: as early Christianity developed from the small localized churches of the Pauline communities to more established city congregations, the bishops of the third and fourth centuries struggled to claim their place in the empire.[9] Those living during and after Constantine's monumental acceptance of Christianity were especially prone to this melee for positions of authority. The Luciferians and the Donatists were both fourth-century schismatics who followed orthodox Trinitarian theology; Ammianus[10] recounts that the struggle between Damasus and Ursinus for the bishopric of Rome in 366 CE escalated into an actual battle, in which 137 people were killed in a single day in the Basilica of Sicininus. Damasus also was accused of hiring thugs to intimidate (leading on occasion led to the death of) his Christian opponents.[11]

This was the context in which newly powerful bishops used burial locations as a way to centralize their authority: whoever controlled the past through the cult of the saints controlled the future of Christianity. The graves of the important Christian dead were not the primary front of these intra-Christian battles, yet they were one enduring facet of the battles. The pure physicality of the locations of the graves of the important

7. Cf. Suzanne Dixon, who argues that burial texts and artifacts are evidence only of burial and that they should not be taken as accurately demonstrating living society. Susanne Dixon, *Reading Roman Women: Sources, Genres and Real Life* (London: Duckworth, 2001), 17.
8. See also Maureen A. Tilley, *Donatist Martyr Stories: The Church in Conflict in Roman North Africa* (Liverpool: Liverpool University Press, 1996).
9. See especially H. A. Drake, *Constantine and the Bishops: The Politics of Intolerance* (Baltimore, MD: Johns Hopkins Press, 2000).
10. Ammianus Marcellinus, *Res Gestae* 26.3.
11. Marcellus and Faustinus, *Lib. Pre.* 22 (PL 13. 98).

dead, and later the shrines of the martyrs – whole or in pieces – ensured that they were visible to the masses in a decidedly visceral fashion. Those who controlled the locations of the martyr's graves were able to control the cult practices that were associated with them. The control of the cult practices in turn ensured that the established episcopate remained in its position of power. Damasus demonstrates this clearly through his ambitious usage of inscriptions to establish a tradition of a non-existent unity within the church which served to solidify his own position at the head of that unified church. Conversely, as we shall discuss in Chapter Four, Athanasius of Alexandria argued against the use of martyrs' remains as cult locations, especially when it served his own political agenda: when he did not control the cult centers, he argued that they were unnecessary; but when he did control those centers, he argued that it was inappropriate to translate (the movement of a corpse from one location to another) the relics. Burial was not the only means by which bishops sought to establish a cultural memory to cement their political and religious power. However, those who emerged victorious – or more importantly were *remembered* as victorious – were those who crafted Christian cultural memory at the tombs of the saints.

The present work is about struggle: the struggle to control, the struggle to dominate, and the struggle to determine how the graves of the important Christian dead would be used to fabricate an image of Christianity which would ultimately determine the direction of the church in the fifth and sixth centuries. I focus on the structures and the practices that developed around the physical remains of the martyrs, as well as how those remains were distributed, and ultimately how they were visited by pilgrims. To this end I use some scant archaeological work, but more often have relied upon written descriptions of those structures.[12] This literary perspective is in part an accident of what materials have been preserved, or more importantly preserved in (more or less) their original format: it would be wonderful to be able to examine the catacombs of Rome as they were originally formed and organized, but due to the very importance of those locations, and their subsequent beautification, it is almost impossible to glean the sort of material that would allow us to re-create their original appearance. I am aware that a textual emphasis has certain limitations; however, the focus of this work is not about the structures themselves, but rather the cultural memory that was created around them and the graves that they contained, and it is entirely possible that descriptions of the monuments (even when they

---

12. See note at the start of the Bibliography.

venture into the hyperbolic) allow a modern reader to see what was considered to have been an important feature, which might be unavailable through a purely archaeological approach.

Through an analysis of letters, various church histories, and sermons, we can understand how the martyr's graves were understood by those who sought to control them in the later fourth century. We can also see how those who controlled the pens that wrote those documents sought to present the activities at the shrines of the martyrs; either those that they approved of and wanted to see repeated or those that they deemed reprehensible or heretical. Consequently, this is something of a hybrid work: it is about space rather than narrative, although those spaces are understood through the narrative that was crafted around them.

Exploring the desire of the episcopate to control the practices that were part of the worship at martyrs' shrines necessitates drawing on material concerning groups only known to us by what was written about them by their opponents. The most useful of this material comes from North African bishops who wrote against two groups with a considerable affinity for devotion to the martyrs: Donatists and Meletians.[13] Such material has obvious limitations, but even if we cannot claim, for example, that Augustine's diatribes against his Donatist neighbors reflect the normative behavior of those same Donatists, we can be confident that the authors of those texts believed in their rhetorical examples. Consequently, when Augustine argues against the Donatist Circumcellions,[14] it may be the case that the behavior ascribed to this group occured, either as a widespread practice or only sporadically; or perhaps something like it happened which was subsequently taken out of context, both for veneration as well as criticism by Donatists and Catholics respectively. However, it is also entirely possible that the group's alleged practices, or anything like it, never happened at all.

Either way, there is one thing that we can know for certain: Augustine used the idea in his writings as a means of criticizing his opponents. He also hoped that his argument would be convincing to whoever was

---

13. They drew the boundaries between themselves and the "Catholic" church based on the latter's reincorporation of *lapsi* after the persecutions of the early fourth century, rather than due to any strict theological differences. William H. C. Frend, *The Donatist Church: A Movement of Protest in Roman North Africa* (Oxford: Clarendon Press, 1952); *Martyrdom and Persecution in the Early Church* (Oxford: Oxford University Press, 1965); Tilley, *Donatist Martyr Stories*.

14. See e.g. Augustine, *Gaud.* (PL 43: 705ff). According to Augustine the Circumcellions were a group that traveled from place to place and were reputed to practice self-induced martyrdom through tossing themselves off cliffs, or initiating fights so as to suffer death at the hands of those they attacked.

hearing/reading it. It would have been significantly less convincing if there had been no popular belief that these things were taking place, but even if the heresiological material is a complete fabrication it remains important for the current endeavor, given that the arguments took place in the context of discussions concerning the martyrs and their centrality to Christian identity. They demonstrate the role of martyrdom, martyr shrines, and the veneration of martyrs precisely because they were meaningful to the audience that heard them, and as such reveal the power of the activities surrounding the martyr cult as a battleground for power in the fourth century. As Harold Drake notes: "The martyrs won […] a respect on the popular level which the apologist could never have hoped to achieve,"[15] and it was this popularity that meant that Augustine had to address Donatist martyrs in his arguments against the group, even though by doing so he further bolstered their popularity. The usage of the past as a means of controlling the present is a recurrent theme in this work; this includes fictitious "pasts" that were presented as having taken place. The presentation of these historically dubious events underscores their importance in the rhetoric regarding the martyr cult, and the desire to control the cultural memory which encompassed it.

The founder of the International Catacomb Society, Estelle S. Brettman, compiled an enticing volume entitled *Vaults of Memory*.[16] Here, among the images and research of the catacombs, she presented the Roman catacombs as if they were a blank repository that simply recorded history as it was; as if within these catacombs, or indeed with any vault, any archive, there was no intentionality in their creation. The image that she created implied that the dead commemorated in the epitaphs, or the poor uninscribed corpses, were simply waiting for the impressions of history to be pressed upon them. However, this understanding of both the catacombs and the archival process ignores the active choices made by those with the power to control those archives. Indeed, one thing that we know was that the things which were remembered – the items stored in the vault – were those that were intentionally placed in the vault to ensure their remembrance. They were stored for safe-keeping in an archive by those who had the desire and the power to do so.

The analysis of any archived material must include a critical awareness of the power dynamic involved in the determination of which material has been collected and stored in that archive. While we look

---

15. Drake, *Constantine and the Bishops*, 99.
16. Estelle S. Brettman, *Vaults of Memory: Jewish and Christian Imagery in the Catacombs of Rome, An Exhibition* (Boston: International Catacomb Society, 1985).

to the past as a means of understanding and structuring the present, it is always a mediated past that we encounter – and the archiving of the past is not determined by chance. The roots of the "archive" can be traced to *arkeion*, which is also the root for "architecture" and "archon"; as such it is the house that stores the documents of power, and is related to the power of remembrance:

> The meaning of "archive," its only meaning, comes from the Greek *arkeion*: initially a house, a domicile, an address, the residence of the superior magistrates, the *archons*, those who commanded. The citizen who thus held and signified political power were considered to possess the right to make or represent the law. [...] There is no political power without control of the archive, if not memory. [17]

The archive is a seat of power, a location of documents or information that serves to establish the power of those who control it. Thus, whoever choses the items in the archive has the power to choose (or manipulate) the memory that is preserved therein. In this regard graveyards, catacombs, and churches are like more traditional archives: they are not passive receptacles, but are constructed by those with the authority to control their contents. The collective memory, as it is preserved in public monuments, in the seats of power, is the building material for the creation of a group's identity; as Richard Miles put it in the introduction to *Constructing Identities in Late Antiquity*: "The formation and contestation of identity are fundamentally about power, the power to represent."[18]

Throughout this work I have been influenced by Michel Foucault's understanding of power. For Foucault the power to represent is a creative force, but for it to exist at all it must be used. As summarized by two interpreters:

> Power is not a commodity, a position, a prize, or a plot: it is the operation of the political technologies throughout the social body. The *functioning* of these political rituals of power is exactly what sets up the nonegalitarian, asymmetrical relations.[19]

Foucault suggests

> an 'analytics' of power: that is, [inquiries] toward a definition of a specific domain formed by relations of power, and toward a determination of the instruments that will make possible its analysis. [...T]here is no power that is exercised without a series of aims and objectives."[20]

---

17. Jacques Derrida, *Archive Fever: A Freudian Impression* (trans. Eric Prenowitz: Chicago: University of Chicago Press, 1995), 2, 4.
18. Miles, "Introduction," 5.
19. Hubert C. Dreyfus and Paul Rabinow, *Michel Foucault: Beyond Structuralism and Hermeneutics* (2nd ed.: Chicago: University of Chicago Press, 1983), 185.
20. Michel Foucault, *The History of Sexuality*. Vol. 1: *An Introduction* (trans. Robert Hurley: New York: Vintage 1990 [1978]), 81.

Foucault presents power as a force that is proportional "to its ability to persuade, incite, influence, direct, impress or control the conduct of others."[21] Yet it does not directly act upon others:

> [W]hat defines a relationship of power is that it is a mode of action which does not act directly and immediately on others. Instead it acts upon their actions: an action upon an action, on existing actions or on those which may arise in the present or the future. [... A] power relationship can only be articulated on the basis of two elements which are each indispensable if it is really to be a power relationship: that "the other" (the one over whom power is exercised) be thoroughly recognized and maintained to the very end as a person who acts; and that, faced with a relationship of power, a whole field of responses, reactions, results, and possible inventions may open up.[22]

Power contains within itself the ability to produce truth and reality, but again there must be a willingness to accept that newly minted truth and reality.[23] Peter Burke argues that "[s]peaking is a form of doing, that language is an active force in society, a means for individuals and groups to control others or to resist such control, for changing society or for blocking change, for affirming or suppressing cultural identities."[24] Due to the relationship between individuals and groups in the enactment of power, one cannot simply attribute any one particular outcome to any particular individual.[25] In the case of the current work, however, we can see how individuals drew upon the extant rhetoric of burial so as to influence others. Yet they could not act unidirectionally; they needed the acquiescence of those they wanted to influence.

The bodies of the saints, and the ability to determine what can be remembered through them and performed in their presence, were technologies of power in the fourth century, and were used to great effect. It is important to observe, however, that this technology would have been fruitless had those who were controlled not been receptive to being influenced through messages associated with the important dead. The

---

21. Isaak Dore, "Foucault on Power," *UMKC Law Review* 78 (2009–10): 738.
22. Michel Foucault, "Afterword: The Subject and Power," in H. C. Dreyfus and Paul Rabinow, *Michel Foucault: Beyond Structuralism and Hermeneutics* (2nd ed.: Chicago: University of Chicago Press, 1983), 220. See also Michael Gallagher "Foucault, Power and Participation," *International Journal of Children's Rights* 16 (2008): 395–406.
23. See Colin Gordon, "Introduction," in *Power*. Vol. 3 of *The Essential Works of Foucault 1954–1984* (by M. Foucault, ed. James D. Faubion: New York: New Press, 1994), xi–xli, xix.
24. Peter Burke, *The Art of Conversation* (Ithaca, NY: Cornell University Press, 1993), 26.
25. Dore, "Foucault on Power," 740. See also Caroline Schroeder, who uses this understanding of power dynamics to interpret Shenoute's discourses on the body. Caroline T. Schroeder, *Monastic Bodies: Discipline and Salvation in Shenoute of Atripe* (Philadelphia: University of Pennsylvania Press, 2007), 5ff.

crafting of the images of the important dead, through the control of their corpses, proved to be tremendously effective in realizing the desire to shape the self-identity of fourth-century Christianity (relative to a perceived shared past), especially when it was combined with an affinity for the ritual activities which surrounded that cult. The willingness of pilgrims to subsequently transmit this information, independently of the episcopate, both reinforced and subverted the original desire of those who crafted the original meaning.

The power to represent was crucially important to the formation of identity and memory in the emergent Church. Identity and memory were intricately bound; without memory there could be no identity.[26] Or, perhaps more precisely, if there was no memory, one had to be created in order to form an identity. However, almost all memory was created to one degree or another – as the memory of an individual could be manipulated (either by the individual or some outside force), the collective or cultural memory of a society too could shift over time.[27]

Maurice Halbwachs, the father of modern collective memory studies, argued that memory is essentially fluid, an idea that has been contrasted by Jan Assmann and Barry Schwartz, who both argue that while memory is malleable, it is not entirely flexible.[28] In the current work I take the latter position: memory is anchored to moments in the past that were then reinterpreted in light of any particular present. One of the ways that memory can be tied to the past is through the construction of monuments, which serve to remind a population of what (they are told) is important to remember about that past. For example, when Damasus created his image of Hippolytus as a "schismatic" who returned to the fold of the Catholic Church, Damasus did not invent Hippolytus out of whole cloth, but rather re-created his memory (and the memory of others) through the addition of an elegant inscription on his tomb. The moments of history that are chosen to be remembered form the way

---

26. See Barbara Misztal, *Theories of Social Remembering* (Maidenhead, UK: Open University Press / McGraw-Hill Education, 2003), 1.

27. For a discussion of the malleability of memory see Daniel L. Schacter, *The Seven Sins of Memory: How the Mind Forgets and Remembers* (New York: Houghton Mifflin, 2002). A number of New Testament scholars have also discussed the problems of memory, most notably John Dominic Crossan, *The Historical Jesus: The Life of a Mediterranean Jewish Peasant* (New York: Harper One, 1991).

28. Maurice Halbwachs, *On Collective Memory* (ed. and trans. Lewis A. Coser: Chicago: University of Chicago Press, 1992); Jan Assmann, "Collective Memory and Cultural Identity," *New German Critique* (Spring/Summer 1995): 125–33 (trans. John Czaplicka); Barry Schwartz; "Memory as a Cultural System: Abraham Lincoln in World War II," *American Sociological Review* 61 (1996): 908–27; *Abraham Lincoln and the Forge of National Memory* (Chicago: University of Chicago Press, 2000).

that a community becomes visible to itself as well as to those outside. Jan Assmann suggests: "Which past becomes evident in that heritage and which values emerge in its identificatory appropriation tells us much about the constitution and tendencies of a society."[29] The choices of which "history" people determined important enough to be remembered can provide insight into what was (or what was hoped to be) important for any particular population. Yet in accordance with Halbawchs, the memory work can only occur within a community which constantly reminds itself about itself. The decision over which past to preserve was never a passive process: it was one that always involved decisions and an exertion of authority. The chosen memories also served to reinforce the power of those who had the ability to represent those memories in the first place, yet through a language that must have been available for everyone to understand:

> Memories are processed through language, which provides the conventional and customary meanings that then refract back onto the memory. Through retelling – whether narrative, performative, representative, even liturgical – memory accrues meaning through discursive and embodied repetition.[30]

Cultural memory, especially as it is reflected (and shaped) through monumentalization, was not something that "just happened." Monuments did not just organically create themselves whenever an event of momentous import occurred. Rather, they were created for specific purposes, by specific people in specific societies. Indeed many of these memories may never have happened at all. While it is not the purpose of this book to test the historical veracity of any of the particular claims by the episcopate or Church historians (but rather to see how their use of such narratives served a primarily political agenda), one must be aware of the possibility (probability, in some instances) that these stories were complete fabrications.[31] By placing memory in monumental (plastic) form, it could be molded so as to more accurately represent the memory that individuals wanted to be remembered (not necessarily the one that is remembered at the time of the memorialization), so that memory can then be echoed back to the memorializer in the form of the monument thus creating the desired memory. When we look to the graves and monuments of the past, we long to rediscover our present foreshadowed therein.

---

29. Assmann, "Collective Memory," 133.
30. Elizabeth A. Castelli, *Martyrdom and Memory: Early Christian Culture Making* (New York: Columbia, 2004), 11.
31. For a discussion on the manufacture of traditions see Bruce Lincoln, *Discourse and the Construction of Society: Comparative Studies of Myth, Ritual, and Classification* (New York: Oxford, 1989); Eric Hobsbawm and Terence Ranger, eds., *The Invention of Tradition* (Cambridge: Cambridge University Press, 1983).

In recent years there has been an increase in scholarship examining the role of burial as a means of understanding identity in the late Roman Empire. While the historian Valerie Hope presents the most interesting usage of the understanding of the "rhetoric of commemoration," Suzanne Dixon argues that burial representations should be understood to reflect only the evidence for the way that people wanted to be remembered in burial and that it is incorrect to draw conclusions about the living in society from those monuments.[32] I disagree: the way that a society chooses to represent itself can tell us how it wants to understand itself, and how it wants the future to remember it. From this we can notice trends in that society which may not afford a view into the status of an individual's life as it was lived, but do tell us clearly how that individual (or whoever erected the monument) wanted to be remembered.

Monumentalization is both a reflection of society as well as a reflection for that society, as has been demonstrated effectively by Barry Schwartz, Ian Morris, Kirk Savage and James Edward Young.[33] This monumentalization and creation of identity through burial was especially effective for the Christian community, due to the distinctly Christian association of the living with the remains of the dead, the developing cult of the dead, and *ad sanctos* burial. It also flourished in the emergent Church, due to the prevalence and importance of memorialization in the world in which it arose.

Savage points out in his essay on commemoration and freed slaves after the American Civil War that public monuments do not arise as if by an act of nature to remember the past, but, rather, they are constructed by those who have the power to influence society to erect such monuments.[34] This is echoed by Young in his work on Holocaust memorials. He notes that the versions of the Holocaust that are remembered in every country are often in conflict with each other. None of these monuments remember the past "as it really was," but instead re-create the past in such a way that casts the best light on the country doing the memorializing.[35]

---

32. Dixon, *Reading Roman Women*, 23. See also Hope, "Inscription and Sculpture."

33. James Edward Young, *The Texture of Memory: Holocaust Memorials and Meaning* (New Haven, CT: Yale University Press, 1993); Kirk Savage, "The Politics of Memory: Black Emancipation and the Civil War Monument," in *Commemorations: The Politics of National Identity* (ed. John R. Gillis: Princeton: Princeton University Press, 1994), 127–49; Ian Morris, *Death-Ritual and Social Structure in Classical Antiquity* (Cambridge: Cambridge University Press, 1992); and probably the most interesting and sophisticated work on the subject comes from Schwartz, "Memory as a Cultural System"; *Abraham Lincoln*.

34. Savage, "Politics of Memory," 127–49.

35. See Young, *Texture of Memory*, for a fascinating study of the various uses of Holocaust memorials and the way they differ from country to country. They tell us at

These works on monuments may be some of the best and most explicable works on cultural memory. They situate the creation of the monuments in a specific time, and trace the intentions of those responsible for those monuments. At the same time it is possible to see how the monuments are used in the future, by those whose memory is shaped by them. Graves, likewise, are sites of social memory: the meaning of the events recorded there are understood by a society only in light of other events, and both what and how we remember are a function of the society in which we situate ourselves.[36]

As we shall see in the case of the memorials and monuments set up by Constantine and Damasus, the object (in this case the remains of the martyr) is both present, and no longer mute. The addition of the epitaph by Damasus allows the martyr to speak, but only with the words that Damasus provides. The objectification of an item on display does not effectively silence that item. It might not speak fully for itself any more, but in some regards it is only through the action of display (which is not an unintentional act) that an item may be able to speak at all, even if those words are influenced by those with the power to effect that display.

Ian Morris's *Death-Ritual and Social Structure in Classical Antiquity* uttered a call for Classical scholarship to no longer forget the burial of an individual as a means of understanding social structure. All too often, he argued, scholars have opted for either literary sources or those provided by archaeology. His response was that neither one nor the other is preferable, but that scholarship should use everything available for analysis. To this end he took a Geertzian perspective on ritual, that it is both a model *of* and *for* society.[37] Morris focused a considerable amount of

---

least as much about those who wish to memorialize the Holocaust as the Holocaust itself: "In every nation's memorials and museums, a different Holocaust is remembered, often to conflicting political and religious ends" (ix). He makes an interesting point about how the very act of setting up memorials to a certain extent liberates us from the need to remember, as the memorial does the work for us. While this may be the case for the Holocaust, it seems to have been decidedly the opposite for the martyr shrine. While both Holocaust and martyrdom were traumatic events, the horror of death is not found in martyr stories nor is it in their shrines. I do not mean to say that the stories did not contain gruesome depictions of the executions of the martyrs or that the shrines did not have imagery of that as well; but martyrs were to be remembered as examples of faith, and their death through martyrdom was, for the faithful, a wonderful event which many sought to replicate – unlike the Holocaust. Persecution, then (especially after Constantine), was something to which the church sought a connection. See also Young's *At Memory's Edge: After-Images of the Holocaust in Contemporary Art and Architecture* (New Haven, CT: Yale University Press, 2000).

36. Eviatar Zerubavel, *Time Maps: Collective Memory and the Social Shape of the Past* (Chicago: University of Chicago Press, 2003), 6.

37. See also Schwartz, *Abraham Lincoln*.

energy specifically on the rituals surrounding the burial. However, while this was, perhaps obviously, one of the important contextual elements to consider, one must also look at what was done with the grave after the burial. How did the living continue to interact with the departed, and were they commemorated, ignored, or forgotten?

As mentioned earlier, only a few scholars have dealt with identity creation and burial in the early Church. The first of these is Ann Marie Yasin. She explores basilica burials in North Africa, seeking to offer a counter-example to the traditional scholarly understanding of *ad sanctos* burial.[38] She argues that basilica burials show no organized chronological focus on being buried near to the remains of the martyrs. For Yasin it was not the proximity to the saint that was important, but the ability to be remembered by those in attendance at the church; the saints' remains only helped draw people to the church.[39] My goal, however, is not to look at the practice of *ad sanctos* burial *per se*; I see it as a side effect of the usage of the remains, and the location of those remains, by the early Church. This focus on *ad sanctos* burial as a symptom is not something that I have found to be to be at the center of any of my readings on pilgrims and pilgrimages, the archaeological material, or the scholarship on martyrdom.

The second author to have explored this subject is Dennis Trout.[40] His work on the reinvention of meaning associated with burial locations by Damasus focuses primarily on the inscriptions that the fourth-century bishop of Rome left on the graves of the saints, so as to invest them with a sense of continuity with Rome itself. While this is a work that is useful for my current endeavor, my own work does not replicate Trout's as my intention is to reach beyond the desired meaning to explore how that meaning was received. His work focuses on the fourth century, with the figures of both Damasus and Paulinus of Nola. In his work on Damasus he focuses a great amount of attention on the way that Damasus uses Virgilian prose to connect the new Christian presence with the traditions of Rome. While this has some importance for my argument, it does not address intra-Christian dialogue nor does it explore the broader uses of burial and identity creation.

---

38. Ann Marie Yasin, "Commemorating the Dead – Constructing the Community: Church Space, Funerary Monuments and Saints' Cults in Late Antiquity" (MA thesis, University of Chicago, 2000); "Funerary Monuments and Collective Identity: From Roman Family to Christian Community," *Art Bulletin* 87 (2005): 433–57.

39. Yasin, "Commemorating the Dead," 241.

40. Dennis Trout, "Christianizing the Nolan Countryside: Animal Sacrifices at the Tomb of St. Felix," *Journal of Early Christian Studies* 3 (1995): 281–98; *Paulinus of Nola: Life, Letters, and Poems* (Berkeley: University of California Press, 1999); "Damasus and the Invention of Early Christian Rome," *Journal of Medieval and Early Modern Studies* 33 (2003): 517–36.

Marianne Saghy agrees with Trout in that Damasus set about to tie-in the new Christian orthodoxy with the history of Rome, noting how Damasus "contributed his own novel theology of martyrdom to the Catholic spirituality of the fourth century, and discovered a medium of divine affirmation for his uncertain position as bishop."[41] This may well be the closest work to my own study. However, Saghy's analysis focuses exclusively on the figure of Damasus, and while Damasus is perhaps the clearest example of the manipulation of burial structures in the construction of a Christian collective memory for political purposes, he is not the only one who approached burial in this way. As such, he needs to be seen within the broader context of the development of Christian attitudes toward both the dead and the Christian community as a whole.

Elizabeth A. Castelli has convincingly examined hagiographies and martyrdom accounts to explore the idea of martyrdom as a central theme in the construction of Christian cultural memory in the emergent Church.[42] However, while in the current work I also draw on some of these hagiographical works, my focus is concerned with the physical space inhabited by the corpses of the martyrs, rather than with literary accounts of martyrdoms. These physical locations, perhaps due to the efficacy of the literary works, contained enough gravitational pull to draw pilgrims into their orbits. Initially, this affected just the local population, but just as any celestial object gains mass and has a stronger gravitational pull once it has incorporated those objects closest to it, the shrines of the saints too accumulated a strong enough local following that they began to draw from a trans-local population.

Finally, when one deals with any topic relating to the martyr cults of the late fourth century and beyond, one must acknowledge the work of Peter Brown, especially *The Cult of the Saints*.[43] Brown convincingly argues against the previously held idea that there had been a two-tiered system of belief, that of the intellectual elites and that of the vulgar masses (who were supposedly influenced by their pagan background). The rise of the martyr cult, he suggests, was because of the great influx of wealth into the coffers of the church in the late fourth century and the need to spend it in a publicly acceptable fashion, rather than because of the mass influx of new converts. The control of the martyr shrine also allowed the newly

---

41. Saghy, "*Scinditur in partes populous*," 273.
42. Castelli, *Martyrdom and Memory*.
43. Peter Brown, *The Cult of the Saints: Its Rise and Function in Latin Christianity* (Chicago: University of Chicago Press, 1981).

powerful bishops of the fourth century to solidify their power. While Brown does a beautiful job of demonstrating how active the episcopate was in the development of the martyr cult, his work has a few flaws that I hope to rectify here. The first is that through his rejection of the bottom-up model, he comes dangerously close to simply inverting it, in effect concluding that it was the bishops and not the "common believer" who was in complete control of the cult of the saints. Instead, we need to look at the development of the cult of the saints in light of the dialogic dynamic that is always present in uses of power. The cult needed both the bishops and their flock to become what it became. Another issue that one encounters in Brown's work is that he does not deal with how the development of the cult of the saints progressed; rather, he presents material (seemingly effortlessly) from the third through fifth centuries, with little attempt to account for change over time.

This book offers an approach to the martyr cult that is more about the cult and less about the martyr. Chapter One sets the stage for the development of the Christian usage of the martyr's grave in the fourth century. To that end, it describes several pertinent features of Roman burial practices: the polluting nature of the corpse, the desire of the deceased to be remembered, the importance of location, and the intentional creation of meaning through the tomb structure. I also examine the various groups that were responsible both for the care of the dead as well as for their commemoration: families and voluntary associations. This discussion sets the stage for an understanding of Christianity's adaptation of these practices in the second and third centuries, especially the modification of the church's role as a new family of Christ and how that adaptation related to their concern for their own dead.

From this starting point, Chapter Two then moves on to examine how two seminal early fourth-century figures, Constantine and Damasus, helped to determine the development of the veneration of the martyrs. Constantine was responsible for the construction of numerous church structures, and explicitly developed the basilica as a seat of Christian power. Many if not all of these structures incorporated pre-existent martyr veneration, and Constantine sought to harness that power for his own purposes. Ultimately, Constantine would design his own funerary monument in Constantinople and through his translation of the relics of Stephen and Luke lay the foundation for a trans-local understanding of the remains of the important dead. Damasus, the bishop of Rome, following Constantine sought to address the challenges of maintaining control by presenting a unified image of the church though the inscriptions that he placed around the tombs of the martyrs.

Once the stage had been set by Constantine and Damasus, later bishops sought to control the martyr cult as it developed elsewhere in the empire during the late fourth century. Chapter Three examines how some of those bishops – such as Athanasius, Augustine, and Ambrose – approached the cult of the martyrs in ways that addressed their own leadership challenges. Other contemporary bishops, such Paulinus of Nola, whose leadership was not associated with such political contests, embraced the martyr cult with less concern about their own authority within the participation of the martyr cult.

Not everyone in the empire in the fourth century was a proponent of martyr veneration and the attention that Christians paid to their corpses. Christians faced criticism from those outside Christendom, as well as from those Christians who felt that the practices at the martyr shrines during the all-night vigils (which involved loud music, drunken revelry, and the comingling of the sexes) were extreme enough to warrant the prohibition of martyr veneration. Others felt that implicit in the cult was worship of the martyrs, which was too similar to the polytheism of the non-Christian gentiles. Chapter Four examines how various groups rejected the martyr cult, as well as typical Christian responses to that rejection.

Christians occasionally traveled to specific places associated with the history of their tradition prior to the fourth century. In particular, Palestine drew Christian travelers from the late second century. It was only by the end of the fourth century, however, that there was a significant rise in the number of Christians who could be classified collectively as "pilgrims." Initially, most pilgrimages were to the "Holy Land," to visit sites associated with the life and death of Jesus. Chapter Five traces the development of the pilgrims' interest in such prestigious locations, but also focuses on martyr shrines visited by pilgrims. Pilgrimage to martyr shrines could range from traveling to shrines outside the walls of a city on feast days, to a long-distance journey to visit important shrines hundreds of miles away. Pilgrims' travel created a network of memory associated with the martyrs. Ultimately it was the pilgrims who solidified Christian cultural memory at the graves of the saints by sharing what *they* considered to have been important within this network.

The current work follows a rise of interest in the cult of the martyrs and an interest in the sacred geography of Christianity in the fourth century. However, it stands apart from previous scholarship in that it attempts to trace the development of the martyr cult from its origins in Roman familial burial commemoration to the point where it becomes one of the central features of Christian churches. I do not trace the development of the martyr cult past the early fifth century (roughly 100 years after the conversion of Constantine). This period is determinative in the direction that the martyr cult would take, and it was in this period that the role of the martyrs (and their shrines) was established as a central feature of Christian identity. The martyr cult was one of the most strongly contested battlefields for control not only of the remains of the saints, but also for Christian identity. That identity was squarely situated above the bodies of the important dead.

Chapter One: To Begin

The Life of the Dead is Set in the Memory of the Living

> Being religious is a quality which every single person can impose on a site of his own free will by burying a corpse in a place which he owns.[1]

> For the life of the dead lies in the memory of the living.[2]

Care and commemoration of the dead was not, initially, a specifically Christian practice. There is little evidence for specifically Christian burial customs in contradistinction to those of their non-Christian gentile neighbors. Christians, of course, would eventually develop their own explicitly Christian iconography and sepulchral norms. In the Church's treatment of the special dead, they would ultimately begin to craft their own identity situated at the tomb of the martyr. But these practices were built upon existing Roman models for the care of the dead.

Roman burial was generally not associated with the practice of the imperial cult or the worship of a particular temple or god (even if it was believed that failure to properly care for the dead would have dire consequences for the empire). Rather, burial practices and commemoration were primarily a private endeavor undertaken by close groups who were composed either of family members or associations which modeled themselves on the family structure. Burial practices, as Brown aptly summarizes, were

> among the most notoriously stable aspects of most cultures. […] They cannot be neatly categorized as "pagan" or "Christian," "popular" or "superstitious." This is because, whatever their origins may appear to have been to a modern scholar, the customs surrounding the care of the dead were experienced by those who practiced them to be no more than part and parcel of being human.[3]

For the Roman population (inclusive of the emergent Christian community), then, the question that we need to ask is: what were these practices

---

1. Marcianus, in Justinian, *Digest* 1.8.6.4 / *Inst.* 2.1.9. Trans. in Jan H. A. Lokin, "The Work of Penelope: The Composition and Decomposition of Roman Law," in *Antiquity Renewed: Late Classical and Early Modern Themes* (eds. Z. R. W. M. von Martels and Victor Michael Schmidt: Leuven: Peeters, 2003), 25 n. 8.

2. Cicero, *Phil.* 9.10, trans. Gesine Manuwald, *Marcus Tullius Cicero: Orationes Philippicae III-IX* (Berlin: Walter de Gruyter, 2007), 285.

3. Peter Brown, *The Cult of the Saints: Its Rise and Function in Latin Christianity* (Chicago: University of Chicago Press, 1981), 24.

that were "part and parcel of being human"? This chapter discusses some general aspects of Roman commemorative practices, especially those that would ultimately lead to unambiguously Christian practices in the third and fourth centuries. The locations of the remains as well as the ceremonies that ministered to the deceased's spirit were important aspects of the care for the memory of the deceased. The care of the memory of the deceased was as important as the belief that the care of the spirits could give them peace after death. One of the fundamental aspects of this care was the regular pilgrimages made by the family (or its surrogates) to the graveside, in order to care for the dead and commemorate their life.

For Christians and non-Christian gentiles the placement of the tomb held considerable importance, both for the construction of the memory of the individual as well as for the collective memory of the society. Of course the memory of the burial location would not last more than a generation or two if there was no lasting monument to mark the grave. As such the physicality of the monument, and the text inscribed thereon, was of tremendous import to allow that memory to transcend the life of the individual and their immediate family. Some graves, especially of the important dead, gained special prominence, and were granted privileges by society (as pertains for example to location, funds for construction, and visitations by non-family members). Often these graves sought to present a grander and broader image of the Roman world. The graves of the emperors were often constructed to depict the empire as their builders (either the emperor himself or his family after his death) wanted it to be remembered, with an eye toward the future: "These monuments were unabashedly propagandistic; for the most part their *raison d'etre* was to promote an individual and his family, proclaiming their message through inscriptions, sculpture, and sheer physical presence."[4] However, it was not only the emperors who sought to project an idealized image of their life through the medium of their tomb. Many of the most elaborate tomb structures came from those who sought to claim a level of legitimacy in death (through their commemoration) that they did not have in life.[5]

The discursive act of memorializing the deceased was situated at the gravesite, and augmented by the rituals of the living for their dead. Without an observer, a spectator, a witness to the sepulture there could be no memory. The tomb addressed viewers and reflected the graves around it, while at the same time it attempted to set itself apart from nearby

---

4. Penelope J. E. Davies, *Death and the Emperor: Roman Imperial Funerary Monuments from Augustus to Marcus Aurelius* (Austin: University of Texas Press, 2004), 8.

5. Most of Valerie Hope's work supports this; see for instance, "Trophies and Tombstones: Commemorating the Roman Soldier," *World Archaeology* 35 (2003): 79–97.

monuments. Graves "performed in dialogue with other tombs of this period."[6] Without the passersby to listen to and interpret that dialogue, the monuments would be mute: a tomb "acquires meaning only through those who look at it; it may speak, but it is always dependent on the passerby to read it aloud."[7] Consequently, location, as we shall see, was tremendously important if one wanted to be remembered: the greater the foot traffic near a memorial, the greater the chance for remembrance. However, even those who were buried in out-of-the-way locations could count on their family and descendants making local pilgrimages at various points during the year. To be human meant to take care of your dead when you could: to bury, care for, and remember them.

Romans and the Afterlife: An Afterlife of Memory

> Honour is paid, also, to the grave. Appease the souls of your fathers and bring small gifts to the tombs erected to them. Ghosts ask but little: they value piety more than a costly gift: no greedy gods are they who in the world below do haunt the banks of Styx.[8]

While there were images in Roman poetry of an afterlife, such as Virgil's Limbo, Hell, and the Elysium Fields, the concept does not seem to have gained much of a following outside the poetic community. There is little evidence of the poetic descriptions of the afterlife in Roman burial inscription or burial art.[9] Despite the lack of archaeological evidence for the poetic afterlife in Roman burials, there was a general understanding of a form of spiritual afterlife: the afterlife was typically perceived to be good, with a decent degree of individuality after death.[10] There was also a general belief that those who had passed into that afterlife could continue to affect the lives of the living if they were not treated properly, even if such interactions were quite rare.[11] In the late Republic the mournful

---

6. Lauren Hackworth Petersen, "The Baker, His Tomb, His Wife, and Her Breadbasket: The Monument of Eurysaces in Rome." *Art Bulletin* 85 (2003): 231. In this case: "The monument's unconventional use of architectural form and decoration arose from a visual strategy for Eurysaces to make himself memorable." See also Penelope J. E. Davies, "The Politics of Perpetuation: Trajan's Column and the Art of Commemoration," *American Journal of Archaeology* 101 (1997): 49.

7. Davies, *Death and the Emperor*, 8.

8. Ovid, *Fasti* 2.9.533–6 (Frazer and Goold, LCL 253).

9. J. M. C. Toynbee, *Death and Burial in the Roman World* (Baltimore, MD: Johns Hopkins University Press, 1996 [1972]), 37.

10. Toynbee, *Death and Burial*, 38, notes that from the end of the Republic there was a rise in the belief in individuality.

11. "The dead subsisted, then, as nebulous, impalpable beings, perceived by the senses only exceptionally." Franz Cumont, *After Life in Roman Paganism* (New Haven,

festival of the *Parentalis* (from February 13–24)[12] was dedicated to the care of dead parents, who were remembered in a state of semi-existence near the location of the burial of their ashes.[13] These ashes would have also been provided with "such necessities as the soul might need after death"[14] to at least to make it feel at home, even if the deceased could not use these objects. The *manes*, or spirits of the dead, needed regular feeding, either on the anniversary of their death or during the annual festival. If these offerings were not properly taken care of, the dead could become most problematic: Ovid, writing in the early to mid-first century, comments that *manes* not fed properly escaped the grave to spread death and destruction throughout the city:

> But once upon a time, waging long wars with martial arms they did neglect the All Souls' Days. The negligence was not unpunished; for 'tis said that from that ominous day Rome grew hot with the funeral fires that burned without the city. They say, though I can hardly think it, that the ancestral souls did issue from the tombs and make their moan in the hours of stilly night; and hideous ghosts, a shadowy throng, they say, did howl about the city streets and the wide fields.[15]

The funerary meals for the dead were the most universal of all Roman religious ceremonies, demonstrating the widespread belief in the need for commemoration and libation for the dead.[16] While participation in other rituals varied, the care of the dead was nearly ubiquitous and strikingly uniform. Despite the focus on the participation of the individual or familial group, failure to properly care for the dead could have dire consequences for the city or the empire, as we saw above. These rituals crossed religious and social divides; the care of the dead united the empire.

Not only was the soul of the common dead commemorated during the *Parentalis*, as well on the anniversary of their death; the important

---

CT: Yale University Press, 1922), 4. See also Edward Champlin, who observed that at least in the wills he examined there was no idea of any individual imagining him/herself as a spectral being. This is the lone voice challenging the ubiquity of the belief in a spiritual afterlife in the non-Christian Mediterranean; Edward Champlin, *Final Judgments: Duty and Emotion in Roman Wills, 200 B.C. – A.D. 250* (Berkeley: University of California Press, 1991).

12. Toynbee (*Death and Burial*, 63) states it lasted until the February 21.
13. M. R. Ogilvie, *The Romans and Their Gods in the Age of Augustus* (New York: W. W. Norton, 1970), 75. See alslo Toynbee, *Death and Burial*, 37; David I. Smith, *Learning from the Stranger: Christian Faith and Cultural Diversity* (Grand Rapids, MI: Wm. B. Eerdmans, 2009), 42.
14. Ogilvie, *The Romans and Their Gods*, 104.
15. Ovid, *Fasti* 2.9.547–54 (Frazer and Goold, LCL 253).
16. Cumont, *After Life*, 55.

dead also received (should they merit it) special treatment. Upon the death of an emperor it was within the power of the Senate to deify that emperor through the ceremony of *apotheosis*. Herodian relates that an eagle was released during the ceremonial "cremation" of a wax effigy of the emperor. The eagle was believed to take the soul of the emperor to the heavens, after which he was worshiped among the other gods.[17]

Monuments

> A dead man shall not be buried or burned in the city.[18]

There were three central Roman notions on death and burial. The first was that death brought pollution and demanded acts of purification. Paulus observed in his *Opinions* (late second or early third century CE) that: "You are not allowed to bring a corpse into the city in case the sacred places in the city are polluted."[19] Paulus's reasoning about the desecration of sacred locations adds an explicitly religious dimension to this prohibition, decreed by the *Law of the Twelve Tables*. Second, the Romans felt that that to leave a corpse unburied had unpleasant repercussions on the afterlife of the deceased, who would subsequently inflict his or her own unpleasantness upon the living population.[20] Finally, monuments were an important way for the deceased to ensure their memory lasted long after their death.

Monuments, and more importantly the corpses that they memorialized, had to be separated from the homes of the living. The most fundamental aspect of Roman law concerning the treatment of the dead was

---

17. Herodian, *Hist. Emp.* 4.2.10–11. On the *apotheosis* of emperors see Simon Price, "From Noble Funerals to Divine Cult: The Consecration of Roman Emperors," in *Rituals of Royalty: Power and Ceremonial in Traditional Societies* (ed. D. Cannadine and S. Price: Cambridge: Cambridge University Press, 1987), 56–105.

18. Cicero, *De Leg.* 2.58, trans. in Valerie M. Hope and Eireann Marshall, *Death and Disease in the Ancient City* (New York: Routledge, 2000), 92.

19. Paulus, *Opinions* 1.21.2, trans. in Valerie M. Hope, *Death in Ancient Rome: A Sourcebook* (New York: Routledge, 2007), 129.

20. Toynbee, *Death and Burial*. John Bodel deals with common burials and the undertakers and executioners who may have dealt with them. There may have been roughly 30,000 people who died in Rome annually, with possibly 1500 turning up annually that were unclaimed and unwanted. From 100 BCE to 200 CE, then, there would have been some nine million corpses produced by the city, which had to be buried in one way or another. These were unceremoniously and anonymously dumped in a mass grave at the Esquiline Hill, outside of Rome. John Bodel, "Dealing with the Dead: Undertakers, Executioners and Potter's Field in Ancient Rome," in *Death and Disease in the Ancient City* (ed. Valerie M. Hope and Eireann Marshall, London: Routledge, 2000), 128–51.

that it was illegal to bury the remains of the deceased inside the walls of the city. Cicero's observation, that a "dead man shall not be buried or burned in the city" is from Table 10 of the *Twelve Tables*. These laws were part of the very foundation of Roman civilization; consequently, the prohibition was very strongly held, and Christians (as I will discuss in Chapter Four) were attacked for the appearance of violating this rule. Corpses in the Hellenistic world fit into a Durkheimian realm of taboo, of the otherness that should be avoided, which served as a focus for rituals.[21] Those whose occupations forced them to be in frequent contact with corpses were indelibly tainted by that contact. Undertakers and executioners had to live outside of the walls of the city, so as to avoid contaminating the city with their ritual impurity. Whenever they entered the city (which was frequently) they were forced to be clearly identifiable so that the general population would not be contaminated by them.[22] The remains of Roman citizens maintained some additional sort of sanctity, as unlike non-Roman remains it was illegal to tamper with those of a citizen.[23]

The landed gentry were not only interested in being buried in conspicuous locations surrounding cities. Those who had farms desired to be interred on their property, perhaps indicative of a strong tie between Romans and their land.[24] The sixth-century surveyor Siculus Flaccus observed that the stones that marked the boundary from one farm to another were often confused with burial monuments.[25] The taboo against mingling living areas with areas for burial remained strong even when there would have been no strict legal prohibition against it. There was no wall around the agricultural property to bury the dead beyond, yet the same customs remained even without that visual barrier. Corpses, even here, remained external, in between; if one was entering an individual property, just as when entering a public city, one was first greeted by the necropolis.

The desire for the dead to survive through the memory of the living was of paramount importance. This was not antithetical to the presence

---

21. Especially his definition of religion: "A religion is a unified system of beliefs and practices relative to sacred things, that is to say, things set apart and forbidden." Émile Durkheim, *The Elementary Forms of Religious Life* (trans. Karen E. Fields: New York: Free Press, 1995 [1912]), 46.
22. John Bodel, "Dealing with the Dead," 131.
23. Toynbee, *Death and Burial*, 48, 73ff.
24. Stephen L. Dyson, *Community and Society in Roman Italy* (Baltimore, MD: Johns Hopkins University Press, 2000), 144.
25. Siculus Flaccus, *De Cond. Ag.* 139.23–6.

of the graves, which were clearly separated from the homes of the living. While it is true that the Roman burials were an extra-urban phenomenon, they were not external to the city out of a desire to hide the graves or forget the dead. Quite the opposite was the case: the roads approaching a Roman city were lined with tombs. Travelers were greeted by Romans graves long before they reached the *pomerium*. These tombs, situated so as to be as visible as possible, worked to demonstrate the social (desired, if not actual) hierarchy within the city. The tombs of emperors and others with the money or fame to warrant noticeable memorials would have been impossible to miss.[26]

The construction of monuments to the deceased was the primary way that individuals, families, or groups ensured their immortality. Monuments had a liminal stature in the Roman world. Not only did they physically surround the city, demarking the boundary between the urban and rural; they connected the here-and-now with the past that they recalled, as well as the future that they looked toward. They transcended time, projecting an image of the past into the future through a monument that is always in the present. This was most clearly called to mind when the epigrams called out to the reader to remember the deceased. The witness was called to look back to the life of one who died in the past, but also often unmistakably told to look forward to their own death at some unknown time in the future (even if the epitaph does not explicitly demand that from the viewer): "from the viewer's perspective *monumenta* link together all of time."[27]

Marcus Terentius Varro (116–27 BCE) describes the terms associated with memory and monuments thus:

> *Meminisse*, "to remember," comes from *memoria*, "memory," since there is once again movement back to that which has stayed in the mind; this may have been derived from *manere*, "to remain," like *manimoria*. And thus the Salii when they sing "O Mamurius Veturis" signify a *memoria*, "memory." […] From the same word comes *monere*, "remind," because he who reminds is just like memory; so are derived *monumenta* "memorials," which are in burial places and for that

---

26. On the emperors' tombs and the desire for memory, see Davies, "Politics of Perpetuation"; Catharine Edwards, *Death in Ancient Rome* (New Haven, CT: Yale University Press, 2007).

27. Mary Jaeger, *Livy's Written Rome* (Ann Arbor: University of Michigan Press, 1997), 17. Valerie Hope also discusses the epitaph of Allia Potestas (CIL VI 37965) which at line 43 observes that the epitaph will keep Allia Potestas alive so long as the epitaph survives. See Valerie M. Hope, "Remembering to Mourn: Personal Mementos of the Dead in Ancient Rome," in *Memory and Mourning: Studies on Roman Death* (ed. Valerie M. Hope and Janet Huskinson: Oxford: Oxbow Press, 2011), 177.

reason are situated along the road, so that they can remind those who are passing by that they themselves existed and that the passersby are mortal.[28]

Again, it was through the usage of burial monuments that the dead and their family had their opportunity (with the aid of sufficient funds) to project their identity into the future. This memory, while probably tied with the actual life of the individual, clearly was a creation of the individual or their family with the aim of presenting a specific image of the deceased for eternity. Freedmen and soldiers often created monuments that were incongruous with their station in life.[29] Their tombs were regularly more elaborate, and consequently more expensive, than the tombs of those who could have afforded the monuments more easily. Through these monuments their heirs sought to secure some sort of legitimacy in death that they had been unable to attain in life.[30]

The tombs and structures that surrounded the cities and farms in the Roman Mediterranean served to create the memory that the deceased and their family wanted to endure for perpetuity. The physical locations reminded those coming to the grave as the *telos* of their travel, as well as those who were simply passing by, about the deceased and what was deemed to have been important about their lives. Taken together, all of these monuments also informed the foreigner and the local alike about the history of those wealthy or important enough to be memorialized, cementing the cultural memory through the commemoration of the dead.

Roman monuments fell into several categories, ranging from the individual monument, with an upright stone slab or *stelai*, to elaborate *columbaria*. The *columbaria* were large chambers with many niches set into the walls for whole bodies or cremated remains in urns. These communal burial chambers tended to be set up by wealthy householders for their families and servants, or were used by voluntary associations for the burial of their members. Between the *columbaria* and the individual

---

28. Varro, *De Ling. Lat.* 6.49, trans. in Jaeger, *Livy's Written Rome*, 15–16. Jaeger uses the Spengel and Spengel edition of *De Ling. Lat.* (1885).
29. For a discussion on gladiators' representation on monuments, see Valerie M. Hope "Fighting for Identity: The Funerary Commemoration of Italian Gladiators," *Bulletin of the Institute of Classical Studies* 44, Supplement 73 (2000): 93–113. For a discussion on how soldiers presented themselves considerably more elaborately (especially those who earned their freedom through service) than their contemporaries, as an attempt to gain status in death that they did not have in life see her "Trophies and Tombstones: Commemorating the Roman Soldier," *World Archaeology* 35 (2003): 79–97.
30. Maureen Carroll, *Spirits of the Dead: Roman Funerary Commemoration in Western Europe* (New York: Oxford University Press, 2006), 247.

monument were family tombs which were still communal in their nature, but held only a few dozen remains as opposed to the later and larger *columbaria*. Typically both the family tomb and the *columbaria* would have privileged locations for the illustrious dead, the patriarch of the family, or the wealthy individual who funded the *collegia* that used the *columbaria*.[31]

In addition to these structures there were also the rectangular house tombs of the middle empire, as well as large circular and polygonal tombs, tower tombs, Ghirza (a local type of tomb found at Ghirza with temple and obelisk tombs), provincial tumuli (round low structures), and the Eastern tombs with rock-cut facades found in Jerusalem and Petra.[32] The tombs and crypts had great variety, ranging from a minimal plot of land consecrated for burial with an area for a picnic-like memorial meal, to full dining rooms with adjacent kitchens able to feed a large group of mourners.[33] Frequently the sarcophagi themselves were equipped with openings or pipelines leading down to the remains, which enabled the mourners to give the food offerings directly to the dead.[34]

Not all monuments to the dead were situated prominently above ground, along the major roads. Romans also injected their memory into the earth through the use of *hypogea*, *columbaria*, and, most famously, catacombs. The catacombs were a late addition to the Roman burial milieu. They were a "public underground necropolis of relatively large religious communities, namely those of Jews and Christians, in Rome and Italian cities outside Rome."[35] These are not to be confused with the *hypogea*, which were small and privately owned. The catacombs were egalitarian (even the very poor could be buried there) and sprawled out with an unsystematic design which tended to have several layers, each one dug beneath the last. Catacomb usage (for either Jewish or Christian communities) probably arose from the *columbaria* that were used both by burial associations and wealthy families as early as the first century BCE.[36] Radiocarbon dating has determined that the Jewish catacombs were initiated by the first

---

31. For the sheer amount of data of Roman graves and grave structures, Toynbee's *Death and Burial* remains an indispensable text (101ff).
32. Toynbee, *Death and Burial*, 199.
33. Toynbee, *Death and Burial*, 119–26.
34. For more information on the elaborate funerary meals see Graydon F. Snyder, *Ante Pacem: Archaeological Evidence of Church Life Before Constantine* (Revised ed.: Macon, GA: Mercer University Press, 2003), 41; Toynbee, *Death and Burial*, 62; Caroline Walker Bynum, *Resurrection of the Body in Western Christianity, 200–1336* (New York: Columbia University Press, 1995), 53.
35. Toynbee, *Death and Burial*, 234.
36. Carroll, *Spirits of the Dead*, 261.

century CE, which counters the belief that the Christian catacombs predated those of their Jewish neighbors.[37] There is debate among scholars as to whether or not there was the comingling of graves; however, for the most part it is accepted that in the early period there was no expectation of exclusivity regarding burial.[38] This non-exclusivity in burial practices is further reinforced by the fact that there was no explicit Christian prohibition of burial with non-Christians until the time of Charlemagne in 782.[39]

There are some 35 or 36 known Christian catacombs lining the major ancient highways that radiate from Rome, some of which are pre-Constantinian, such as the oldest portions of the Catacomb of Saint Callistus (the Sacrament Chapel) and part of Lucina Catacomb (the Double Chamber). The catacombs were used for more than the disposal of the remains of the dead. It was here that the extended Christian community gathered to remember their dead. While the idea that they were the locations where Christians hid from the Roman persecutions is almost certainly false, these catacombs were visited by the living in order to honor the dead in much the same way that non-Christian Romans gathered at the graves of their important dead. Despite the issues of group size (space was limited, so large groups would have been impossible), it is clear from the graffiti and structures present in the Catacomb of Priscilla that memorial meals for the dead were practiced there.[40]

Catacomb burial flourished through to the early fourth century. However, catacombs stopped being expanded by the end of this century, at which point the majority of burials were taking place in conjunction with new basilicas. When Jerome discussed his visits to the catacombs late in the century, it is clear that these locations were no longer being

---

37. Leonard V. Rutgers, "Radiocarbon Dates from the Jewish Catacombs of Rome," *Radiocarbon* 44 (2002): 541–7.

38. Carroll, of modern authors, is nearly alone when she argues that at least as far as catacomb usage goes there was no comingling (*Spirits of the Dead*, 261). Mark Johnson, "Pagan-Christian Burial Practices of the Fourth Century: Shared Tombs?" *Journal of Early Christian Studies* 5 (1997): 37–59 and Éric Rebillard, *The Care of the Dead in Late Antiquity* (Cornell Studies in Classical Philology 59; Ithaca, NY: Cornell University Press, 2009) observe that the six Jewish catacombs seem to have been exclusively Jewish, but that was more likely a matter of familial decision and family burial than a religious distinction; however, Boyarin argues against a clear distinction between Jewish and Christian groups, especially during the first several centuries – exactly the period of catacomb development which could imply that even these included some Jewish Christians. Daniel Boyarin, *Dying for God: Martyrdom and the Making of Christianity and Judaism* (Stanford, CA: Stanford University Press, 1999).

39. Rebillard, *Care of the Dead*, 29.

40. Carroll, *Spirits of the Dead*, 263

used for interment and perhaps were only infrequently visited, not yet locations for pilgrimage other than the macabre fascination of schoolboys:

> While I was a boy at Rome being educated in the liberal arts, on Sundays I used to tour the tombs of the apostles and martyrs with others of the same age and inclination and frequently to enter the crypts, dug deep into the earth, that sheltered – on the walls on either side of us as we entered – the bodies of those buried there. Because everything was so dark, so that the saying of the prophet was almost fulfilled, "let them descend living to the dead."[41]

The catacombs continued to be places of pilgrimage until the translation of relics of the saints caused them to be ignored and then ultimately forgotten by the ninth century.

Monuments to the Important Dead

The most striking monuments in and around Rome were, and continue to be, those that were erected for the important dead: especially, yet not exclusively, emperors and their families. These grand monuments were constructed by those with the most wealth and power, and with potentially the greatest stake in how they would be remembered. Memory for an emperor was not simply a desire to escape the oblivion of anonymity, but also had very practical repercussions for the family and their hopes for dynastic successors. Their monuments sought to cement the claims of their heirs:

> Having identified this motive for the funerary monument's design, one perceives that the tomb was not simply a monument to a dead ruler, but, perhaps more significantly, an accession monument as well, erected either by an emperor for himself out of concern for his descendants or by an heir to validate his claim to the throne.[42]

The form of the monument may well also have been intended to force the viewer to re-enact the funerary rituals, while at the same time providing an image of the empire that the emperor most wanted to be

---

41. Jerome, *Ezech.* 557.254 (PL 25.0345A-B), trans. in Michael Roberts, *Poetry and the Cult of the Martyrs: The Liber Peristephanon of Prudentius* (Urbana: University of Michigan Press, 1993), 158–9. For more information on Jerome's student years in Rome see J. N. D. Kelly, *Jerome: His Life, Writings, and Controversies* (New York: Harper & Row, 1975), 21–3.

42. Davies, *Death and the Emperor*, 74. We will see in the next chapter that for Constantine the construction of shrines was a monument for himself, while the epitaphs of Damasus were an attempt to claim to be the heir to the respect and power of the martyrs.

remembered for. Trajan's Column, for example, forced the viewer to circumambulate in order to view its frieze, which spiraled from the base toward the top.[43]

The monuments to the emperors ensured a particular memory, not only of the emperor, but also of their image of Rome. For instance, the Mausoleum of Augustus was not only a tomb but also a war monument that celebrated the life of Augustus and presented for history the military prowess of Rome. Through the association of this monument with the *apotheosis* of Augustus, the monument was "a vital means of guaranteeing his descendants divine patronage, and thus setting them above potential pretenders to the throne."[44] Likewise, those emperors who died early, leaving behind less than glorious memories, were buried hastily, without fanfare, in tombs that may have commemorated their family but presented no image of Rome. Nero, who expressed the desire that his body should be immediately cremated so that it would not be desecrated, was interred in a family tomb in Domitii. Caligula's body was likewise cremated, and so hastily done that it was only halfway burnt, and was buried in a shallow grave. It was only later, after his sisters returned from exile, that they had it exhumed and properly reburied in a tomb.[45]

It was not only the emperors' and their families' tombs that held a special status in the minds of the Romans. There is a tradition that Virgil's tomb was venerated as a cult center and locus for pilgrimage.[46] Another report states that Pliny "was the proud owner of one of Cicero's villas, and of the ground where Virgil [was buried]. He used to keep the great poet's birthday with a scrupulous piety, and he always approached his tomb as a holy place."[47]

Who Cares for the Dead?

What the monument should be, as the word itself suggests, should be aimed more to the memory of posterity, than to the present time of grace.[48]

---

43. Davies, *Death and the Emperor*, 127ff. See also above n. 24.
44. Davies, *Death and the Emperor*, 172.
45. Davies, *Death and the Emperor*, 17. For a discussion on the pitfalls of cremation see David Noy, "'Half-Burnt on an Emergency Pyre': Roman Cremations Which Went Wrong," *Greece and Rome* (Second Series) 47 (2000): 186–96.
46. R. D. Williams, "Changing Attitudes to Virgil: A Study in the History of Taste from Dryden to Tennyson," in *Virgil* (ed. D. R. Dudley: London: Routledge and Kegan Paul), 119.
47. Samuel Dill, *Roman Society from Nero to Marcus Aurelius* (London: Macmillan, 1905), 165.
48. Cicero, *Nonius* 32.17, author's trans.

The Family

The family was the primary institution in charge of the burial and care for the memory of the deceased. It was up to the family, or the extended household including freedmen, freedwomen, and slaves (if the family could afford it) to ensure that the proper rites were carried out immediately following the death of the individual, as well as to pay for the construction and procurement of a tomb, including the inscription, if any.

The family was also responsible for the care of the tomb, and commemoration of the death of the individual. They would share meals, which ranged from relatively simple offerings to the deceased to elaborate feasts. These memorial repasts to the dead took place *at the location of the tomb*. They were not instances where the family gathered together to commemorate the loss of their loved one inside the safety of their homes, or in the comfort of their own dining rooms. Instead, they traveled outside the city walls, to the specific location of the remains of their family member, in order to share the meal with the departed.

This travel of individuals or groups of family members from their homes to the specific location of the graves of their dead in order to participate in ritualistic meals should be considered a form of pilgrimage. Granted, this pilgrimage did not require much sacrifice, or involve the pilgrim traveling a tremendous distance; however, it did involve a shift in boundary, a transition through a limen to be in one specific location in order to engage in a specific ritual that was required of the family. The requirement may not have been decreed by law, but it was ensured by custom. I will argue in subsequent chapters that this local pilgrimage to the graves of the dead by their family was quite possibly the humble beginning of the Christian pilgrimages to the shrines of the saints to celebrate not the day of their death, but rather the day of their birth into their heavenly life.[49]

Voluntary Associations

There is a degree of debate surrounding exactly how expensive it would have been to bury a corpse in the Mediterranean world but was certainly something that not every family could afford. It may have been as inexpensive as 10–20 drachmae in the late Hellenistic period.[50] Or the total cost of interment, inclusive of more than the purchase of a simple

---

49. See Yasin, "Funerary Monuments"; "Commemorating the Dead."
50. Thomas Nielsen et al. "Athenian Grave Monuments and Social Class," *Greek, Roman and Byzantine Studies* 30 (1989): 412.

monument, could have been priced well out of the reach of the majority of the population, somewhere in the 100–500 drachmae range.[51]

Due to the expense of, and the desire for, individual burials (and the memorialization that came with them), a relatively new group became a prominent player in the burial of Romans in the first several centuries of the Common Era: voluntary associations, or *collegia*.[52] Associations existed that were primarily focused around a particular profession, religious group, or collection of people who took care of the burial of their members, not unlike an insurance policy, with the added benefit of getting together to eat and drink periodically in memory of the other members of the group.[53] For ease of organization, John Kloppenburg divides these groups into Sacerdotal Colleges (or Sacred Sodalities) and Private Associations.[54] The former were characterized by elite membership and were established by an act of the senate; the latter had no official status, and tended to have a non-elite membership. There were also three subgroups found within both groups: *Collegia tenurorum* (burial),[55] *Collegia*

---

51. Graham J. Oliver, "Athenian Funerary Monuments: Style, Grandeur and Construction," in *Epigraphy of Death: Studies in the History and Society of Greece and Rome* (ed. Graham J. Oliver: Liverpool: Liverpool University Press, 2000), 59–80.

52. Debate exists regarding the members of *collegia*, and what their motivations were. Essentially, the debate concerns whether the very wealthy would have participated in these groups, and, if they did, whether they also participated in the communal burial that they offered. See Jinyu Liu, *Collegia Centonariorum: The Guilds of Textile Dealers in the Roman West* (Leiden: Brill, 2009) 271ff. For a discussion on the applicability of *collegia* to Pauline communities (including a good introduction to *collegia*), see Richard S. Ascough, *Paul's Macedonian Associations: The Social Context of Philippians & 1 Thessalonians* (Tübingen: J. C. B. Mohr, 2003); Philip Harland, *Associations, Synagogues, and Congregations: Claiming a Place in Ancient Mediterranean Society* (Minneapolis, MN: Fortress Press, 2003); Wayne A. Meeks, *The First Urban Christians: The Social World of the Apostle Paul* (2nd ed.: New Haven, CT: Yale University Press, 2003); John Kloppenburg and Stephen Wilson, eds., *Voluntary Associations in the Graeco-Roman World* (New York: Routledge, 1996).

53. Ramsay MacMullen, *Enemies of the Roman Order: Treason, Unrest, and Alienation in the Empire* (Cambridge, MA: Harvard University Press, 1966), 174 discusses this as essentially burial insurance.

54. John S. Kloppenburg, "Collegia and *Thiasoi*: Issues in Function, Taxonomy and Membership," in Kloppenburg and Wilson, eds., *Voluntary Associations*, 16–30.

55. There is little debate regarding the existence of voluntary associations in Roman society which were formed solely for the commemoration of their dead members. However, despite this concord, there is some degree of disagreement about how early they began to function explicitly and primarily as funerary societies. Carroll (*Spirits of the Dead*, 44) argues that there was a functioning *collegia* which existed for the purpose of the burial of its members from the Society of the Cult of Silvanus (*Lex familiae Silvani*) as early as 60 CE. This is several hundred years earlier than Kloppenburg asserts.

sodalicia (religious) and professional associations.⁵⁶ Burial may have been accomplished through a common fund that each member paid into on a monthly basis, or it may have been an offering made by the individual members of the community once one of their members died.

Samuel Dill correctly notes that: "The primary object of a multitude of colleges, like that of the worshippers of Diana and Antinous at Lanuvium, was undoubtedly [...] the care of the memory of their members after death."⁵⁷ This work of memory was performed through the dutiful interment of the dead as well as through the frequent (typically at least monthly) communal meal held by the *collegia* in honor of their deceased members. These affairs had a reputation for being, or at least descending into, drunken debaucheries. Describing similar practices among the Christians, Tertullian was quick to point out that the money given by Christians for the care of their members was not spent "upon banquets nor drinking parties nor thankless eating houses."⁵⁸ Philo of Alexandria likewise was critical of the debauchery of the associations when he observed that these groups were only interested in drunkenness and "outrageous conduct."⁵⁹ Both of these instances were criticisms of *collegia* by those who sought to distance themselves from the tarnished reputation of such societies, primarily because the common features (e.g. consumption of meals, burial of members) that they shared with the *collegia* would have led outsiders to fail to distinguish between them. Consequently in this case Philo and Tertullian were forced to draw boundaries around their practices that were not self-evident.⁶⁰

These groups became responsible for the physicality of the burial and disposal of the corpses. They also provided a location and an organized means for the commemoration of the individual. It may seem that *collegia* had replaced the role of the family insofar as the care of the dead is concerned, and this, in many regards, was the case. Often, however, the families of the deceased were still involved in the decision-making process surrounding the care of their corpse.⁶¹ There was often a good deal of co-operation between the family and the association, where either the

---

56. See also Liu, *Collegia centonariorum*.
57. Dill, *Roman Society*, 259.
58. Tertullian, *Apol.* 39.3–6 (PL 1.0740A; Glover LCL 250).
59. Philo, *In Flacc.* 136, trans. in Ramsay MacMullen, *Roman Social Relations, 50 B.C. to A.D.* (New Haven, CT: Yale University Press, 1974), 284.
60. See Frederik Barth, *Ethnic Groups and Boundaries: The Social Organization of Culture Difference* (Long Grove, IL: Waveland Press, 1998).
61. John Patterson, "Patronage, Collegia and Burial in Imperial Rome," in *Death in Towns: Urban Responses to the Dying and the Dead, 100–1600* (ed. Steven Bassett: Leicester: Leicester University Press, 1995), 23.

family would contribute their input to the burial of the individual in the *columbaria* or the association would contribute money to the family to supplement the costs associated with burial.[62]

No matter who undertook the care of the dead, there was a noticeable decline in the number of grave-markers toward the end of the third century throughout the empire.[63] One has to wonder if it was simply a coincidence that during precisely this period of decline in the general interest in memorializing the dead, we start to see the first instances of specifically Christian burials. Did the emergent Christian church, a marginalized group which was beginning to express its identity both to itself as well as to the larger Roman world, now pick up the tools of memorization that had been previously used as a means of gaining status in death that they did not have in life? These tools of the rhetoric of burial fit well in the hands of the Christians who wielded them, in their own distinctive style, and in their own distinctive locations.

Christian Differentiation, Isolation, Self-Expression

> When the anniversary of their death comes around, we make ritual offerings for the dead as birthday honors.[64]

There is no evidence that suggests the burial practices of the first Christians were unlike those of their Jewish and gentile neighbors. Christians would have been cremated or buried as per the custom of the geographic and ethnic circles in which they lived. There is little to no evidence for a specifically Christian form of burial or burial practices in the New Testament.[65] Burial of the dead throughout the Mediterranean was a common social phenomenon and not one explicitly relegated to the practices of any

---

62. See Jonathan Scott Perry, *The Roman Collegia: The Modern Evolution of an Ancient Concept* (Leiden: Brill, 1999), esp. Chapter Four, where he collects nearly 40 inscriptions depicting such co-operation between family and association.

63. Ramsay MacMullen, "The Epigraphic Habit in the Roman Empire," *American Journal of Philology* 103 (1982): 233–46.

64. Tertullian, *Cor.* 3.3 (PL 2.0079A-B), trans. in Nicola Denzey, *The Bone Gatherers: The Lost Worlds of Early Christian Women* (Boston: Beacon, 2007), 135.

65. Perhaps the only exception is Paul's discourse in 1 Cor. 8:1ff about the consumption of food sacrificed to idols, which may have been aimed at the participation of Christians in the consumption of memorial meals for the dead. See also Charles A. Kennedy, "The Cult of the Dead in Corinth," in *Love and Death in the Ancient Near East* (eds. John H. Marks and Robert M. Goods: New York: Four Quarters, 1987), 227–36; Meeks (*First Urban Christians*, 162) argues that it was highly likely that these early Christian communities continued the memorial meals: "Nothing would seem more natural than for Christians of Paul's groups, for whom common meals were already so important, to hold funeral meals for deceased brothers as well – either separately, or as part of the Lord's Supper."

individual cult. It was not until the end of the second century that specifically Christian sepulchral art began to be produced.[66] As we have seen, burial was a means by which an underclass could present itself as important and worthy of respect. Consequently, it would be in keeping with the practices of other Roman subgroups that the early Christians would seek self-expression and perhaps more importantly legitimacy through sepulchral art. But I would also argue that it made sense for Christians to take time in developing their own language of burial which simultaneously recalled, and deviated from, the practices of their neighbors. This delay would be especially noticeable, as there was no specific theological significance to their initial burial practices.

While the practices, at first, were not significant theologically, it is important to note that Christians fundamentally altered the Roman understanding of death. While there was the belief in the spirits of the underworld, as made clear by the ubiquity of the phrase *"Dis Manibus,"* there was never any real desire to depict the dead as "members of a new and separate afterlife."[67] Christians, on the other hand, approached death in two distinct ideas. One was that the individual was not dead, but merely sleeping. Paul, in the first century, is the earliest known Christian writer to discuss the notion that the departed Christian brethren are in this state (1 Cor. 15:18ff). This view would ultimately become the most prevalent in Christian literature, and one way in which burial inscriptions are identified as Christian is through the usage of language referencing death as sleep. Once Christian burial became more established, rather than dedicating the dead to the spirits of the underworld, they were more often proclaimed to be "resting here" or "sleeping here": *"hic dormit."*[68] Second, in concert with this understanding was the idea that it was possible for the soul of the deceased to be in the company of God awaiting the resurrection. The deceased, and especially the martyred saint, existed

---

66. Of course it is always difficult to interpret these images concretely; see Ross Kraemer, "Jewish Tuna and Christian Fish: Identifying Religious Affiliation in Epigraphic Sources." *Harvard Theological Review* 84 (1991): 141–62.

67. Valerie M. Hope, *Roman Death: Dying and the Dead in Ancient Rome* (London: Continuum, 2009), 39. This can be seen, especially through the desire for the important dead to act on behalf of the living, and the occasional transformation into "ancestors." However, it is notable in that their role in death is decidedly focused on the living as opposed to existing in a new state *post mortem*.

68. See Carroll (*Spirits of the Dead*, 272) for a discussion of the usage of *"hic dormit"* in Christian epigraphy. She notes that Christian epitaphs, "do not read as pagan epitaphs often do, as bitter lamentations of the loss of life" (273). It may have been only in death that Christians believed that life began, as is evidenced by the celebration of the "birthdays" of the martyrs.

in two distinct locations simultaneously: sleeping in the grave and awake in the presence of God in heaven. This dual nature of the dead would eventually become tremendously important in developing of the understanding of the efficacy of being in the presence of the martyr's remains. Through prayer at the graves one could interact with the resting martyr, who was simultaneously in the presence of God.

The Origins of Christian Burial

> Duty to remember the martyrs or duty to support the destitute, the duty to bury the dead played a significant role in the construction of a Christian identity throughout the third century and at the beginning of the fourth. [69]

The presence of Christian burial is extremely well attested in ancient Rome: there are between 30,000–35,000 specifically Christian epitaphs, which come from as early as the late second or early third century. Initially, Christians were buried next to their pagan and Jewish neighbors with no theological or soteriological mandates for an exclusively Christian burial or burial location; there would not have been any hesitation in burying Christians with their non-Christian neighbors, and even after Christians developed "cemeteries" and catacombs in the second or third century where they were exclusively buried[70] there were no doctrinal prohibitions against private Christians who wished to be buried with those outside of the *ekkelesia*.[71]

Christianity as a Voluntary Association

Much of the modern scholarship looking at the relationship between *collegia* and the emergent Church has been done by New Testament scholars, and has focused almost exclusively on Pauline communities.[72] Even

---

69. Rebillard, *Care of the Dead*, 100.
70. Caroll, *Spirits of the Dead*, 261. However, the exclusive nature of Christian burial is a matter of debate, as is the clear identification of Christian iconography; Kraemer, "Jewish Tuna." Also, the issue of exclusivity is not as clear cut as it might have been. Mark Johnson in his work on the possibility of pagans and Christians being buried together provides a good introduction to the various canonical laws, or more specifically the lack thereof, surrounding the specific locations of Christian burial. Johnson ("Pagan-Christian Burial Practices," 38), examines exclusivity in both Christian and Jewish contexts and concludes that it was more likely a matter of a close group being buried together than an issue of theological importance.
71. Cf. Carroll, *Spirits of the Dead*, 161.
72. For a discussion on this see: Ascough, *Paul's Macedonian Associations*; Pieter W. Van der Horst, *Ancient Jewish Epitaphs: An Introductory Survey of a Millennium of Jewish Funerary Epigraphy (300 BCE – 700 CE)* (Kampen: Kos Pharos, 1991), 118.

if the comparison between the emergent Church and voluntary associations is not perfect, it aids us in our quest for a greater understanding of the world in which these communities developed, how these communities viewed themselves in general, and how they were viewed by outsiders with regard to their burial practices in particular. The analogies between *collegia* and the early Church, both Pauline and working into the second and third century, far outweigh the minor divergences.[73] I am inclined to argue that those who dispute the similarities may be attempting to shield the early church from the taint of association with non-Christian gentile practices.

Ann Marie Yasin argues that the analogous structure to which we should compare the early Christian groups is not the *collegia*, but rather the family.[74] However, as we have seen, especially regarding burial, this is a false dichotomy. Both the early Christian communities and those who joined voluntary associations sought to replicate the role of the family in the remembrance and the commemoration of their dead. It is true that the parallel between the early churches and *collegia* is not precise, but neither is a comparison with the family. While the Church took care of many of the functions of the family, it was not as if participation in the Church eradicated all familial loyalty. Ramsey MacMullen has dismissed Yasin's notion that the collective identity of the group outweighing familial identity was unique to Christians, observing the "ubiquity of *mausolea* and *hypogea* built close to basilicas by families that could afford them, keeping themselves to themselves."[75] The truth seems to have been somewhere in between: the church provided a focus for burial, in much the same way as did the *collegia*. In neither case, however, did the group practice completely eliminate the desire for individual memory. When they had the money, the individual or their family sought to distinguish themselves from the larger population for the preservation of their own memory. I will discuss Augustine's analysis of *ad sanctos* burial in Chapter Three; however, it is worth noting that for Augustine the only thing that burial near the saint did for an individual was to allow them to be *remembered* (and prayed for) as an individual (by members of the group – both the local group as well as the group who visited the site only because of the presence of the saint) more than if they had been buried elsewhere.

---

73. E.g. in Meeks, *First Urban Christians*.

74. Yasin, "Commemorating the Dead," Cf. Carroll, *Spirits of the Dead*, 264; Valeriy A. Alikin, *The Earliest History of the Christian Gathering: Origin, Development and Content of the Christian Gathering in the First to Third Centuries* (Leiden: Brill, 2010), 17.

75. Ramsey MacMullen, "Christian Ancestor Worship in Rome," *Journal of Biblical Literature* 129 (2010): 597–613; see also Yasin, "Funerary Monuments."

Yasin too quickly claimed both that Christian identity overwhelmed the desire for the individual to be remembered as an individual, and that this desire was unique to Christianity. However, MacMullen in turn too quickly dismissed the idea that Christians saw themselves as a new family and structured their burial around normative behavior for the familial unit. Even within familial *hypogea* and the larger *columbaria* there were locations of greater or lesser prominence. These conspicuous locations went to the important dead of the family. Similarly, in many, if not all, Christian catacombs and burial basilicas there were locations where the important dead (martyrs, saints, bishops) were interred. The important feature that both the early Christian burial practices and those of the *collegia* shared was the fact that they collectively took care of their dead. They venerated them as a group, which exceeded yet built upon the previous Roman tradition of hereditary tribute.

It also needs to be considered whether or not Christian groups saw themselves as voluntary associations: there is one theory that asserts they may have intentionally organized themselves as *collegia* in order to gain legal status for the administration of their cemeteries, although this is regarded as improbable.[76] In the few instances where Christians explicitly make reference to *collegia* (and burial within that group) the Christian authors attempted to define the boundaries between these groups by casting the non-Christian groups in a negative light. Even then, however, there were no absolute prohibitions against a Christian being a member of other *collegia*. Cyprian complained that in addition to offering sacrifices to idols during the persecutions in the mid-third century, Martialis (a Spanish bishop) also visited the *collegia* and ate at their banquets. Not only did Martialis dine with these groups, but he also buried his sons "among profane sepulchers," in essence burying them with those outside of the Christian community.[77] Here, then, we have a Christian bishop, Martialis, who frequented the banqueting of the *collegia* and buried his son in association with them. While Cyprian was not pleased with this behavior, it was only once Martialis became a *lapsi* and sacrificed to idols that he needed to be removed from the episcopal seat. His association with *collegia* was looked down upon, but was not sufficiently inappropriate for his removal from office. One can conclude

76. Rebillard, *Care of the Dead*, 47.
77. Cyprian, *Ep.* 67.6. Cyprian refers to these groups as "strangers," yet if Martialis had been feasting with them, it is unlikely that he meant strangers in the sense of the unknown, but rather in the sense that they were not part of the Christian community. This is also echoed in the contemporaneous Commodianus, *Inst.* 2.29.12–13. See Rebillard, *Care of the Dead*, 51.

from this that it was not expected that the burial of Christians, in the mid-third century, had to take place with their own group, or even that the Church would take care of the burial of all of its members (whether they liked it or not). Christians – even bishops and their families – were free to bury their dead however they pleased; it was noteworthy, but not forbidden, when they ignored their Christian family and buried them "among profane sepulchers."

The Koimeterion Debate

From at least the time of Tertullian and Hippolytus there was an understanding that (at least some) Christian communities took care of their dead collectively. There has been, however, significant debate as to where it was that these early groups buried their brethren. Typically we think of groups burying their dead in a cemetery that was collectively owned by that group for that purpose. Indeed, this practice eventually would become the norm for the Christian community. The term "cemetery" developed out of usage by early Christians, although the meaning that they ascribed to the term, especially in the early third century, is by no means clear; however, we can be sure that the modern concept of a cemetery is decidedly anachronistic when applied to the third century, and as such cannot be used accurately in the Roman context. Traditionally, the Greek *koimeterion* (and its Latin derivative *coemeterium*) has been translated as "cemetery," although its roots more strongly imply a resting place, or dormitory – which coincides well with the Christian notion of death as sleep. The earliest usage of the term can be found in Tertullian and Hippolytus, although it is clearly picked up by the fourth century as exemplified in Eusebius.

Hippolytus is commonly attributed to have the made first recorded usage of the term in reference to a Christian cemetery in his diatribe *Philosophumena*[78] (often translated as *Refutation of all Heresies*), against Callistus. In Book 9, Hippolytus recounted how the then-Bishop Zephyrinus – having apparently been duped by the trickster Callistus – turned to Callistus for help with the clergy, and also set him in the position of overseer of the cemetery (*koimeterion*):[79]

---

78. This is a text that had previously been attributed to Origen, but seems now to be universally attributed to Hippolytus and should be dated to early in the second century. Zephyrinus was bishop of Rome from 199–217, and was succeeded by Calistus.
79. See also Carroll, *Spirits of the Dead*, 3.

After [Victor's] falling asleep, Zephyrinus having had [Callistus] as a coadjutor in the management of the clergy, honoured him to his own detriment, and sending for him from Antium, set him over the cemetery.[80]

Here Hippolytus described the succession of Roman episcopal authority, from Victor's death ('falling asleep') to Zephyrinus, who acted quickly in appointing Callistus to oversee the *koimeterion*. Ever since Giovanni Battista de Rossi in the mid-nineteenth century it has been assumed that the *koimeterion* discussed here is the catacomb that bears the name of Callistus. This catacomb includes the important "Crypt of the Popes" and is generally dated between the latter half of the second century and the first half of the third.[81] If this was the case (that the formation of the first catacomb was decreed to be overseen by a church authority), then the care of the dead and the role of the catacomb was clearly important to the third-century church. The construction of this catacomb would have been long before the cult of the Martyrs was in full bloom, but it undoubtedly laid the seed for burial to have been an ecclesiastically controlled phenomenon.[82]

Recent scholarship, however, has called into question this convenient reading of the *Philosophumena* on a number of grounds. Eric Rebillard convincingly argues that, not only was there no episcopal oversight of the care of the dead at this early date, but also that De Rossi was philologically lazy.[83] *Koimeterion/coemeterium* never referred to what we think of as a cemetery, but was rather the individual tomb where the individual

---

80. Hippolytus, *Haer.* 9, trans. F. Legge, *Philosophumena; or The Refutation of All Heresies* (London: Society for Promoting Christian Knowledge, 1921), 128.
81. Giovanni Battista de Rossi, *La Roma sotterranea cristiana* (Rome: Cromolitografia Pontificia,1864). Amy Hirschfield calls a good deal of De Rossi's work into question, arguing that the use of the catacombs was a trope for justifying and creating a cultural memory specifically for nineteenth-century Christians: "The authors of much of the past academic and popular writing about the catacombs viewed them as sites of connection to a venerated religious past that could be used to legitimize the religious present." Amy K. Hirschfield, "An Overview of the Intellectual History of Catacomb Archaeology," in *Commemorating the Dead: Texts and Artifacts in Context: Studies of Roman, Jewish, and Christian Burials* (eds. Laurie Brink and Deborah A. Green: New York: Walter de Gruyter, 2008), 12. In the nineteenth century, an understanding of the past was created as a way of bolstering the religion of the time; consequently, modern scholarship must take a good deal of the conclusions that were made with a healthy grain of salt.
82. Snyder accepts this view, stating that this "sets a date for the public appearance of Christianity" and noting that the church having property was a matter of public record. Snyder, *"Ante Pacem,"* 159.
83. Rebillard, *Care of the Dead*, 2ff.

Christian rested (slept).[84] Through an analysis of Tertullian's *Apologia*[85] and John Chrysostom's *De Coemeterieo et de Cruce*,[86] where Chrysostom at Antioch used the *koimeterion* to refer to one tomb out of many possible tombs, Rebillard concludes: "In the middle of the fourth century, for the Christians of Antioch, it is clear that the word *koimeterion* does not mean 'cemetery'."[87] Clearly, this does not mean that there were not some dead who were overseen by Callistus; only, that it was not the entirety of the catacomb now known as that of Callistus. There was the possibility that this property was that of the family of Pope Zephyrinus that may have been given over to community use through the traditional Roman understanding of patronage.[88] This is a distinction without a difference. Either way, Hippolytus demonstrated that Zephyrinus was concerned with the resting places of (at least) the important dead and was establishing episcopal control over them, through the appointment of Callistus to oversee the *koimeterion*, whether the property was owned collectively by the church or privately by Zephyrinus's family.

Tertullian first used the term *koimeterion* for the Christian location for burials in his treatise *De Anima*,[89] which probably dates to early in the third century. He recounted a story, that he proclaimed was "well-known," of a corpse "voluntarily" making room in a "cemetery" for another that wished to be buried there.[90] If *koimeterion* only referred to the resting places of the important dead, why is it that in the evidence from Tertullian no mention is made of the mobile corpse being noteworthy for any reason other than the fact that it made room for a partner? Likewise, when Eusebius discusses the *koimeterion* he does not explicitly refer to

---

84. Rebillard, *Care of the Dead*, 4–7.
85. However, in this case it seems clear that 39.5–6 indicates that while there may not have been explicit episcopal oversight of burial, there was a common fund for charitable giving, and part of that fund was to be used for the burial of the poor. This problematizes the idea that the burial of the common dead at the end of the second century was entirely left in the hands of the family of the deceased.
86. PG 49.393.
87. Rebillard, *Care of the Dead*, 7; Carroll, *Spirits of the Dead*, 261, looks to the same texts, specifically Tertullian, *Ad Scapulum* 3.1 and *Apol.* 39.5–6, as well as Origen's *Hom. Jer.* 4.3.16, to determine that there were Christian cemeteries in Alexandria during the third century
88. Carroll, *Spirits of the Dead*, 261; Paul F. Bradshaw et al., *The Apostolic Tradition: A Commentary* (Minneapolis, MN: Fortress Press, 2002), 191; Carolyn Osiek, "Roman and Christian Burial Practices and the Patronage of Women," in *Commemorating the Dead*, (eds. Laurie Brink and Deborah A. Green: New York: Walter de Gruyter, 2008), 246.
89. See Carroll, *Spirits of the Dead*, 2.
90. Tertullian, *An.* 51. For other early uses of the term, see Hippolytus (*Com. Dan.* 4.51) and Origen (*Hom. Jer.* 4.3.16).

martyrs or *martyrium*. According to Eusebius,[91] the Emperor Valerian (reigned 253–260) forbade Christians from gathering at or entering what are so-called cemeteries, and it is often assumed that this prohibition was quite possibly out of concern over the cult of the martyrs. However, given Eusebius's enthusiasm for the cult of the martyrs, one would expect him to have made reference to the martyrs in the *koimeterion*, if the only usage for *koimeterion* was in reference to the resting places of individual martyrs; yet he did not.

Rebillard cites at length a text from John Chrysostom which makes explicit reference to a gathering at a *martyrium* and then notes that the place is also called a *koimeterion* due to the fact that the corpses are not dead, but resting.[92] This analysis is instructive, although I am not convinced of the entirety of his argument and it would seem to be that the identificiation of *martyrium* and *koimeterion* might not be as clear-cut as Rebillard supposes. However, even if *koimeterion* did not refer exclusively to the burial locations of the special dead, as noted previously we must be careful not to equate the term with a walled and isolated cemetery in a modern city.

John Bodel agrees with Rebillard's conclusion that Christian burial in the third century could not have been something that Christians sought to perform outside of the confines of traditional Roman burial.[93] That is to say, there must have been a comingling of Christians and non-Christians in the same burial compounds due to the sheer numbers of Christian dead in the third century.[94] Also, there was no corporate ownership of cemeteries by Christians: "[T]here were no official Christian funerary societies or indeed specifically funerary *collegia* of any sort, and the notion of a central 'Church' at this date, let alone of an official cemetery 'owned' by a church, is doubtful."[95] I am not entirely convinced by his conclusions that there *must* have been comingling of graves in the catacombs in equal portions during the third century, [96] and he himself does not seem too convinced either when he notes that people associated with a particular cult "might

---

91. Eusebius, *H.e.* 7.11.10.
92. Rebillard, *Care*, discussing John Chrysostom, *Coemet.* (PG 49.393).
93. John Bodel, "From Columbaria to Catacombs: Collective Burial in Pagan and Christian Rome," in *Commemorating the Dead*, 179.
94. For a discussion of the legality of burial mingling, and the conclusion that there could have been no legal prohibitions of such, see Johnson, "Pagan-Christian Burial Practices."
95. Bodel, "From Columbaria to Catacombs," 202–3.
96. Bodel, "From Columbaria to Catacombs," 186.

band together in death in collective cemeteries."[97] Yet, one cannot convincingly argue that there was no comingling of graves either – indeed, there is significant evidence to the contrary.

What distinguished early Christian burial churches from other types of ancient collective funerary monuments was the nature of the community commemorated. Inclusion in the group was based not on blood ties, rank, offices, or profession, but on membership in a church. The collective memorials, whenever they developed, and by whomever they were owned, did not merely commemorate individual departed Christians but reinforced the collective identity of the church community. The individuals expressed their new identity, their new "family", in *memorium* through their burial.

Burial of the Poor

> The last and most important duty of piety is the burying of strangers and the poor.[98]

Christian groups set up common funds for the burial of those who could not provide for their own burial. At the time, this was nearly unprecedented: even the *collegia* required payment from their members, whereas the Christians would care for their fellow members regardless of their ability to contribute fiscally. The early second-century text *The Apology of Aristides* observed with pride the fact that not only did Christians give to the poor, they buried them as well.[99] Aristides noted here that Christians contributed to a communal fund for the care of the poor, including burial. He was also quick to observe that their burial was taken care of carefully. Even the indigent Christian was afforded a proper burial; he or she was not unceremoniously dumped into the communal mass grave at Potter's Field as were the many unwanted corpses of Rome. Tertullian argued in his *Apology* that burial of the poor was an act of charity commensurate with other acts of kindness toward those who cannot take care of themselves. The money given to the common fund was not spent on drinking, "but to support and bury poor people, to supply the wants of impoverished boys and girls, the aged veteran, or to relieve the shipwrecked sailors, those who have been banished to the prisons in the Metellan islands on account of their faith."[100] In much the

---

97. Bodel, "From Columbaria to Catacombs," 192.
98. Lactantius, *Div. Inst.* 6.12.25. (PL 6.633B), author's trans.
99. Aristides, *Apol.* 15.
100. Tertullian, *Apol.* 39.3–6 (PL 1.467B–468A), author's trans. Despite these passages

same way as it was a function of a family to provide for the burial of its members, so too did the Christian community care for its members. Despite this, we shall see in Chapter Three that those opposed to the reverence paid to martyrs at their tombs, and even those who sought to promote that reverence, were quick to point to the drunkenness of the crowds as detrimental to the martyr cult. Tertullian attempted to draw a boundary between the practices of the church and other groups with their own common funds (i.e. the *collegia*), which may not have been clear to the outside observer, and which may have in many cases been an exaggeration: the burial of the poor and feasting and drinking may not have been mutually exclusive.

There is one other early text which clearly demonstrates the understanding of a communal burial location, and specifically notes the presence of the poor as well as episcopal participation in the distribution of funds for the burial of the poor. This is *The Apostolic Tradition*, an anonymous text that is typically attributed to Hippolytus.[101] Chapter 40, which deals with burial, does not exist in the Latin manuscript, so is probably not from the earliest layer of the text, but exists in some other versions. According to the text:

> Do not let them overcharge people to bury a man in the cemeteries. For it is the property of every poor person. Only let the one who digs be given the wage of the worker with the price of the tiles. And those who are in that place, who take care [of it], let the bishop support them, so that [the burial place] shall not become burdensome to any who come to those places.[102]

We can see in all of these accounts that the general focus on the burial of the poor was not out of a particular interest in burial as a specifically

---

which discussed the burial of the common Christians, John Bodel ("From Columbaria to Catacombs," 182) argued that bishops prior to Constantine were not interested in the burial of the common poor.

101. *The Apostolic Tradition* went through a complex editing process including several layers and consequently does not represent the practices of any one early Christian community (Bradshaw et al. *Apostolic Tradition*, xi).

102. Trans. Bradshaw et al. *Apostolic Tradition: A Commentary*, 192. This is translated from the Sahidic Coptic version. Similar content is found in both the Arabic and Ethiopic versions, as well as in two derivatives: the *Canons of Hippolytus* (generally thought not to have been written by Hippolytus) and the *Testamentum Domini*. The latter advises individuals to provide burial locations if they have one, and for the church to allow the poor the use of a burial location *if* it has one. This "if" implies that the text must have been written for a large intended readership, and that there were some church communities that did not have a common burial location, but there were others (emphasis on the plural) that did. In other words, he was writing both for groups who had communal burial plots and those that did not.

Christian phenomenon, but rather as an act of charity.[103] The church became the benefactor or patron of those members who could not afford burial on their own. Not all Christians by the third century were buried by or with their Christian brethren, and many continued to be buried with their family or voluntary association. The burial of the important dead, however, was performed collectively by their co-religionists.

The Burial of the Important Christian Dead

Many recent works have covered the place of martyrdom in emergent Christianity.[104] The origin of Christian martyrdom, like many origin stories, is shrouded in debate, and is not necessarily a debate that I am interested in engaging with fully at the moment. The history of Christian martyrdom traces its roots to the *ad hoc* persecution of Christians by Nero, and then the subsequent and more systematic persecutions in the ensuing centuries. Our earliest martyr account outside the New Testament, although it does not in fact refer to an actual death scene, comes from Ignatius in his epistle to the church in Rome; here, Ignatius wrote of his desire to be thrown to wild beasts.[105] This passage reveals an understanding that his co-religionists might have an interest in his remains, and he expresses his wish not to bother anyone with that burden. In his retelling of the events Eusebius observes that his wish to be cast to the beasts was honored, yet the reason for that desire was not. After he was torn apart by the beasts the faithful gathered together "the harder portions of his holy remains."[106] Subsequently they were taken to Antioch where, wrapped in linen, they were seen as an "inestimable

---

103. Aristides *Apol.* 14 notes that some of these practices were performed by Jewish populations as well.

104. Indeed almost any work that deals with the formative events of the third, fourth, and fifth centuries has to touch on the topic to one degree or another. Many relevant works are cited elsewhere in this book. For a representative sample see Hippolyte Delehaye, *Les origines du culte des martyrs* (Bruxelles: Bureaux de la Société des Bollandistes, 1912), still considered one of the best works on the subject; Frend, *Martyrdom and Persection*; G. W. Bowersock, *Martyrdom and Rome* (Cambridge: Cambridge University Press, 1995); Boyarin, *Dying for God*; Ulrich Volp, *Tod und Ritual in den christlichen Gemeinden der Antike* (Supplements to Vigiliae Christianae 65; Leiden: Brill, 2002); Vasiliki M. Limberis, *Architects of Piety: The Cappadocian Fathers and the Cult of the Martyrs* (Oxford: Oxford University Press, 2011); Candida Moss, *Ancient Christian Martyrdom: Diverse Practices, Theologies, and Traditions* (New Haven, CT: Yale University Press, 2012); *The Myth of Persecution: How Early Christians Invented a Story of Martyrdom* (New York: HarperOne, 2013).

105. Ignatius, *Ep. ad Rom.* 4.

106. Eusebius, *M. Ign.* 6 (PG 5.987B–988A), trans. Alexander Roberts et al., *ANF* 1:131.

treasure." In many, if not most subsequent martyr narratives, this desire by the Christian community to gather the remains (even soaking up the blood) of the martyrs would become a central feature.

Those who could not be martyrs themselves were inundated with stories and tales of martyrs. They were discussed as early as the late first or early second century in Rev. 6:9, where the author describes seeing the souls, under the altar, of those who had died violently as a witness to Jesus.[107] It is interesting that the author makes a connection between martyrs and the altar at such an early date, as it was not until several centuries later that there was a consistent connection between altars and the graves of martyrs.[108] But even before the physical presence of the martyr was felt in the church structure, martyr accounts were being read to Christian congregations in the second century.[109] In the middle of the third century, Cyprian observed that it was the responsibility of the clergy to care for the burial of martyrs, which may be a sign of the importance of the remains of the martyrs, or of the power of the clergy.[110]

The martyrdom of the individual transformed violence and death into a means of creating meaning in a universe in desperate need of having order imposed on it. As Castelli aptly states: "By turning the chaos and meaninglessness of violence into martyrdom, one reasserts the priority and superiority of an imagined or longed-for order and a privileged and idealized system of meaning."[111] It must be remembered that the threat of martyrdom was not as pervasive as is frequently imagined (both now and then), yet this did not diminish its effectiveness as a focal trope for the emergent church.[112]

This system of meaning was produced through the retelling of martyr acts which exemplified those who had overcome the physical body and suffering of this world, dying in spectacular displays of defiance and faith. The hagiographic material was important, but so too was the

---

107. I do not want to enter into the debate concerning the dating of Revelations here; however, I personally lean towards the later-date end of the spectrum, in part because of the association between the altar and martyrs.

108. It was possible that the Eucharist was performed at the graves of the martyrs at least as early as the late second century. See Alikin "The Earliest History," 103.

109. *M. Pol.* 20 and *M. Perp. et Fel.* 1.5 indicate the reading of these tales within the Church (see also Alikin "The Earliest History," 171).

110. Cyprian, *Ep.* 12.2.1.

111. Castelli, *Martyrdom and Memory*, 34; Stephanie L. Cobb, *Dying to Be Men: Gender and Language in Early Christian Martyr Texts* (New York: Columbia University Press, 2008). See also Lucy Grig, *Making Martyrs in Late Antiquity* (London: Duckworth, 2004). Grig pushes that date back through the fourth and fifth centuries.

112. On the overstatement of persecution see most recently Moss, *Myth of Persecution*.

construction of martyr shrines, which may have been the first Christian building endeavors. Initially these shrines were small memorial chapels, or *cellae memoriae*.[113] However, the first graves to the martyrs were not necessarily elaborate structures, but were more likely indistinguishable from the graves for the common Christian.[114] As the common Christian's graves were indistinguishable from the common Roman graves, these early martyr graves could have been easily overlooked. Indeed, Ambrose's "discovery" of the graves of Protasius and Gervais in 386 corroborates the idea that Christians (at least in Milan) did not believe that all of their martyrs' graves were well marked. Aside from the Arians, who had political reasons for not trusting Ambrose, there appeared to have been no hesitation among his congregation to accept that bodies from unmarked graves were truly those of martyrs.

Martyrs were also buried in the Christian catacombs, once these began to be constructed. Here too martyrs were laid in simple graves without apparent elaborate inscriptions or decoration. There is some evidence of pilgrim graffiti surrounding various niches, and others would eventually have inscriptions placed over them, even if they did not initially have inscriptions when the corpse was interred.[115] Despite the evidence for martyrs' graves in the catacombs, "the martyr cult developed more above the ground in special edifices called *martyria*."[116] Initially these were housed in small buildings, which both marked the grave of the martyr and provided room for the local community to gather.[117] Snyder describes two pre-Constantine *martyria*, one in Bonn, Germany, and the other in Salona, Croatia. The *martyrium* in Bonn was a small roofed room (3.25 × 2.55 m) which contained two *mensae*. From the incorporation of a bowl into one of the *mensa* as well as pictorial representations, it is clear that food was shared with the community, living and dead. The food was also distributed to the poor. While no martyr's body was discovered at the *martyrium* in Bonn, Snyder observes that it was most likely built next to a non-masonry building which housed the martyr's tomb.[118]

The site at Salona was built around the graves of several martyrs who were believed to have been killed during the Diocletian persecution

---

113. Gillian Mackie, *Early Christian Chapels in the West: Decoration, Function and Patronage* (Toronto: University of Toronto press, 2003), 9.

114. Joseph Donella Alchermes, "Cura Pro Mortuis and Cultus Martyrum: Commemoration in Rome from the Second through the Sixth Century" (PhD thesis, New York University, 1989), 10.

115. Alchermes, "Cura Pro Mortuis," 34.

116. Snyder, *Ante Pacem*, 164.

117. Mackie, *Early Christian Chapels*, 9.

118. Snyder, *Ante Pacem*, 164–6.

(ca. 304). The initial graves were not elaborately decorated, although the subsequent *ad sanctos* burials were inscribed with various notations indicating that they were buried in that location in order to be next to the graves of the martyrs. A small structure was erected in order for the *refrigerium* meals to be celebrated. Snyder observes, however, that it is difficult to date the construction of the building, and due to the distance from Rome he is skeptical that it was an imitation of Constantine's building endeavors.[119]

Eventually *martyria* would serve two purposes: not only did they mark the location of the graves of the martyrs (and thereby preserved their memory), they also organized the space around that grave for the function of the pilgrims (initially from the surrounding area) who visited those locations.[120] One must be careful not to suppose that these places just happened spontaneously. As MacDonald correctly observes, "[P]lace is constructed in the intersection of material conditions, political realities, narrative, and ritual performance."[121]

I want to suggest, therefore, that the martyrs served in the early Church as the important dead of the community, and consequently such martyrs should be viewed as an extension of the Roman important dead. Prior to Constantine they did not have the status of the deceased emperor; rather, they were the important dead within a familial unit. As the church came to fill, or even replace, the functions of the family, so too then did the shrines of the martyrs become the center of those family units as they continued their traditional role of commemorating the dead. The veneration of the saints in this regard was not something radically new to the Christian community, but rather continued previous Roman practice. However, now it was not only the biological family that visited the graves of their important dead, but also the larger spiritual family of the Christian community.

Conclusion

Burial locations and the sarcophagi contained therein both generated and reflected ideas about the community that created them. They indicated the feelings of the community at the time of the death of the indi-

---

119. Snyder, *Ante Pacem*, 166–71. See also J. B. Ward-Perkins, "Memoria, Martyr's Tomb and Martyr's Church," *Journal of Theological Studies* 17 (1966): 20–37.

120. See Andre Grabar, "From Martyrium to the Church: Christian Architecture, East and West," *Archaeology* 2.2 (1949): 97.

121. Mary N. MacDonald, "Introduction: Place and the Study of Religions," in *Experiences of Place* (ed. Mary N. Macdonald: Cambridge, MA: Harvard, 2003), 13.

vidual, but at the same time they also constructed meaning for the future; pre-Constantinian iconographic representations of comfort and rebirth served to remind the community what it (or those with the power or money) deemed to be important.[122] They presented images from sacred literature, reinterpreting them in light of their own current situation and representing them to themselves. As the emergent Church drew upon the practices associated with the commemoration of the dead, through the catalyst of persecution at the hands of the Romans, it began to place an increased emphasis on the remains of the martyrs.

It is true that during the third century and the construction of the Catacomb of Saint Callistus, the body and its burial may not have played a central role in Christian theology; however, it did play a strong role in the *popular* practice of Christians.[123] The location of the grave was the location of the bodies of the fallen brethren, and occasionally the location of the remains of the martyrs who had died as a witness to their faith. It comes as little surprise that these privileged locations would then have been the location of the creation of a Christian identity, of the seat of the Christian cultural memory, as well as a place through which earthly issues of power were negotiated. However, it must be emphasized that this seat of memory was not a uniquely Christian innovation. The location of burial and the structure of the monument had been an important means by which Roman society had sought to (re-)create the memory of their loved ones, as well as structure their own history with an eye toward the future. In subsequent chapters I will discuss how this location of cultural memory underwent dynamic changes both in the grandeur of the monuments and also in the contest for what behaviors were seen as appropriate at the grave and shrine.

I would like to take a moment and offer a brief reflection on why it was the location of burial or relics that solidified Christian popular practice,

---

122. Snyder, *Ante Pacem*, 26ff. Snyder lists 12 signs used by Christians prior to the fourth century, most of which are symbols of comfort: the lamb, anchor, vase, dove, boat, olive branch, Orante, palm, bread, Good Shepherd, fish, and vine with grapes. Kraemer, "Jewish Tuna," notes that many of these are of course also seen on Jewish graves; consequently, clear identification is more difficult than simply identifying a fish.

123. See Brown, *Cult of the Saints*, 2, on the hazards of putting too strong an emphasis on a two-tiered construction of ancient Christianity. This is not my intention here. The body of the martyr and commemoration thereof may have been important to the episcopate (as it developed). It was not, however, something that the bishops felt was their responsibility to care for until such a time as the martyr cults themselves were perceived as a rival locus of religious power, at which point they embraced it so as to control it.

and not other factors. Or to put it another way, why these practices and locations were the ones that were as significant as they were: one does not see the same degree of debate and controversy surrounding other important practices (e.g. baptism or *agape*) as we see surrounding the cult of the martyrs. Death is universal. Death and the meaning associated with death is something that must be navigated. Ian Kines observes that:

> Human societies are moulded by their dialogue with death: frameworks, by which individuals and communities establish their own world-picture, are stretched and then defined by the need to comprehend and incorporate mortality.[124]

While I make no claims to be able to speak for all of human society everywhere, I can confidently assert that in Roman society during the early centuries of the Common Era, death, the treatment of corpses, and the commemoration of the dead were items of significant concern. This social concern may be especially true as there was, as Judith Perkins put it, an "increased emphasis on the body in the late Republic and early Roman Empire."[125] According to Perkins this emphasis on the body developed directly into the body as a suffering body. It was through this emphasis not only on the body, but especially on the body as a body that suffers that ultimately gave Christianity a good deal of its authority and even appeal to the broader Roman population who if they knew anything at all about Christians it was that they suffered and died for Christianity, precisely because that was the way in which Christians described themselves, both to themselves and to others.[126] The representation in early Christian narrative of a community of sufferers and the persecuted worked not simply to represent a realistic situation so much as to provide a self-definition that enabled the growth of Christianity as a whole.[127]

Through the popularity of the (hagiographic) narratives that Christians told about themselves, they came to identify their movement with suffering and death. Hagiographic material was rife with images of the death and dismemberment (in graphic detail) of those who had died for their faith. Ultimately it does not matter if all of the hagiographic material is historically accurate. Such material was taken to be valid and used

---

124. Ian Kines, "Dialogues with Death," in *The Archaeology of Death* (eds. Robert Chapman et al.: Cambridge: Cambridge University Press, 1981), 83.
125. Perkins, *Suffering Self*, 6. Here Perkins is drawing upon Foucault's *The Care of the Self*. Vol 3 of *The History of Sexuality* (trans. Robert Hurley: New York: Vintage 1988 [1984]).
126. Perkins, *Suffering Self*, 211.
127. Perkins, *Suffering Self*, 12

accordingly. It was this narrative of suffering and death that came to be a dominant feature in the identity of Christians.[128]

Christians came to identify with suffering, and the sporadic instances of extreme suffering came to be interpreted not as humiliating executions but rather as happy endings that did not signal the death of the individual, but rather their crowning achievement and efficacious entrance into the presence of God, the ultimate victory over corporal failures. The death of the martyr was celebrated, by the late second century, annually as the martyr's "birthday" rather than the anniversary of his or her death.[129] Annual festivals surrounding the "birthday" of the martyrs was not the only early Christian ritual that could be tied with death. Indeed, possibly one of the earliest of all Christian rituals, baptism, also focused on death: "from the standpoint of the Mediterranean ritual world, therefore, baptism according to Romans 6 was an imaginary funeral."[130] Death was part of the very nature of the ritual world of the early Church, and it should come as no surprise that those who died for that Church should likewise achieve crucial significance, as they had overcome their mortal body and been reborn in the presence of God.

Once the martyrs were interred the locations of their graves could become infused with a purpose and importance that was closely tied with the martyrdom of the individual, but this did not happen in all cases. The commonly held belief that there were unmarked martyr graves meant that they could readily be "discovered," as we shall see with Ambrose late in the fourth century. Yet other memorials were known from a very early date, and I will discuss some of these locations in detail in the subsequent chapters. When they were known (or believed to have been known) and remembered, the graves of the important men and women were the first physical locations that were seen as sacred by Mediterranean Christians. They were constructed as space, and then the rituals which surrounded this space were constructed and ultimately would reflect the power dynamics in subsequent centuries as various ecclesial and political figures sought to establish their power upon the martyrs' graves.

Future work may well delve more deeply into the question of why it was that the martyrs' graves, and ritual acts carried out in their proximity, came to play so large a role in the development of Christianity in

---

128. Perkins, *Suffering Self*, 200.
129. Tertullian, *Cor.* 3.3 (PL 2.0079A).
130. Richard E. DeMaris, *The New Testament in its Ritual World* (Cambridge: Cambridge University Press, 1981), 64–5.

the fourth century. This work aims primarily to explain the *how* of that development as opposed to the *why*. However, I will hazard a cautious hypothesis on the latter question: the graves of the martyrs were the perfect combination of pre-existing Roman practices (associated with commemoration), they were popular with the church faithful who were inundated with hagiographic material, and perhaps most importantly they were nearly virgin territory for the construction of Christian identity. The development of rituals, narrative, and space were the perfect medium for influential leaders to exploit.

Chapter Two: To Build Up
The Erection of Shrine and Reputation

> The "stars" that held the attention of a fourth-century Christian were the tombs of the martyrs, scattered like the Milky Way throughout the Mediterranean.[1]

> All the Temples of Rome are covered with soot and cobwebs, the city is shaken to its very foundations, and the people hurry past the crumbling shrines and surge out to visit the martyrs' graves.[2]

Beginning in 303, the Emperor Diocletian initiated Rome's most dedicated persecution of Christians, confiscating their property (including cemeteries), imprisoning many, and making martyrs out of others. These persecutions served only to further solidify the idea among the Christian community that theirs was a religion destined to suffer, and they were destined to suffer with and for it. Out of that suffering Christians hoped to secure their place in heaven. During this time many followed the instructions that Tertullian laid out over a hundred years earlier, earning the "crown of martyrdom" rather than offering incense to the emperors or handing over their sacred literature.

On April 30, 311 the Emperor Galerius issued an edict in Nicomedia which granted an indulgence to Christians, freeing them from further persecution and granting freedom to those in prison.[3] However, Galerius neither returned the property that had previously been confiscated, nor could he stop all of the persecutions that continued under Maximinus in the East (Egypt, Palestine, and Asia Minor). When Constantine defeated Maxentius on October 28, 312 persecutions of Christians effectively came to an end. It was not until two years after Galerius' edict that Christian properties were returned to them, when Licinius and Constantine issued the Edict of Milan.[4]

---

1. Peter Brown, *The Making of Late Antiquity* (Cambridge MA: Harvard University Press, 1978), 100.
2. Jerome, *Ep.* 107.1 (PL 22.677), trans. in Cythia White, *The Emergence of Christianity: Classical Traditions in Contemporary Perspective* (Westport, CT: Greenwood Press, 2007), 107.
3. Lactantius, *Mort.* 34.
4. Lactantius, *Mort.* 48. See also Eusebius, *v. C.* 2.39–40. It is worth noting that Eusebius presents Lincinus as a despised villain and not the one who issued the edict

Prior to the early fourth century, martyrdom was held up as an exemplary way to die, something that ordinary Christians were urged by their leaders to seek or accept willingly.[5] The bloody and graphic accounts of their deaths were read aloud in churches so as to inspire others with the dedication and faith of the martyrs. How then were the Christians to retain their identity as a persecuted church, once Christianity became the religion of empire?

Many have argued that the role of the ascetic monk may have eventually taken the place of the martyr, as an ideal and the heir to the image of overcoming the obstacle of the physical body. This process, however, did not fully happen until the fifth to sixth centuries.[6] To see oneself as being part of a group that is no longer being persecuted, but has been persecuted in the past, is not necessarily the same as overcoming the obstacle of the physical body. The archetype of the martyr epitomized the Christian ideal of resistance and struggle against persecution, and their remains became objects of veneration both at the time of their death, and especially once the persecutions came to an end. Eventually even the sacred relics of the ascetic would be venerated at shrines. The style of that veneration came directly from the previously established cult of the martyrs. The fact that the style of veneration drew upon the martyr cult denotes the importance of the martyrs and their shrines in the lives of Christians in the fourth through sixth centuries.

Graves and other *memoria* became the newly decorated archives of the bygone time, the glorious age of the Christian heroes: the martyrs. The cult and the places around which the cult centered came to be one of the primary locations where powerful Christians exerted their control over the construction of Christian memory in the fourth century. The speech acts performed at the graves of the martyrs carried more weight due to the presence of the martyr; their monumental nature gave them (and their

---

restoring both churches and (explicitly mentioned) property that was not used for worship but was still owned communally by the churches. Eusebius was an ardent proponent of the cult of the saints and as such explicitly discussed the return of the glorious martyr shrines to the Church.

5. But perhaps not *too* willingly. The idea of "volunteerism," or voluntary martyrdom, was frowned upon. For a good overview of the scholarship on this topic see Philip L. Tite, "Voluntary Martyrdom and Gnosticism," *Journal of Early Christian Studies* 23 (2015): 27–54. For a discussion on Augustine's dismissal of the Donatist Circumcellions as non-martyrs due to their willingly seeking death see below p. 104.

6. See R. A. Markus, *The End of Ancient Christianity* (Cambridge: Cambridge University Press, 1990); and Peter Brown, "The Rise and Function of the Holy Man in Late Antiquity," *Journal of Roman Studies* 61 (1971): 80–101. For Markus it was precisely the rise of the holy ascetic that served to mark the end of "Ancient Christianity." See also James E. Goehring. *Ascetics, Society, and the Desert: Studies in Early Egyptian Monasticism* (Harrisburg, PA: Trinity, 1999).

builders) tremendous authority, and the power to craft memory around these sites. It was not only the physicality of the location that aided the crafting of the message, but also the ritualistic nature of the commemoration of the martyrs.[7]

Those who built these shrines and inscribed them with meaning would ultimately mimic the martyr, not in their death, but in their intercessory role (by claiming that power for themselves). Just as the martyr was believed to intercede with God on behalf of the Christian, offering prayer to that martyr (in effect bending the ear of God to the plight of the worshiper), so too those who built the shrines made the martyr accessible to those who wished to venerate that martyr. The role of intercessor was tremendously important, and one that would live on in the memory of the community. Aside from the spiritual power that this role provided, it also granted political and social control.

This chapter will examine two of the most important early figures to tap into the power of the martyr cult in the fourth century: Emperor Constantine and Bishop Damasus of Rome. Each, in differing ways, would set the stage for the full development of the Christian use of the physicality of the remains of the important dead as a means of exerting their own image of Christendom and, especially, their place therein. Both had to deal with divisions within the Church, and one of the ways that this was achieved was through control of the physical spaces associated with the martyrs. Through the control of the physicality of the martyrs' remains, they were able to craft the cult of the martyrs into something that allowed them to be the speakers for the dead. They spoke on behalf of the martyrs in both the way that they crafted Christian architecture around the dead, and in the way that the remains became, to a degree that had not been seen previously, the foci of the Christian community. These remains, newly and elaborately enshrined, in turn solidified the power of those who laid claim to them. The graves, tombs, and shrines which were erected for the dead were fashioned by the living to elicit a specific response in those who were living when they were created, but also with an eye toward future generations who would come there to worship. What Constantine and Damasus created at the martyr shrines would shape the way martyrs were revered in the future. In addition, the future power dynamics of the Church and Empire as a whole were directly influenced by the actions of Constantine and Damasus through their use (and promotion of) the shrines of the saints.

Constantine and Damasus thus began to use the bodies of the important dead as a means of expressing and solidifying their power, as well as

---

7. For a discussion on the importance of ritual see Catherine Bell, *Ritual Theory, Ritual Practice* (New York: Oxford University Press, 1992).

cementing the cultural memory that they personally crafted for a Christianity which heretofore had no single memory to which to cling. Through their usage of the memory of the martyrs, Constantine and Damasus were able to shape the very nature of Christian belief in a way that supported their own personal role within Christianity. This would ultimately allow them to influence political, social, and economic forces. This framework set the background for the changes that developed in the latter part of the century with Augustine, Ambrose, Jerome, and Paulinus, all of whom built upon the substructure positioned by Constantine and Damasus.

Despite their role in the rise of the cult of the saints, Constantine and Damasus did not create the cult without antecedents. Marianne Saghy argues that it was because of the basilicas built by Constantine around the tombs of Peter, Paul, and the martyred third-century deacon Lawrence that the cult of the martyrs was able to flourish in Rome: "Constantine did not build upon a living and vigorous tradition of celebrating the martyrs: rather, it was his great imperial 'judgment halls of God' [...] which triggered an interest in the martyrs, and created, at the same time, a convenient spot for glorifying them."[8] While it may be true that the elaborate physical structures surrounding the cult of Peter, Paul, and Lawrence were Constantinian additions, there is considerable evidence for the cult of the saints in previous centuries: there was a long-established interest in the graves of the important dead, and a desire to care for them and associate with them, both in traditional Greco-Roman religion as well as in the Christianity that developed out of it. When he centered his basilicas on the tombs of the martyrs, Constantine was drawing upon the traditions of his Roman predecessors, as well as the importance that the martyrs and saints had in Christianity prior to his reign.

Peter Brown reminds us that "we are dealing with a very old world" when it comes to Rome, in which "changes did not come as disturbing visitations from outside; they happened all the more forcibly for having been pieced together from ancient and familiar materials."[9] Constantine integrated the familiar materials which surrounded the care of the dead

---

8. Marianne Saghy, "Scinditur in Partes Populus: Pope Damasus and the Martyrs of Rome," *Early Medieval Europe* 9 (2000): 275.

9. Brown, *Making of Late Antiquity*, 8. This is also echoed by Markus, *End of Ancient Christianity*, 88–95. Ann Marie Yasin states: "Such material [as Saint Peter's Basilica] constructed directly over the even earlier tombs or memorials of Christian saints bridged the temporal gap between the present of imperially sanctioned and economically ascendant church and its own heroic past of persecuted and victorious martyrs." Ann Marie Yasin, *Saints and Church Spaces in the Late Antique Mediterranean: Architecture, Cult, and Community* (Cambridge: Cambridge University Press, 2009), 1.

in Rome, as well as those which developed surrounding the commemoration of the primarily local martyrs in Christianity. This was not an innovation on his part, as per Saghy: he explicitly drew upon the histories of both (previously opposing) groups and created a new focus for the construction of Christian cultural memory at the tombs of the saints. Likewise, Damasus drew upon Roman epigraphical technique as well as evoking the great Roman poet Virgil in his inscriptions over the martyr's graves. Through this he wanted to tie the Christian Rome of his present to its illustrious pre-Christian past. He also sought to replace Romulus and Remus with another pair of founders: Peter and Paul.[10] Through this act he attached the reputation of Rome to the illustrious founders who had suffered martyrdom there. These actions helped to solidify the centrality of Rome in Western Christendom, and cement Damasus's power as Rome's bishop.

Even as Constantine drew upon previous traditions, his grandiose buildings and focus on the remains of the dead became instrumental in the way that the cult developed later in the century. We can see in both Constantine's building endeavors, and eventually in the epitaphs of Damasus, actions aimed at preserving (or re-creating) the memory of the dead. This recollection of the dead also served to facilitate the creation of the collective memory for the future of Christianity through their commemoration of the cults of the saints. Constantine and Damasus displayed the martyrs, putting them *on show*.[11] They created an image both of the martyrs and, more importantly, of themselves in relation to those martyrs. These acts conveyed a message of harmony and unity arising from the discord and chaos of the past.

Constantine

> To make themselves the master of memory and forgetfulness is one of the great preoccupations of the classes, groups, and individuals who have dominated and continue to dominate historical societies.[12]

---

10. Dennis Trout, "Damasus and the Invention of Early Christian Rome," *Journal of Medieval and Early Modern Studies* 33 (2003): 521.

11. This was done in much the same manner that the Museum of Natural History in New York City put exhibits on show which prompted Mieke Bal's essay on the power of demonstration and those who have the authority (or claim that authority) to present material. Mieke Bal, *Looking In: The Art of Viewing* (Amsterdam: Gordon and Breach, 2001). In both instances, Constantine or Damasus filled a similar constantative role as museum architects and curators where they presented information as the one who possesses knowledge, the one who can inform the viewer about "the truth."

12. Jaques LeGoff, *History and Memory* (trans. Steven Rendall and Elizabeth Claman: New York: Columbia University Press, 1992), 54.

> Public monuments do not arise as if by natural law to celebrate the deserving; they are built by people with sufficient power to marshal (or impose) public consent for their erection.[13]

One dare not approach the subject of power dynamics and their relationship with collective memory present in the fourth century without addressing the abrupt and cataclysmic shift early in the century, ushered in through the legalization of Christianity and subsequent conversion of Constantine. Susan Alcock observes that: "[W]hile social memory is never inert or static, manipulation of the past is most pronounced at times of marked social, religious, or political change."[14] Constantine initiated such a trifecta. It is not surprising, then, that during this period of upheaval, manipulation of the Christian social memory was evident both in Constantine's basilica-building endeavors, which were primarily focused on the cultic locations of the martyrs, as well as in his self-proclamation of apostolic identity through his mausoleum church.

Obviously Constantine's interaction with the church and its bishops did not begin or end with his construction of church structures. It is not the purpose of this chapter to deal with the nuances surrounding every aspect of Constantine's involvement with the Church.[15] However, in the midst of his dealings (if indeed one could posit a singular "Church" at this point) he was responsible for the construction of their first grand structures. The majority of these surrounded the remains of important martyrs and other important graves, and one of the ways that he was influential in the development of Christianity in the fourth century was through these architectural achievements, which bridged the divide between previous Roman monuments to the important dead and the Christian focus on the cult of the martyrs. Through these structures Constantine situated himself as a patron of the martyrs, as well as among the ranks of the apostles themselves through his choice of his own burial location.

When Constantine addressed an assembly of Christian leaders, recorded by Eusebius as Constantine's *Oration to the Saints*, he briefly discussed the veneration given to martyrs which should include: "Songs and hymns, a temperate memorial meal of thanksgiving, without the need for

---

13. Kirk Savage, "The Politics of Memory: Black Emancipation and the Civil War Monument," in *Commemorations: The Politics of National Identity* (ed. John R. Gillis: Princeton: Princeton University Press, 1994), 135.
14. Susan Alcock, *Archaeologies of the Greek Past: Landscape, Monuments, and Memories (W. B. Stanford Memorial Lectures)* (Cambridge: Cambridge University Press, 2002), 32.
15. For further elaboration on Constantine's relationship with the Church see H. A. Drake, *Constantine and the Bishops: The Politics of Intolerance* (Baltimore, MD: Johns Hopkins Press, 2000).

frankincense and fires, but only pure light for the assembled worshipers of God."[16] Throughout the oration Constantine challenged anyone to dispute that the martyrs, through their sacrifice, could not be seen as exemplary in their faith in God. Concerning this passage, H. A. Drake observed: "Constantine's treatment of the martyrs suggests, then, that despite its theological veneer the oration may be read for signs of a more immediate, more political, conflict – for control of the message."[17] It would be convenient, for this work, to posit an early date for this speech, from which we could speculate about a shift in Constantine's attention, subsequently directed toward the martyrs. However, it is nearly impossible to date the "Oration" to any specific date, or even to a specific period in the life of Constantine.[18] Despite the ambiguity surrounding the date of the speech, Drake could have (although he did not) as easily have discussed Constantine's architectural treatment of the martyrs in exactly the same way that he treated them in the *Oration to the Saints*. That is to say, Constantine sought to control the message of the martyrs, and thereby also sought to control the immediate political message through his architectural endeavors surrounding those martyrs. Thus, political power was sought or established through both textual and spatial exertions of ideological control. These architectural endeavors revolved specifically around the construction of basilicas, which housed the martyrs' remains and, perhaps more importantly, the cult that surrounded those remains.

As a religious structure, the basilica was a Constantinian innovation which drew upon previous Roman tradition for its inspiration. Constantine's use of the *genes* of the basilica for his early church structures was a deliberate way to raise the status of Christianity to the highest levels of the Empire. He did not present the Christian basilicas as new temples. Indeed, the physical presence of a Christian church building was not seen as fundamentally the same thing as a temple. The disparity between temple and church (and, by extension, basilica) was primarily because the Christian god was not believed to reside in the church, while the god of the temple was believed to be actually present therein. Constantine deliberately chose the form of the basilica for two reasons, both of which dovetailed nicely with traditional Christian practices: first, the open floor plan of the basilica served admirably as a meeting hall, for congregational worship as well as for the funerary function that would eventually become a central feature as expressed by "funerary basilicas" (essentially, "U"-shaped

---

16. Constantine, OC 12 (PG 20.905), trans. Mark Edwards in *Constantine and Christendom* (Liverpool: Liverpool University Press, 2003).
17. Drake, *Constantine and the Bishops*, 305.
18. For the problems of dating this speech see H. A. Drake, "Suggestions of Date in Constantine's Oration to the Saints," *American Journal of Philology* 106 (1985): 335–49.

covered cemeteries).[19] Second, as the pre-Christian basilica was also the seat of imperial power by incorporating the basilica within Christianity, Constantine established the church as the "throne room of the Emperor of Heaven, comparable to the sanctuary where the living god-emperor received the obeisance of his subjects."[20] Eventually, Constantine would proclaim in 333 that any individual, at any point in a trial, could demand and was entitled to be heard by an ecclesiastical tribunal.[21] Consequently, the basilica became not only a seat for the "Emperor of Heaven," but in fact a judgment hall for earthly concerns before a Christian tribunal.

Constantine focused the majority of his architectural energy on the construction of churches and basilicas which were connected to the cult of the martyrs (and often served as burial locations for those desirous of *ad sanctos* burial). However, the first church structure that Constantine built in Rome was instead focused on the destruction of the memory of an entity that had supported Maxentius against Constantine: the Equestrian Guard (*equites singulares*). Early in his reign Constantine sought to use architecture as a means of presenting his version of history. To build the Lateran Basilica (started in 313 and probably completed in 320), Constantine razed the Equestrian Guard's barracks. This was part of the process by which Constantine sought to present himself as the liberator of Rome, and establish his predecessor as a tyrant. The Lateran Basilica ultimately served as the cathedral in Rome for more than a millennium.[22]

The vast majority of Constantine's other basilicas were constructed near or over the tombs of the martyrs. One additional exception was

---

19. See Ramsey MacMullen, "Christian Ancestor Worship," 601; Richard Krautheimer, "The Constantinian Basilica," *Dumbarton Oaks Papers* 21 (1967): 115–40.

20. Krautheimer, "The Constantinian Basilica," 127. For more on Constantine's construction in general see Richard Krautheimer, *Corpus Basilicarum Christianarum Romae* 5 vols (Vatican City / New York: Pontifico Instituto de archeologia Christiana / Institute of Fine Arts, 1937–77); *Early Christian and Byzantine Architecture* (4th ed: New York: Penguin Books, 1986); Paul Corby Finney, "Early Christian Architecture: The Beginnings (A Review Article)," *Harvard Theological Review* 81 (1988): 319–39; J. B. Ward-Perkins "Memoria, Martyr's Tomb and Martyr's Church," *Journal of Theological Studies* 17 (1966): 20–37. Gregory Armstrong provides a review of the 23 known Constantinian Churches (and several more ambiguous churches) in "Constantine's Churches," *Gesta* 6 (1967): 1–9. Halgren Kilde observes that Constantine's churches "were informed by clear social, political and religious agendas. Constantine's churches were symbols of both religious and imperial power." Halgren Kilde, *Sacred Power Sacred Space: An Introduction to Christian Architecture and Worship* (New York: Oxford University Press, 2008), 40.

21. *First Sirmondian Constitution*; see also Drake, *Constantine and the Bishops*, 344ff.

22. For a discussion on the use of this as a destruction of memory see John R. Curran, *Pagan City and Christian Capital: Rome in the Fourth Century* (New York: Oxford University Press, 2000), 76–96.

the Church of the Apostles on the Via Appia, which was the location of a pre-existent cult location dedicated to Peter and Paul. This may well have been the second major structure Constantine erected in Rome, and if it can be dated to the earlier period of Constantine's constructions (perhaps as early as 314) then it is worth noting that Constantine's second basilica also was not centered around the tomb of a martyr, but was located over the catacombs where there was an active cult to Peter and Paul.[23] It is telling that there was a cult center at this site, even if the remains of Peter and Paul had been removed (if they had even been there in the first place). The eventual focus of Constantine's buildings would be on the remains of the saints; however, the physicality of the saints' bodies does not seem to have been his primary focus early on.

The exact dating of the construction of many of Constantine's church structures is far from clear. Both Krautheimer and Armstrong observe that it was not for roughly a decade after the initiation of the Lateran Basilica that Constantine began the construction of the most elaborate of his martyr basilicas in Rome: that dedicated to Peter.[24] According to the *Liber Pontificalis,* Constantine showered lavish gifts upon the Church.[25] Regarding the important locations of the tombs of Peter and Paul, Constantine (at the request of Bishop Sylvester) built a basilica for Peter. In that structure Constantine laid Peter's coffin, which was surrounded by five feet of bronze on all sides, and hung a 68-kg golden cross above the encased coffin.[26] It is notable that Constantine exhumed Peter's coffin, violating the Roman prohibition against disturbing a corpse so as to

23. For an overview of the literature on the shrine to Peter and Paul on the Apian Way see, David L. Eastman, *Paul the Martyr: The Cult of the Apostle in the Latin West* (Atlanta, GA: Society of Biblical Literature, 2011), 71ff. Inscriptions have been found and dated to prior to 260 discussing banqueting in honor of Peter and Paul on the Appian Way near the Catacombs. These inscriptions demonstrate the desire that the Apostles would intercede on behalf of the banqueters.

24. Krautheimer, "The Constantinian Basilica," and Armstrong, "Constantine's Churches."

25. The *Liber Pontificalis* should not be read uncritically, as in many cases it appears to be, if not a work of explicit propaganda from the end of the fifth or beginning of the sixth century, close to it. The dominant theory concerning the authorship of the first section of the book is that of Louis Duchesne, who argues that it was written by a single author who relied on the *Catalogus Liberanus* and the *Papal Catalogue,* writing sometime in the late fifth century; Louis Duchesne, *Etude Sur le Liber Pontificalis* (Paris: E. Thorin, 1887). For our purposes the text of the *Liber Pontificalis* may both tell us about the events of the early fourth century, and shed light on the way that pivotal period in Christian history was (or was desired to be) perceived a century later. In either case, it cannot be seen to be the final word in historical veracity, as we will see shortly as regards its discussion of the construction of the basilica built to commemorate Paul.

26. *Lib. Pont.* 34 (PL 127–8).

move it into its new resting place. With this reburial, the tomb of Peter became a glorious basilica resplendent with precious metals and architecture, the most impressive of Constantine's basilicas in Rome. In the middle of this grandeur, Constantine placed his name and the name of his mother, ensuring that their memory was forever associated with the construction of the basilica, for all to see when they came to honor the apostle. This was not his first construction in Rome, but it was perhaps his crowning achievement in the Eternal City.

The shrine to Paul, the second martyr upon whom the Roman Church would eventually base its authority, may have been built by Constantine or it may have been a pre-existing shrine. The elaborate Basilica that the author of the *Liber Pontificalis* mistakenly attributes to Constantine was constructed at the end of the fourth century, after the existing structure was destroyed (383/384).[27] The larger structure ensured that there was ample room for the numbers of pilgrims who would eventually visit the final resting place of the Apostle to the Gentiles. If the initial Pauline shrine was a Constantinian construction, then due to its small size it would have been completed much more quickly than the Petrine basilica.[28] There has not been any significant discussion as to why Constantine would have initiated such a lavish basilica honoring Peter, but simply rushed a significantly smaller shrine honoring Paul. I suggest three possible reasons for this: first, that the cult of Paul on the Ostian Way was a well-established entity by the 320s, and as such Constantine wanted to ensure that it had a functioning building as quickly as possible; second, that the structure pre-dated Constantine, and there was no reason to add to it when there were so many other structures to be completed (unlikely, as Constantine felt no qualms when he demolished the structure on the Appian Way which housed the banquets that Christians held on behalf of Peter *and* Paul *ad Catacumbas*) before beginning the construction of the Church of the Apostles; third, that this shrine was in fact on private property, as the *Liber Pontificalis* suggests when it recounts that one Lucina reinterred Paul's corpse on her own property after she convinced the bishop to remove both Peter and Paul from their second burial location *ad Catacumbas*.[29] If

---

27. For a detailed discussion of this structure see David L. Eastman, *Paul the Martyr: The Cult of the Apostle in the Latin West* (Atlanta, GA: Society of Biblical Literature, 2011), 72ff.
28. Armstrong, "Constantine's Churches," 3.
29. *Lib. Pont.* 22 (PL 127–8). Due to the prevalence of Lucina in martyr narratives, it is nearly impossible to determine if she was an actual person in any of the individual narratives, or perhaps shorthand for any number of pious women, or even if she existed at all. On the use of "Lucina" as a generic term for a Christian woman associ-

this shrine was indeed on private land, it may have been that Constantine was hesitant to disrupt a private chapel.

Constantine practically surrounded Rome with his church structures, making their presence obvious to all. Charles Odahl suggests that Constantine chose these peripheral locations so as not to offend "pagan" sensibilities, which would have been affronted had he built a Christian monument in the center of the city.[30] However, this ignores the importance of the specific locations that Constantine did choose – namely, those associated with already extant martyr cults. In addition to the structures discussed above, he also built basilicas to Agnes (at the request of his daughter, Constantina) and to Lawrence, and a basilica commemorating both Peter the Exorcist and Marcellinus. Lawrence's basilica is especially notable as it included "stairs of ascent and of descent to the body of the holy martyr Lawrence."[31] Here we have evidence of a clear desire for the body to be accessible to pilgrims. Previously, this must have been a pilgrimage site, of which Constantine wanted to take advantage (or celebrate), while at the same time ensuring that the pilgrims would still be able to continue the previous practice of visiting the actual tomb of the saint. Constantine took pains to ensure that those who wished to visit the corpse of Lawrence could still do so – importantly, the practice of venerating the corpse was not a Constantinian addition to the cult around Lawrence, but rather a tradition that he was maintaining.

The final basilica to be discussed here is the Basilica Apostolorum, which Constantine built for the remains of the apostles and was also the one that would house his own mausoleum in his new capital, Constantinople. Constantine desired that Constantinople should rival Rome in physical splendor, as well as in Christian sanctity. As recounted decades later by Paulinus of Nola, in *Carmen* 19:[32]

---

ated with the saints and specifically their remains see Kate Cooper, "The Martyr, the Matrona, and the Bishop: The Matron Lucina and the Politics of the Martyr Cult in Fifth- and Sixth-Century Rome," *Early Medieval Europe* 8 (1999): 297–317; Nicola Denzey, *The Bone Gatherers: The Lost Worlds of Early Christian Women* (Boston: Beacon, 2007), xv.

30. Charles Matson Odahl, *Constantine and the Christian Empire* (London: Routledge, 2004), 147. He also claims that Constantine deliberately did not choose the traditional temple style when erecting Christian buildings as the temples were "polluted with the stains of pagan idolatry" (148).

31. *Lib. Pont.* 61 (PL 127–8).

32. It is ambiguous if the relics were translated by Constantine himself or his son. Jonathan Bardill places the dates of translation for Andrew and Luke in 336, with Timothy's remains arriving in 356; Jonathan Bardill, *Constantine, Divine Emperor of the Christian Golden Age* (Cambridge: Cambridge University Press, 2011), 369. For a discussion on the translation of these relics and the dating thereof see Cyril Mango,

> When Constantine was founding the city named after himself [...] he should likewise emulate Romulus' city with a further endowment – he would eagerly defend his walls with the bodies of apostles. He then removed Andrew from the Greeks and Timothy from Asia; and so Constantinople now stands with twin towers, vying to match the hegemony of the great Rome.[33]

This translation of Andrew and Timothy is echoed by Eusebius in his *Vita Constantini*.[34] It was in the Basilica of the Apostles, in Constantinople, that Constantine decreed that he be interred once he died, "thereby ensuring that he would become in fact as well as name *isapostolos*, 'the equal to the apostles'."[35] Here Constantine clearly erected a monument for himself which promoted, through the use of the remains of whichever apostles were available to him, the idea that he was at least equal to those sent out by Christ. The memory that he created in those who visited (and eventually those who would come to develop his shrine as a cult center) was that he was with The Twelve, at the center of their communion. Constantine was buried in his basilica in 337.[36]

"Constantine's Mausoleum and the Translation of Relics," *Byzantinische Zeitschrift* 83 (1990): 51–62; David Woods, "The Date of the Translation of the Relics of SS. Luke and Andrew to Constantinople," *Vigiliae Christianae* 45 (1991): 286–92.

33. Paulinus of Nola, *Carm.* 19.329ff. (PL 61.530B–531A), trans. P. G. Walsh, *The Poems of St. Paulinus of Nola* (New York: Paulist Press, 1975), 142. Composed January 405.

34. Eusebius *v. C.* 3.40, 8 (PG 20.905). For a detailed analysis of the dating of the translation of the relics of Luke and Andrew to Constantinople see Woods, "Date of the Translation," cf. R. W. Burgess "The Passio S. Artemii, Philostorgius, and the Dates of the Invention and Translations of the Relics of Sts. Andrew and Luke," *Analecta Bollandiana* 121 (2003): 5–36, especially 29. It is also worth noting that Constantine kept his intentions of being interred in this location secret until he neared his death.

35. Drake, *Constantine and the Bishops*, 11.

36. See Mark J. Johnson, *The Roman Imperial Mausoleum in Late Antiquity* (Cambridge: Cambridge University Press, 2009), 123 on differing theories concerning the dating of the structure and the debate over whether the church stood alone or included a separate mausoleum for the burial of Constantine. Due to the paucity of information (and occasional contradictions in what little exists) there are a variety of theories. Johnson ultimately argues that the basilica as designed by Constantine was a "building that blurred the distinction between church and a mausoleum" (128) but that the mausoleum was later separated from the church, which accounts for the discrepancies in the ancient sources. Johnson also dates the translation of Luke and Timothy to June 22, 336. However, the debate surrounding the dating of the translation and arrival of these remains is far from settled. For my purposes it may not matter if the apostles were interred prior to Constantine, as the message that his mausoleum sends would be clear either way. Ultimately, the fact that Paulinus and Eusebius present, as fact, that the remains were there prior to Constantine is sufficient to demonstrate the cultural memory of their presence.

Constantine's construction of his own shrine is notable. After engaging in the construction of basilicas for over two decades, Constantine decided to build one in his new eastern capital of Constantinople with a dedicated mausoleum for the apostles, including himself. Not only was he actively controlling the way he would be remembered, through the incorporation of the remains of the apostles; he was ensuring that there would be an active cult presence. He claimed for himself something as close to divinity as his new religion would allow. Jonathan Bardill may have gone a bit too far when he suggested that Constantine did not see himself as an additional apostle but rather as Christ, the figure that the apostles revolved around.[37] Or if he did, Constantine's claim might not have been astonishing to his audience, which was used to the notion of a divine emperor.

The idea that an emperor would be considered divine by the time of Constantine was nothing new; indeed, by the end of the second century it had become almost a formality.[38] Divinity was traditionally not something that the emperors claimed for themselves – at least not in Rome, although this varied in the provinces – but rather something that was conferred upon them *after their death* through the ceremony of *apotheosis*. Consequently, any cult site that was constructed to honor the newly divine emperor was begun by his heirs.[39] Constantine ensured his own cult center by permanently linking himself to the cult of the martyrs (which he diligently promoted) and more radically claiming, if not divinity, then a privileged place in the presence of God. If one examines the behavior of Christians surrounding the cult of the saints, as well as the behavior of their non-Christian predecessors in relation to various gods, Constantine may well have claimed an equal title to that which other emperors had had bestowed upon them *post mortem*.

We have evidence for the power of the cult that developed around Constantine's mausoleum from Socrates Scholasticus in his *Ecclesiastical History*. Here, Socrates relates what appears to have been the greatest atrocity (among many) that Macedonius, the bishop of Constantinople, committed: the movement of the body of Constantine in 358, after an earthquake

---

37. Bardill, *Constantine, Divine Emperor*, 376.
38. Penelope J. E. Davies, *Death and the Emperor: Roman Imperial Funerary Monuments from Augustus to Marcus Aurelius* (Austin: University of Texas Press, 2004), 10–11. Simon Price calculates that 36 of the 60 Emperors from Augustus to Constantine received posthumous divinity. Simon Price, "From Noble Funerals to Divine Cult: The Consecration of Roman Emperors," in *Rituals of Royalty: Power and Ceremonial in Traditional Societies* (eds. D. Cannadine and S. Price: Cambridge: Cambridge, 1987), 56–105.
39. For a detailed list of shrines constructed by the heirs of the emperors see Davies, *Death and the Emperor*, 11ff.

which damaged the basilica, to another church near the body of the martyr Acacius. There was a strong devotional following of the emperor at his tomb, and after the translation chaos and bloodshed ensued:

> The church where the coffin lay that contained the relics of the emperor Constantine threatened to fall [...]. Macedonius, therefore, wished to remove the emperor's remains, lest the coffin should be injured by the ruins. The populace getting intelligence of this, endeavored to prevent it, insisting "that the emperor's bones not be disturbed [..."], and thus two parties were formed on this question [...]. Macedonius, in total disregard of these prejudices, caused the emperor's remains to be transported to the church where those of the martyr Acacius lay. Whereupon a vast multitude rushed toward that edifice in two hostile divisions, which attacked one another with great fury, and great loss of life was occasioned, so that the churchyard was covered with gore, and the well also which was in it overflowed with blood, which ran into the adjacent portico, and thence even into the very street.[40]

Constantius ultimately dismissed Macedonius, not for the other transgressions (many of them bloody) that Socrates relates, but rather for this removal of the body of Constantine, and the disruption of the cult centered on those remains. One also has to wonder what became of the relics of the apostles which had been translated to the basilica, with whom Constantine had surrounded himself. Sozomen made no reference to their translation, or even concern for their safety. It is entirely possible that the cultic devotion to Constantine, a more recent and immanent hero, had completely eclipsed that of the apostles. If that is the case then even if Constantine only wanted to be the equal to the apostles, the cult which developed at his tomb made him their superior.

There are two aspects of this event that have been overlooked in modern scholarship. First, most of the attention has been focused on the elevation of Constantine to the same stature as that of the apostles. This is a potent observation coming from a Christian perspective, yet for the majority of the Roman population the inverse may have been more dramatic: Constantine elevated the apostles to the level of the emperor. It was only within Christian circles that the apostles had significance; by being interred with the apostles' remains Constantine proclaimed that they were due the honors afforded to the emperor himself.

Second, it has seemingly been overlooked that in his translation of the apostles, Constantine took what had been primarily a local tradition honoring local martyrs and important dead (in much the same fashion

---

40. Socrates Scholasticus, *HE.* 2.38 (PL 69.1008C–1008D), trans. Edward Walford and A. C. Zenos, *NPNF*[2] 2:67. Sozomen, *HE* 4.21 recounts this event with nearly identical language; he however does not include the grotesque descriptions of Macedonius with which Socrates graces his page.

as local family groups would have honored their *own* important dead) and created a trans-local cult. The important Christian dead thus became important for Christianity as a whole, and not just for any particular locality. Constantine broke these regional barriers through his radical translation of the remains of the dead, not from the location where they had died to the location where they had lived, but from their old graves to a new grave at a location with which they had had no association during their lifetime. For both Christianity and the Roman world in general, these translations were a fundamental shift in the treatment of the dead, ultimately paving the way for the widespread translations of not only whole corpses, but also the dispersal of much smaller relics beginning later in the century.

Constantine was not the only figure in early fourth-century Rome who sought to use ecclesiastical structures, especially those surrounding the remains of the martyrs, as a means of controlling the cultural memory of the population and establishing his own control after a period of political upheaval. Damasus fought hard to become the bishop of Rome and engaged in an extensive program of inscribing the resting places of the martyrs of Rome, and in doing so established himself, much as Constantine had, as a patron (servant) of the martyrs.

Damasus

> Death is the sanction of everything that the storyteller can tell. He has borrowed his authority from death.[41]

> [W]e will experience our present differently in accordance with the different pasts to which we are able to connect that present.[42]

According to the first book of the *Collectio Avellana*,[43] during the reign of Constantius there arose a period of discord concerning who would be the rightful bishop of Rome. Liberius was elected in 352, only to be exiled three years later by Constantius. In his place Felix II was then elected (perhaps unjustly) in 355. The sources differ on the end of Felix. The *Liber Pontificalis* presents him as condemning Constantius and dying a

---

41. Walter Benjamin, "The Story Teller: Reflections on the Works of Nikolai Leskov," [1936] in *Illuminations: Essays and Reflections* (by Walter Benjamin, ed. Hannah Arendt and trans. Harry Zohn: New York: Schocken, 1968), 94.
42. Paul Connerton, *How Societies Remember* (Cambridge: Cambridge University Press, 1989), 2.
43. With some collaboration from the *Lib. Pont.*

martyr's death at his hands,[44] while the *Collectio Avellana* presents him as dying peacefully after reigning for eight years. With the death of Felix II, Liberius returned to power and completed his previous position, forgiving those who had turned against him. When he too died,

> the priests and deacons Ursinus, Amantius and Lupus, with the holy people, who had been faithful while Liberius was in exile, went to the Basilica of Julius and called for Ursinus to take the place of Liberius as their bishop. However the liars gathered [at the church] in Lucinis and demanded Damasus take the place of Felix as their bishop.[45]

Ultimately Damasus was victorious, and from the years 366–384 he presided as the bishop of Rome. During this time he was a willing participant in open warfare between differing factions of the Christian community in Rome. He had employed violence in order to gain the episcopal seat; according to the Roman historian Ammianus Marcellinus: "Damasus got the best of the strife by the strenuous efforts of his partisans. It is a well-known fact that on one day one hundred and thirty seven dead bodies were found in the basilica of Sicinius […] and the populace who had been thus roused to a state of ferocity were with great difficulty restored to order."[46] Furthermore, Damasus did not shy away from continuing aggression in order both to retain his position and to squash any and all dissention. He was beset by opposition, particularly from those who would have been loyal to Ursinus[47] and also from the Luciferians.[48]

One way in which Damasus sought to solidify his power was through an expansive program of inscriptions over the tombs of the martyrs. Through his focus on the martyrs, Damasus sought to do three things: first, to solidify power as the sole bishop of Rome, presenting himself as the one who brought the martyrs forward for veneration, and acting as an intercessor with the martyr just as the martyr was an intercessor with God;[49] second, to connect the Christian present of Rome with the city's illustrious past;[50] and third, to secure his position (and the position of

---

44. Whereby the much more sympathetic figure of Damasus gathers his bones and buries them appropriately, *Lib. Pont.* 38.
45. *Avel.* 1.5 (CSEL 35.1, 2, 18–22), author's trans.
46. Ammianus, *Res. Gestae.* 27.3.12.
47. See Curran, *Pagan City and Christian Capital*, 138–42.
48. A relatively minor post Nicene splinter group which, following the opinion of Lucifer of Cagliar, rejected the return to the communion of any bishop who had had anything to do with (even if they recanted) Arianism. One specific instance of violence that occurred between Damasus and a Luciferian priest was recounted in Marcellus and Faustinus, *Lib. Pre.* 22 (PL 13.098).
49. See Saghy, "*Scinditur in Partes Populus*," 273–87.
50. For a discussion of the Roman-ness of the martyrs as presented on fourth-

Rome itself) as the center of Western Christendom, due to Rome's possession of the remains of a host of martyrs, most especially Peter and Paul.

Prior to Damasus's beautification of the burial locations of the Christian important dead, Christian epigraphy was not "even particularly literate."[51] Damasus by comparison brought beautifully worked inscriptions into the catacombs and roads leading to the city.[52] Through his presentation of the martyrs, and his control of their history, Damasus sought the aid of these saints to present a unified front against his political opponents. The martyrs, through the inscriptions Damasus provided for them, spoke to the living in a way that solidified Damasus's control of the Eternal City's Christian community. As Damasus could have inscribed the graves of any of the martyrs who achieved the crown in Rome, it must be observed that he chose only those who subscribed to his understanding of Christianity, thus creating a unified body with himself at its head. When he incorporated Hippolytus, the first "antipope,"[53] he was careful to emphasize Hippolytus's return to the unified church, and to establish himself as that church's rightful heir. Damasus's deliberate emphasis on one martyr over another was a way of determining the limits of sacred space, establishing one shrine as important and letting other graves disappear into anonymity. The demarcation of one space as opposed to another as sacred reflected the interests of those with the power to orient their world in such a manner.[54]

Perhaps no other Christian figure from the fourth century borrowed as much of his authority from death than did Damasus. While he was not alone in retelling the tales of the martyrs, his beautification of their shrines supported his own episcopate and crafted the way that history would remember him. It was not only the Christian dead that Damasus conjured to do his bidding: his poetic epitaphs were heavily influenced

---

century gold-glass bases see Lucy Grig, *Making Martyrs in Late Antiquity* (London: Duckworth, 2004).

51. Maureen Carroll, *Spirits of the Dead: Roman Funerary Commemoration in Western Europe* (New York: Oxford University Press, 2006), 270. Here Carroll is making an observation about the very poor quality of Christian epigraphy. Mark Handley observes that this poor quality could have been the result of a false humility, eschewing ostentation, yet none the less desiring memorialization. Mark Handley, *Death, Society and Culture: Inscriptions and Epitaphs in Gaul and Spain, AD 300-75* (Oxford: British Archaeological Reports, 2003), 33.

52. Saghy, "*Scinditur in Partes Populus*," 273–87.

53. A problematic term, not least of all because there was no such thing as a "pope" at the time, let alone someone embodying the office as we think of it today.

54. See Jonathan Z. Smith, *Map is not Territory: Studies in the History of Religions* (Chicago: University of Chicago, 1993), 104–28.

by both the style and content of Virgil, through which he tied the history of Rome to the contemporary history of Christianity while also connecting the heroes of the age of persecution to his modern era of prosperity.[55] When Damasus cited, or made reference to, the past, he was situating himself alongside his intellectual family, claiming them for himself and by extension rejecting the claims of his rivals – and in this way calling his Christian family into communion with their Roman ancestry. The works of Damasus sought to maintain the unity of the Catholic Church (and by very important extension, his own power), and to bridge the boundaries between the Roman and the Christian. These works, then, focused on physical graves of the Christian dead, but drew upon the traditions of Roman inscription and epigraphy.

The style of Damasus's beautification of the graves of the martyrs made his projects immediately recognizable within the tradition of Roman memorialization. Not only did he use "Virgilian prose": he also conformed to more traditional norms of the types of inscriptions, including the form and lettering.[56] Damasus brought the reverence and the respect given by Christians to their martyrs and important dead into the light of the roads and thoroughfares leading to Rome, where they would have been accessible to both the Christian faithful and the pagan traveler alike. This also had the effect of quickly broadcasting the message/memory that Damasus sought to project over a significant geographic area and with speed that would have been impossible had he limited his endeavors to the erection of larger structures.

Nearly all of Damasus's inscriptions purported to tell information from an authority to a recipient who was expected to accept the information. They were also clearly set up to perform actions which extended well beyond simple edification. The action performed in this case is the creation of a new understanding of the martyr being commemorated, and more importantly an image of a unified church in Rome with Damasus at its head. The epitaphs were not simply expressions of what had happened. Rather, they created a new world of the past, one that might not have had any direct relationship to the events that they were purportedly representing – other than in the mind of those in the position to create them. As we will see below, these inscriptions performed an action; they created a cultural memory of the saints, a cultural memory

---

55. See Trout, "Damasus and the Invention."
56. Trout, "Damasus and the Invention." See also Saghy, "*Scinditur in Partes Populus*"; Maura K. Lafferty, "Translating Faith from Greek to Latin: *Romanitas* and *Christianitas* in Late Fourth Century Rome and Milan," *Journal of Early Christian Studies* 11 (2003): 48. Lafferty notes that this hexameter is also known as the *metrumheroicum*.

in support of the established hierarchy of the Catholic Church. They were not passively recounting the events of the past, but were testaments to active decisions on the part of Damasus.

Marianne Saghy and Peter Brown have both attempted to determine the reasons why the cult of the saints in the early years took the form that it did. Saghy observes that the Damasian inscriptions in particular were used not because of some predetermined importance of the graves of the martyrs, but rather due to simple economics:

> It is therefore likely that the catacombs became the chosen ground of papal "propaganda" not only because of the profound spiritual content inherent in martyrdom, but also because the erection of marble tombstones was a less expensive enterprise than the construction of churches.[57]

Brown takes a diametrically opposed view of the usage of fiscal resources and the rise of the cult of the saints: "The Cult of the saints was a focus where wealth could be spent without envy and *patrocinium*, exercised without obligation."[58]

While one should note that these two authors are looking at two distinctly different aspects of the cult of the saints (the former concerned specifically with the usage of catacomb inscriptions by Damasus, and the latter with the entirety of the cult of the saints), their differences concerning the monetary function in the cult is striking. It is even more striking for Saghy to argue that Damasus was concerned with working on the cheap, considering his episcopal reign began in 366, nearly 50 years after the Edict of Milan, and at a time when the church had significant resources. The *Liber Pontificalis* describes the lavish sums of money that Constantine poured into the construction of basilicas and the estates (and, more importantly, their revenue) which were given into episcopal control.[59] The idea that there were somehow insufficient funds to build structures stretches the bounds of credulity, especially as according to the *Liber Pontificalis* there were sufficient funds for Damasus to build at least one basilica, where he buried his mother and sister and was ultimately himself interred.[60]

I propose a different reason for the implementation of his inscriptions. Damasus was dealing with pressing issues of schismatics within the Roman Church, and according to the *Libellus Precum* was dealing

---

57. Saghy, "*Scinditur in Partes Populus*," 279.
58. Peter Brown, *The Cult of the Saints: Its Rise and Function in Latin Christianity* (Chicago: University of Chicago Press, 1981), 41. See also p. 97 below.
59. *Lib. Pont.* 34.
60. *Lib. Pont.* 39.

with them harshly.⁶¹ He was attempting to stamp out rivals, even bringing them posthumously into the fold of the mother church through the use of martyr shrines. Damasus had the power to place inscriptions upon the tombs of those whom he deemed to be important; he neither randomly nor universally inscribed the tombs of all of the Christian martyrs in Rome.⁶² As the archon of these Christian archives he thus had tremendous power over the image that was presented therein. I do not accept that there was a lack of funding to build new church structures. A more plausible theory is that Damasus was trying to conserve time rather than money. He needed a way to establish himself quickly and effectively as the single leader of a unified church, and his inscriptions served this function admirably. He also needed to be seen as the heir of the martyrs, especially as his opponents were being martyred *by his own hands*. His opponents remained a persecuted minority, and he had replaced the Romans as their oppressor. By directly linking himself to the martyrs of the past he was able to overcome this unfortunate association in the minds of Roman Christians (and ultimately all who would come to Rome to visit these tombs).

One significant difference between the construction of funerary inscriptions and the construction of a structure is that the inscriptions could be completed quickly, with almost instantaneous effect. One needed to be neither a Christian nor a pilgrim to see the inscriptions that Damasus had placed upon the tombs of the important dead: they were part of the monumental parade that lined the roads leading to Rome. Foreshadowing Ambrose's famous discovery of the remains of long-lost saints, Damasus also discovered many "forgotten" martyr tombs. These tombs, of course, would have allowed him the ability to create from scratch the life and message that he wanted to present on their *memoria*.⁶³ These *memoria* allowed the martyrs to be remembered not as they were, but as Damasus intended them to be.

Through his use of a very specific style and type of inscription, Damasus also created epitaphs that would have been immediately recognizable even to those who could not actually read the inscriptions for themselves. The literacy rate in Rome never reached more than ten percent; even so, those who viewed these inscriptions would have recognized them *as inscriptions*. Due the sheer number of inscriptions Damasus

---

61. *Lib. Pre.* 22 (PL 13.098).
62. Prudentius, *Pe.* 11 discusses the sheer number of Christian martyrs in Rome, and how many of their tombs only contain their name, or simply the number of martyrs buried in that location.
63. *Lib. Pont.* 39.

placed around (and under) Rome, and the uniformity he employed in his lettering, even the illiterate viewer would have known both what the inscription was, and, more importantly for Damasus's purpose, who had commissioned it.[64] In addition, the style of the inscriptions themselves was intended to play a significant role in the way that they were received by whoever viewed them, Christian or not:

> The capital script, designed by Furius Dionysius Filocalus, recalls in its proportions the square capitals found on imperial monuments [...]. The delicate finials found at the heads and feet of the new script, however, mark it as something new and distinctive.[65]

Damasus was visually tying the inscriptions with traditional Roman epitaphs, a radical departure from the crudely scored (and frequently grammatically incorrect) inscriptions of the previous centuries. This too was a feature that could be appreciated even by those who were unable to read what the inscription proclaimed.

One example of Damasus reaching out to all travelers to Rome, literate and illiterate, is an inscription that he placed on the Tomb of Hippolytus on the Via Tiburtina:

> Presbyter Hippolytus is said to have remained
> In the schism of Novatus while the laws of the tyrant prevailed
> But when the sword cut the marrow of the pious mother
> Devoted to Christ, he was looking for the kingdom of the faithful.
> When asked by the people which way to choose
> He answered that the Catholic faith should be followed by all
> Thus he deserved to be venerated as our own martyr.
> Damasus tells this story as he heard it, with the approval of Christ.[66]

We can see that Damasus is clearly, intentionally, manipulating historical events in order to relate them to his current concern for his position leading a unified Roman congregation. Allen Brent argues that it would have been impossible for Hippolytus to have been part of the Novatian schism (as presented in the Damasian inscription, and later repeated by Prudentius) due to their relative dates, and that Damasus, as the bishop of Rome, must have had access to documents that would have confirmed

---

64. Ihm's collection presents 62 inscriptions as authentic to Damasus, and another 34 as Pseudodamasine (Damasus, *Inscriptions*).

65. Lafferty, "Translating Faith," 45. For the name of the carver see Damasus, *Inscriptions* #18.

66. Damasus, *Inscriptions* #37, trans. in Saghy, "*Scinditur in Partes Populus*," 284. For an interesting and well-argued discussion of the tensions in the third-century church, of which Hippolytus was a central figure, see Allen Brent, *Hippolytus and the Roman Church in the Third Century: Communities in Tension Before the Emergence of a Monarch-Bishop* (Supplements to Vigiliae Christianae 31; Leiden: E. J. Brill, 1995).

this.⁶⁷ Brent then concludes that Hippolytus must have been a bishop based in Rome, of a second – and equal – Christian community, not the first "anti-pope" or an opponent vying for the same seat as Callistus.⁶⁸ While this is not an unlikely scenario, I am not entirely convinced by this, given that there is no direct evidence of a co-episcopal office in Rome, as in some other cities. Considering the chaos that was caused by the presence of two Roman bishops prior to Damasus securing the seat of Peter, I find it unlikely that there would be no historical record of this during the life of Hippolytus, but it is not an impossibility that some in Rome saw Hippolytus as their bishop, and quite probably that they saw him as authoritative in one way or another. Ultimately for the purposes of Damasus's usage of Hippolytus it does not matter if he had been a rival bishop, a schismatic, or simply a peer from another part of the city. It was not Damasus's intention to accurately record history. Rather, Damasus wanted to unambiguously present Hippolytus as having splintered from the Catholic Church. Damasus then presented Hippolytus as overcoming this schism through his death as a martyr for the universal church. That is the image that fits into Damasus's narrative, a narrative which then presents the bishop of Rome as the unifier of differing factions, the one to bring "unity from discord."⁶⁹ This was the cultural memory that Damasus sought to create through his ability to render the lives of the important Christian dead however he chose.

This inscription is one that had the possibility of being read by all, not just the faithful who approached the Eternal City. Damasus was able to ensure which particular individuals were remembered, as well as the way in which they were remembered. In this case he was able to bring Hippolytus back into the fold of the Catholic Church. Damasus used his position as the writer of these epigrams and constructor of the cultural memory which surrounds them to place the challenges that he faced in his current predicament into the "never-never time of *cum issua tyranny premerent.*"⁷⁰ The inscription placed over Hippolytus's tomb was simply a reflection of the current situation that Damasus found himself in, projected into a fictional past of his own creation, in order to support his own contemporary power, and project that power into the future.

Even as he supplemented the *memoria* of those buried on the roads leading to Rome, Damasus also injected his image of a unified church

---

67. Brent, *Hippolytus and the Roman Church*, 368–9.
68. Brent, *Hippolytus and the Roman Church*, 388.
69. White, *Emergence of Christianity*, 63.
70. White, *Emergence of Christianity*, 368. See also Allen Brent, "Was Hippolytus a Schismatic?" *Vigiliae Christianae* 49 (1995): 215–44.

deep within the catacombs. Many argue (based on the description by Jerome, quoted on p. 29 above) that by this point in time the catacombs were no longer being used and expanded for general burial, but had become centers for pilgrimage. As such Damasus placed his name front and center on the important locations that pilgrims visited. He effectively gave specific locations the episcopal seal of approval, and reminded the viewers that this seal of approval came from Damasus. Just as he did at the roadside monuments, Damasus made sure to include his name in the majority of the inscriptions that he set up,[71] and even those that did not include his name used the same type of inscriptions, lettering, and verse. Consequently the Christian visiting the graves of the martyrs would have become familiar with the inscriptions and he or she would have known (even when the martyr had not been explicitly named) that they were part of Damasus's project. His inscriptions and beautification created a degree of homogeneity among the martyrs' shrines, which would have been visible to both Christians (explicitly within the catacombs) and non-Christians alike. All of this served to create an impression of uniformity and consistency with *memoria* of the past. Thereby he was able to give himself, as the leader of the church, the seal of approval of the martyrs themselves.

Perhaps the most famous inscription erected by Damasus was that placed in the "Crypt of the Popes" in the Catacomb of Callistus:

> Know that here lies united an army of saints, these venerable tombs enclose their bodies, while the Kingdom of Heaven has already welcomed their souls. Here lie the companions of Sixtus who bear the trophies won from the enemy. Here lie the brotherhood of popes who guard the altar of Christ. Here the bishop who lived through a long peace. Here the holy confessors sent to us from Greece. Here young men and children, the elderly and their chaste offspring, who desired to conserve their virginity. Here too, I, Damasus confess I would like to be buried were it not for the fear of disturbing the ashes of these holy persons.[72]

This inscription is addressed to passersby, explicitly to the pilgrims who would be looking for "a host of the blessed." It is precisely because of its location in a crypt which contains the remains of several "popes" that it has become one of the most famous of his inscriptions. This was a place where Christians came to visit the tombs of significant leaders of the Roman Church. Here the important dead (both martyred and not) became one unified group, and in that homogeneity they became nameless in the inscription. Just as in his other inscriptions, Damasus

---

71. In a fashion that was not unlike many of his Roman predecessors who made sure that passersby knew who had erected the monument to the deceased.

72. Damasus, *Inscriptions* #12, trans. in Antonio Baruffa, *The Catacombs of St. Callixtus: History, Archaeology, Faith* (Vatican City: Libreria Editrice Vaticana, 1993), 64.

presented a unified church for all who would seek out the remains of their sainted "ancestors." Damasus explained his own absence from the graves. While he was not present (to the reader) after his death, and of course could not have been present prior to his death, no-one visiting the tomb could have been unaware of him, his name on the inscription made brought him to mind for each and every reader. His explicit reasoning for not desiring to be buried with the bishops of the past, as well as other saints of Christian history (both famous and unknown), was that he would not want to disturb them, apparently with his less pious remains; but of course, he is there with them for all eternity in his insertion of his text into their final resting place.

Damasus acted directly upon the readers, exerting the active role of power, by proclaiming this to be a location of central importance (which they already probably knew – why else would they have been there in the first place?), whereby he sought to create the cultural memory of these important dead. This memory could not have been created unilaterally. It relied on the viewer to make this memory a reality for themselves in their observation of the saints' commemoration. Interestingly, aside from Sixtus, Damasus is the only named individual in the inscription. When pilgrims visited the Crypt of the Popes, they could not help but call Damasus to mind, creating his presence through his proclamation of his own absence.

An unspoken reason that he may have wanted to have been buried elsewhere can be inferred from the fact that he ultimately was buried in a basilica he constructed on the Via Ardeatina. Here he shared space, not with the (more) impressive martyrs and bishops, but with his mother and sister. This would then be a space that more people would visit (due to the more public and accessible nature of the basilica as opposed to the catacomb) and with those increased numbers of visitors he would be the most important of the dead interred therein. His false modesty only survived underground.

Damasus was concerned not only about his own power in Rome, but also with the power of Rome within the rest of the empire.[73] One of the most potent claims that he could make relating to the pre-eminence of Rome was the presence of the remains of Peter and Paul in the city. The control of these remains was tremendously important. For the next two hundred years Rome closely guarded the relics of all of their martyrs,

---

73. See Lafferty, "Translating Faith," for a discussion on how Damasus and Ambrose solidified the power of the Western Church through the use of language and relics.

but most especially those of Peter and Paul. Damasus wanted to make clear the citizenship and possession of these relics when he wrote the inscription placed near the catacombs on the Appian Way:

> Here the saints abided previously. You ought to know this, whoever you are, you who seek equally the names of Peter and Paul. The East sent the disciples, which we acknowledge freely. On account of the merit of their blood and having followed Christ through the stars, they have traveled to the bosom of heaven and the kingdom of the righteous. Rome capably deserved to watch over its own citizens. Damasus records these things for your praise, O new stars.[74]

This inscription did not mark the actual grave of either apostle. When this inscription was put in place the cult centers of Peter and Paul were well established by Constantine. However, this location *ad Catacumbas* was possibly the oldest cult center to Peter and Paul in Rome.[75] This location was most likely known to those outside of Rome, and those coming to the Basilica Apostolorum, which Constantine constructed at this site, would have expected to find relics of Peter and Paul. David Eastman argues that Damasus was not claiming that *hic* in this instance means the specific location of the inscription was important, but rather that *hic* meant Rome itself was the place where the apostles had previously lived.[76] His argument about the efforts of Damasus to present Rome's possession of the remains as an *evocatio deorum* (specifically as gods of the past were called out of their previous city and brought to Rome) is convincing.[77] However, I take issue with his stance that the inscription was placed at this particular location, but really must have meant all of Rome. There was a tradition (fictional or not) strongly attested to both through the archaeological evidence of the cultic activity at this location, as well as in the *Liber Pontificalis*,[78] of the remains of the apostles spending time in this location. Consequently, it would have made perfect sense for some traveler to come to this location to "seek the names of Peter and Paul" and they should know that those two had "once lived here" *in this particular place*. Why else would they have come to *this* location looking for their names in the first place?

Markus Bockmuehl refers to this inscription as "fruity papal hexameter" which presents "a kind of 'Starbucks' history – frothy, sweetened

---

74. Damasus, *Inscriptions* #26, trans. in Eastman, *Paul the Martyr*, 101.
75. Which Eusebius (*H.e.* 2.25.7) possibly dates to as early as 200 C.E.
76. Eastman, *Paul the Martyr*, 103–4.
77. It should be noted that Peter and Paul were not the only foreign martyrs that Damasus made Roman. He also incorporated Saturinus and Hermes, whose inscriptions can be found in *Inscriptions* #46.
78. The *Lib. Pont.* explicitly makes reference only to one inscription out of all of those that Damasus put into place: this one.

and flavored as classical myth."⁷⁹ While Bockmuehl sees this as a negative, this effect was exactly what Damasus intended, and considering the popularity of the beverages served at Starbucks, he may well have performed his task admirably. This inscription is decidedly a work of propaganda which sets the church at Rome as the sole possessor of Peter's and Paul's remains and, thus, of their authority, which then ensured Rome's pre-eminence within the broader Christian community.⁸⁰

In what is known as *Ep.* 19 of his corpus, Paulinus of Nola discussed how Constantine wished to emulate "Romulus's city," and that through the introduction of Timothy's and Andrew's remains Constantinople "now stands with twin towers, vying to match the hegemony of the great Rome."⁸¹ It is entirely possible that this understanding of the twin towers of Rome (Peter and Paul) was an understanding not necessarily of Constantine, but rather of Paulinus projecting his own understanding of the pre-eminence of Rome through those twin towers, back on to Constantine. As we saw earlier, Constantine desired (and ultimately succeeded) in having more than two apostles in his mausoleum, to outshine Rome's possession of Peter and Paul. For Paulinus's early fifth century understanding of the prominence of the relics of Rome, possession of martyr relics was essential if Constantine was going to compete with the "hegemony of great Rome." If my understanding of Paulinus's account is correct, this demonstrates how fully he was influenced by the work of Damasus in the construction of the centrality of the cult of Paul and Peter in Rome.

Damasus did not limit the incorporation of Peter and Paul into his narrative of the pre-eminence of Rome to a few simple inscriptions. He commissioned catacomb paintings, and minted small medals for pilgrims to purchase during their time in Rome with the apostles' faces on them. Several gold glass bases survive which probably date to his rule, which presented Peter and Paul in communion. One even explicitly included his own image alongside the other two, whereby he was granted apostolic approval through his presence with theirs. These gold glass bases were ultimately used as decorations within the catacombs, pressed into the enclosures of tombs therein.⁸²

---

79. Markus Bockmuehl, "Peter's Death in Rome? Back to Front and Upside Down," *Scottish Journal of Theology* 60 (2007): 3.

80. For a discussion of the nearly universal acceptance of this claim, see Eastman, *Paul the Martyr*, 101.

81. Paulinus of Nola, *Carm.* 19.329ff. (PL 61.530B–531A); trans. Walsh, *Poems*, 142.

82. See Lucy Grig, "Portraits, Pontiffs, and the Christianization of Fourth Century Rome," *Papers of the British School at Rome* 72 (2004): 203–30; Denzey, *Bone Gatherers*, 178–9. Denzey also argues that Damasus emphasized male saints over their female counterparts.

By drawing upon the "epigraphic habit" of the Roman world, Damasus explicitly created a Christianity that tied itself to the classical heritage of Rome, and also claimed for itself the future of Rome. The presence and passion of Peter and Paul in Rome allowed Rome to claim them as her own, adding new stars to the heavens that have always looked down on the Eternal City. Who better to present and claim these new stars than Damasus?[83] It must be noted that from the biblical account Peter and Paul were not always on the best terms. Consequently, once again the image that Damasus presented was one of unity from discord. The apostles were together as one in Rome, as the church which had been divided into two factions was once again one Catholic Church, under the direction of one bishop. On a broader level Rome itself was now synonymous with Christianity; the city which had previously persecuted the Church was now forged anew by Damasus's pen.

Damasus's usage of the martyrs was similar to that of Constantine, in that he sought to use their power to solidify his own. However, where Constantine constructed elaborate church structures, Damasus turned his attention to the commemoration of the martyrs through his use of inscriptions and epigrams. This technique served Damasus well, as it allowed him to both act more quickly than he would have been able to had he focused on the construction of churches, as well as to cast a much broader net. His inscriptions were found everywhere, from the roads leading into Rome to the depths of the catacombs.[84] His audience became the faithful of the church as well as anyone entering Rome for less ecclesiastical purposes. Damasus successfully placed his mark for everyone to see, a mark that heralded him as the authority on the lives of the martyrs, and the only one who could claim to be their direct descendant. He was able to act as an intercessor with the martyr, as the martyr was believed to have been able to act as an intercessor with heaven.

Conclusion

As we have seen in this chapter, two important fourth-century Christian leaders (one emperor and one bishop) sought to consolidate their

---

83. For a detailed discussion of Damasus's inscriptions see Dennis Trout, *Damasus of Rome: The Epigraphic Poetry. Introduction, Texts, Translations, and Commentary* (Oxford: Oxford University Press, 2015); Rebecca Leigh Littlechilds, "The Epitaphs of Damasus and the Transferable Value of Persecution for the Christian Community at Rome in the Fourth-Century AD" (MA thesis, University of Victoria, 2009).

84. Curran notes that Damasus's inscriptions "help physically unite the sites beyond the walls into an almost unitary Christian hinterland of Rome" (Curran, *Pagan City*, 146).

power by using the bodies of the martyrs. Constantine and Damasus used different means to put the remains of the important Christian dead on display. For Constantine this was through the construction of elaborate monuments to the important dead of Rome, providing previously existing cult centers with new and elaborate structures for the continued worship therein. In these new structures, especially at the most influential sites – the basilicas dedicated to Peter and Paul in Rome, and his own mausoleum in Constantinople – the Christian population could not help but observe who it was who acted as the patron to the saints: Constantine.

Through enthusiastic construction projects using the rhetoric of burial – which traced its roots to pre-Christian Roman practices – Constantine ensured that he would forever be associated with Peter, the Rock of the Church. In no less of an apostolic manner Constantine built towering basilicas upon that rock which combined imperial authority with his new religion. In his own burial Constantine demonstrated that he considered himself to be the patriarch of his new family, surrounding himself with the apostles. Through his usage of the basilica shrine, he presented the martyrs, the Christian special dead, in a light which echoed the role of imperial power. His solidification of his own power was drawn using decidedly Roman lines. However, these lines were arranged in a specifically new and a specifically Christian design. His own memorial demonstrated his desire to be interred with the remains of the apostles where he identified himself (visually) as the central figure in the emergence of Christianity. He could no longer claim divinity (or expect it to be granted posthumously) due to his Christian faith, but he clearly comes as close to it as possible, creating a cult center at his own mausoleum. One of the major contributions that Constantine initiated in his interaction with the cult of the martyrs was not only his elevation of himself to equality with the apostles, which is another way for an emperor to gain a cult following after his death once *apotheosis* was no longer available, but more strikingly what his becoming the equal to the apostles does *for the apostles*.

Modern scholarship has focused on the claim Constantine was making for himself in relation with the apostles. The role of the apostles for the modern audience has been firmly established near the top of the Christian hierarchy. For Constantine to claim to be the equal to the apostles means that he was also claiming that the apostles were *equal to the emperor*. Constantine's monument established that the apostles' role in the empire was no less than his own, and that of his predecessors (who at this time still had an imperial cult). Not only was he claiming a religious role for himself, but he was instituting a *political* role for the apostles. Constantine formulated the graves and shrines to the martyrs and apostles, drawing upon Roman imperial formulas and combining them with the emphasis on the familial nature of honoring the graves of the dead. The martyrs and apostles were the ancestors with whom Constantine sought to identify himself through burial commemoration. This identification raised the status of those who had been executed by the empire to the level of the ancestors of his imperial dynasty.

Damasus had other matters to attend to, specifically the need to consolidate his own power in a period of significant discord. After struggling to become the bishop of Rome, Damasus skillfully intertwined two competing narratives at the sites of the martyr's graves. Rather than building many elaborate structures, he chose the more expedient path through the beautification of the widespread and visible memorials to the martyrs of Rome. He wove together Virgilian verse with the Christian cultural memory of suffering and persecution. Through this he created the fabric of late fourth-century Rome as still being the inheritor of Romulus and Remus as well as Peter and Paul. He did not, however, indiscriminately commemorate every martyr buried in Rome, but rather chose those who best demonstrated the image of the past that most succinctly codified the united Catholic Church of the present. Damasus successfully brought possible schismatics (or more importantly those remembered as such) back into the fold though the intentional misrepresentation of history, as we saw in the case of the Hippolytus inscription. In nearly every case, constantly drawing upon previous Roman practices, Damasus let the reader know who it was that presented the epitaphs for their edification. At the same time he surrounded himself with the martyrs, soldiers who would defend him against his contemporary rivals.

In much the same way that Constantine sought to claim the apostles as his personal ancestry through his construction of the Basilica Apostolorum in Constantinople, Damasus sought to solidify the place of Rome within the empire, at a time when its power was waning. Through equating Peter and Paul to Remus and Romulus, Damasus wove the martyred apostles into the fabric of the city. By claiming the location of execution and final resting place for Peter and Paul he claimed Peter and Paul for Rome, establishing it as the heir to the Rock of the Church.

Both of these individuals set the stage for the future use of the martyrs and their shrines. We shall see in the next chapters the ways in which the martyr shrine continued to be a battleground upon which the Christian powerful sought to craft and present the cultural memory of Christianity, and simultaneously sought to stamp out practices performed at these shrines which may well have undercut their power.

Chapter Three: To Control

The Places and Practices Associated With the Remains of the Saints

No sooner is a great man dead than legend is busy with his life.[1]

As the fourth century drew to a close Christianity gained a dominance that would have seemed impossible a century before. It was at this point more than at any previous time in it its history that Christianity had to struggle to determine its own identity. During the sporadic persecutions of the early fourth century Christians had a common opponent, whom they could all identify themselves against. After the end of the persecutions, that opponent was no longer the threat that it had been and an old problem gained new traction: internal schisms. As Damasus had before them, several bishops from either side of the Mediterranean sought to use the cult of the martyrs as a means of solidifying their control, and mitigating the competing claims of their opponents. They also had to confront various unsavory practices that were popular at the graves of the martyrs. Here too the martyrs were invoked so as to bring a new sobriety to the celebration of the important dead.

The building blocks of the fourth century's usage of burial of the saints as one of the primary means by which the emergent Church sought to explicitly create its own identity and communicate that identity to itself were not pulled out of thin air , but were laid by the likes of Constantine and Damasus. Yet, the structures of memory that were built with these blocks differed depending on the architect. The way that Constantine and Damasus used them was decidedly different from that of Augustine, Ambrose, or Paulinus. However, none of them could have built their mnemonic structures as they did without some of the framework that was laid for them by their predecessors, which were themselves built upon general Mediterranean attitudes toward the dead. The major figures discussed in this chapter all approached the usage of the remains of the saints differently. They each sought to support their power through differing approaches to the cult of the saints. As H. A. Drake observed, at the beginning of the fourth century "it is obvious that there was not just one, monolithic church, but a church that spoke with many voices,

---

1. Albert Schweitzer, *The Quest of the Historical Jesus* (trans. W. Montgomery et al.: Minneapolis, MN: Fortress Press, 2001 [1906]), 75.

through the mouth of bishops who had more than theology to scream about."[2] He has clearly demonstrated that the bishops of the fourth century were struggling to claim their place in the empire. With the advent of the fourth century there were numerous issues with "heresies" and schismatics, which demonstrated that the struggle was not only for doctrinal dominance, but also for political supremacy. While the graves of the important dead were not the primary battleground for these struggles, in many cases those who emerged victorious were those who successfully forged the cultural memory of their followers at the tombs of the saints.

The martyr's remains introduced two aspects of intention. The first concerned what was to be done with the remains, with the emphasis on how they were to be buried, where they were to be buried, and finally – as we saw with Damasus – how that burial was to be decorated; this last element influenced how visitors to the tomb viewed both the martyr as well as (more subtlety) whoever had the power to present the image of the martyr. The second aspect dealt with what sort of behavior was acceptable at these shrines, and perhaps whether scandalous behavior might invalidate the cult of the saints entirely. Due to the dramatic rise in converts to Christianity in the late fourth century, and their desire to continue practices that they might not have associated with one particular cult or another, the episcopate had to determine how to manage behaviors that either may have subverted their own power (e.g. private devotion to the martyrs outside the boundaries of episcopal control), but also those behaviors that they considered unbecoming of a Christian congregation.[3] Even if the shrine was located centrally and presented beautifully, the way in which the martyr cult was viewed became dependent, almost entirely, on how those who gathered at the memorial behaved. Bad behavior, drunkenness, fornication, loud music, and possibly even murder, become issues that various bishops felt they needed to address. To be fair, the notion of murder at the shrines was most likely hyperbolic, yet considering the size of the crowds that could amass, it is not inconceivable that accidental death could have occurred during these late-night vigils (which almost certainly featured the other irregularities listed).

The cult of the saints had a strong following throughout the Mediterranean world, although there were regional differences in the way that

---

2. H. A. Drake, *Constantine and the Bishops: The Politics of Intolerance* (Baltimore, MD: Johns Hopkins Press, 2000), 31.
3. As we saw in Chapter One, the care of the dead did not differ significantly based on one's other interactions with the divine. It was nearly universal throughout the population, much as there is an American way of death. Jessica Mitford, *The American Way of Death Revisited* (New York: Vintage, 2000).

it was incorporated into Christian practice during the fourth century. In Rome it was eagerly embraced by the episcopate as a means of legitimizing its power. In North Africa (including Egypt), however, the cult of the saints was quickly embraced by branches of the Christian community that would be deemed "heretical" by the Catholic Church (e.g. Donatists). Because of the associations of the cult of the saints with these other Christian groups (which were, at times, being persecuted by the Catholic Church), the Catholic episcopate in North Africa were more careful in their approach to the cult of the saints than were their European contemporaries. That does not mean, though, that the episcopate in North Africa did not use the cult of the dead as a means of establishing its own power and attempting to eliminate the claims of its rivals.

This chapter will examine how several key figures at the end of the fourth century sought to use the cult of the saints as it had been initially shaped by Constantine and Damasus, to solidify their own power or the power of the Catholic Church against those that they considered to be heterodox. The usage of the cult of the saints was not uniform, just as many of the practices that were acceptable at the graveside were not. However, the use of the martyr's body was an important (proxy) battleground for several significant debates in which the late fourth-century Christian community found itself engaged.

The intentional actions of Ambrose, who, through the dissemination of the remains of martyrs that he personally (re-)discovered, cleverly spread both the presence of the Church of Milan as well as his own influence much further than would have been possible without his use of the cult of the saints. At the same time, however, he was leery of the popular practices associated with the cult and sought to bring them firmly under episcopal control. His former student Augustine, the recipient of some of those remains, held varying views of the cult of the saints over his lifetime, ranging from displeasure over the drunken crowds at martyr shrines, to defending those same crowds against opponents, to a full embracement of the importance of the martyr's sepulture. While Augustine has been accused of inconsistency, rarely did he resort to seeing the actual remains as a sort of magical talisman. Even when he recounted miracles associated with martyr relics, for him they were a means of instruction, as well as a way of tying his local church, through the intentional promotion of translocal relics, to the broader Christian community centered in Rome.

Paulinus of Nola's focus on the cult of Saint Felix was highly influential in the creation of Nola as a site for an annual pilgrimage on Felix's "birthday." Paulinus, also a recipient of Ambrose's generosity, was unambiguously in favor of the cult of the saints. He composed a body of poetry to commemorate Felix, as well as inscriptions that graced the new cult center at Nola and at a new basilica established at Primuliacum in Aquitaine by his close friend Sulpicius Severus (see below p. 110). The latter, a devotee of Martin, adds to our discussion through his correspondence with Paulinus as well as through the way that he composed the *Life of Martin* and the occasional tensions that arise therein. Jerome, who is important in his recounting of going (sneaking?) into the catacombs on Sundays, is also important in his vehement defense of the cult of the martyrs.

Finally, we will turn our attention to Egypt, where in the fifth century Apa Shenoute was leery of the cult of the saints, or at least the way in which it was practiced in Egypt during his (extremely long) lifetime. However, a careful examination of his texts *Since it Behooves Christians* and *Those Who Work Evil* allows us to observe that he was not against the cult of the saints as a whole but was extremely critical of the logical conclusion of the actions started by Ambrose. He vehemently opposed the "discovery" of saints' bodies, or the inclusion of bones in a church that might have belonged to someone other than a martyr, or even might not have been human. He also opposed people who spent lavishly on the construction of martyr shrines while allowing the poor to go hungry. These things, Shenoute simply could not abide. In this light he was actually a proponent of the cult of the saints: but a cult that was not corrupted by empty platitudes and forged relics.

Ambrose of Milan

> Whom are we to esteem as the princes of the people but the holy Martyrs? Among whose number Protasius and Gervais long unknown are now enrolled, who have caused the Church of Milan, barren of martyrs hitherto, now as the mother of many children, to rejoice in the distinctions and instances of her own sufferings.[4]

One of the most important innovations to the cult of the martyrs came from the bold actions of Ambrose, the bishop of Milan. In direct opposition to an imperial decree, early in 386, he began to disperse the saints' relics that he was in control of, specifically those of Protasius and Gervais. There is no evidence for what would become a common feature of the cult of the martyrs, prior to Ambrose: the division of the bodies which were then sent throughout the empire. The only real caveat to this is the treatment of the ashes of the Forty Martyrs.

Before we discuss Ambrose's discovery of Protasius and Gervais, and the subsequent treatment thereof, we need to examine how Ambrose himself was the recipient of the tradition of the proto-relic trade. There is some evidence that groups in Egypt were disturbing martyr tombs

---

4. Ambrose, *Ep.* 22.7 (PL 16.1021C), trans. H. de Romestin et al., *NPNF*[2] 10:437.

and placing their bodies on movable stretchers. Furthermore, there was evidence as early as 311 of a dispute concerning a woman who was prone to kissing a bone of a martyr prior to taking the Eucharist. Here, however, the woman, Lucilla, kept the bone for her own personal usage:

> Lucilla [...] was said to kiss the bone of some martyr or other – if, that is, he was a martyr – before the spiritual food and drink, and, since she preferred to the saving cup the bone of some dead man, who if he was a martyr had not yet been confirmed as one, she was rebuked.[5]

Even though Optatus was arguing against the Donatists, his concern here was not the fact that she had in her possession the bone of a martyr, or the practice associated with the bone, but rather that it was perceived to take precedence over the Eucharist and that it may not even have been from a martyr at all. By 367 there was strong debate about the ability to determine martyr relics from the remains of common people.

The first instance of the translation of a martyr, with the possible exception of the translation of relics to Constantinople, is generally considered to have happened in 351. According to Sozomen's *Church History*, the Caesar Constantius Gallus (who established Antioch as his residence) was so zealous that he built a temple to the martyr and bishop (of Antioch) Babylas in Daphne (a suburb of the city), in order to purge Daphne of its "pagan superstition and the outrages of profligates."[6] Gallus then had the tomb of Babylas moved into the temple of Apollo. While Sozomen does not describe where Babylas had previously been interred (presumably in Antioch), the new temple and burial location was apparently close enough to the oracle at Daphne that the oracle fell silent. This ultimately proved problematic for Julian, who later tried to consult the oracle. At first he was greeted with silence. Julian eventually determined that the problem was the presence of Babylas's remains and demanded that the Christian community remove them. In what could have been a confrontation, the Christians sang songs of praise as they peacefully took away the remains of their martyred bishop.[7]

Further evidence of martyr translation (or at least movement of their bodies) prior to Ambrose comes from Athanasius's *Festal Epistles* for the years 369 and 370 respectively.[8] In these letters Athanasius condemned relic worship, not because there was anything inherently wrong with the honor given to the martyr or saint, but rather because he objected to the

---

5. Optatus, *Contra Parmenianum Donatistam* 16 (PL 11.916B), trans. Mark Edwards, *Optatus: Against the Donatists* (Liverpool: Liverpool University Press, 1997), 15–16.
6. Sozomen, *HE* 5.19 (PG 67).
7. Sozomen, *HE* 5.19 (PG 67).
8. Athanasius, *Ep. Fest.* 41, 42.

treatment of the remains by the Meletians. According to Athanasius they exhumed martyr bodies that they had discovered, and then carried them on stretchers from place to place. This may not have been too far removed from traditional Egyptian practices, which may have included keeping the mummified corpse of the deceased in the home. Cicero observed that Egyptians kept their dead in their homes after embalming them.[9]

The translations listed above, however, were not seen as gifts given by one location to another. The trade of the remains of the martyrs has its first clear roots with Basil of Caesarea in 373–374. In a letter without any clear addressee, although it is typically seen as being addressed "to a trainer [of martyrs]," Basil requests that the relics of martyrs be sent to the recipient's native land.[10] The verbiage here is interesting, as it begs one to wonder if these martyrs were also originally from Caesarea. If this is the case, then the return of the remains would have been much more in accordance with traditional customs (e.g. the bodies of the dead were often returned to their homeland for proper burial – as with the case of Hippolytus's corpse when it was returned to Rome after he died in exile). However, as Basil expressed in another letter that their hearts were heavy, due to the fact that no more martyrs were being produced.[11] Because of this lack of martyrdom in Caesarea, Basil is exuberant about the violent nature of the struggles of the martyrs beyond the Danube. The martyrs' struggle against the barbarians was a physical manifestation of the struggle against (non-Christian) opponents, which recalled the glory days of open persecution and martyrdom. He lamented the apathy of his congregation, noting that there was no martyrdom, because those who were injuring Christians in Caesarea were the Christians themselves. He hoped that with the return of martyrdom God would become reconciled with his congregation and lead them back to a righteous path. It would seem that Basil's request was granted when he wrote in 373 to Ascholius of Thessalonica and observed that Ascholius had honored his homeland by sending it a martyr, quite possibly Sabbas the Goth.[12]

Basil was not only a recipient of martyr remains. Basil wrote in 370 to a fellow bishop, Arcadius, that he desired to find relics for Arcadius in part so that he could "participate in the saint's distribution of blessings."[13]

---

9. Cicero, *Tusculan Disuptations* 1.45. See John Wortley, "The Origins of Christian Veneration of Body-Parts," *Revue de l'histoire des religions* 1 (2006): 19. See also Lucian of Samosata, *On Funerals,* 3.170.
10. Basil, *Ep.* 155.
11. Basil, *Ep.* 164.
12. Basil, *Ep.* 165.
13. Basil, *Ep.* 49, trans. in Jill Burnett Comings, *Aspects of the Liturgical Year in Cappadocia (325–430)* (New York: Peter Lang, 2005), 112.

Around 375, at the request of Ambrose, Basil sent the body of Bishop Dionysius back to Milan, where Dionysius had previously been the archbishop prior to his exile to Caesarea at the hands of Constantius. In the letter that accompanied the remains to Milan, Basil[14] made two observations worthy of note here. First, he recorded that there was discord among his congregation about the translation of the relics. Second, he was quite explicit in his proclamation that these were in fact the real relics of Dionysius, offering as proof the fact that his congregation did not want to give them up, but did so to bring joy to the congregation of Ambrose. It would seem that even by 375 there was a fear (or perceived fear on Basil's part) that there might be substitution of less holy bones for those of the martyrs.

Basil also apparently gave some of the ashes of the Forty Martyrs to a group of nuns who later gave (some of) them to Gaudentius of Brescia.[15] The presence of the relics of the Forty Martyrs is interesting, as Sozomen related a different discovery story about the Relics in 450 (at least 60 years after they had been given to Gaudentius). Sozomen recounted how the relics had been kept by a woman, Eusebia, in her garden outside the walls of Constantinople, essentially in her private collections. At the time of her death, she had the relics placed near her own tomb, and gave the property to an order of monks. These monks then kept the secret of the martyr's relics (as per her wishes), not even divulging their presence when they sold the property. Eventually, a *martyrium* was built over the property to a different martyr, Thyrsus. In the fifth century, the Empress Pulcheria received a vision from Thyrsus, commanding her to excavate the long-forgotten relics of the Forty Martyrs and re-inter them near his own tomb. The lapse from their primary interment to the vision of Pulcheria was no more than the lifetime of one of the monks, who, upon questioning, recalled where the location might have been. The excavations were carried out and the relics discovered with the tell-tale sweet odor emanating from the casket where they were discovered beneath the *martyrium*. Sozomen himself was present at the public festival wherein the relics were placed near those of Thyrus.[16] One of the four ways of legally dealing with a corpse according to Roman law was to burn it; consequently, the ashes of the martyrs "could be legitimately kept above ground, visible and accessible."[17] That is to say, the ashes of the deceased were acceptable to distribute and divide in a way that the corpse or pieces of a corpse

---

14. Basil, *Ep.* 197; see also Comings, *Aspects of the Liturgical Year*, 112.
15. Gaudentius of Brescia, *Serm.* 17 (PL 20.959ff).
16. Sozomen, *HE* 9.2 (PG 67.844).
17. Wortley, "Origins of Christian Veneration," 5–23.

would not have been. Basil violated no norms through his division of the ashes of the Forty Martyrs.

The distribution of the relics may have been a feature of the Eastern Church, which seems to have been much looser with the distribution of primary relics than the Western Church. Basil observed that many towns and villages had relics of the Forty Martyrs by the 370s.[18] We also see soon afterwards that John Chrysostom, in a sermon late in the fourth century or early in the fifth century, discussed how the Egyptians had many martyrs and freely sent them throughout the country.[19] Gaudentius was also notable in that he may well have returned from his pilgrimage to Jerusalem (ca. 387) with relics of John the Baptist, although he does not elaborate concerning what sort of relics these were.[20]

Ambrose was the recipient of other martyr relics than those sent by Basil. According to the *Martyrologium Hieronymianum* he received the remains of the apostles John, Andrew, and Thomas.[21] This would mean that Andrew's relics had been moved from Constantinople to Milan in 386. These then were the relics that he probably incorporated into his "Roman" basilica.[22] It is odd that he does not mention these very prestigious names when he recounts the consecration of the basilica in a letter to his sister.[23] The absence of any other reference to their presence in his works casts some degree of doubt upon whose relics he incorporated into that structure. One other hypothesis concerning the relics Ambrose used in his "Roman basilica" comes from Daniel Williams, who uncritically comments that those relics came from Rome itself.[24] This is most likely not the case, as Roman bishops jealously guarded their relics. However, there is little doubt that Ambrose received some relics and placed them into the basilica; he laments that there were no local martyrs for veneration in Milan.

---

18. Basil, *Mart.* (PG 31.521).

19. John Chrysostom, *Pan. Aeg.* (PG 50.693). Both John and Basil are discussed in Gillian Clark, "Translating Relics: Victricius of Rouen and Fourth-century Debate," *Early Medieval Europe* 10 (2001): 167.

20. Gaudentius of Brescia, *Serm.* 17 (PL 20.259ff).

21. One is skeptical of placing too much historical veracity on this. However, several other bishops who were known to have received relics from Ambrose also had those of Andrew in their collections (e.g. Paulinus, Gaudentius, and Victricius).

22. Richard Krautheimer, *Three Christian Capitals: Topography and Politics* (Berkeley: University of California Press, 1983), 80 n. 23.

23. Ambrose, *Ep.* 22 (PL 16.1019).

24. Daniel H. Williams, *Ambrose of Milan and the End of the Nicene-Arian Conflicts* (Oxford: Clarendon Press, 1995), 219.

Finally Neil McLynn presents us with one final point of note on the relic trade or martyr translation.[25] He boldly asserts that Felix and Nabor were themselves brought to Milan, from Lodi, by the previous bishop, some 60 years earlier (which would put the translation around the surprisingly early date of 326). McLynn appears decidedly apologetic when he suggests that Felix and Nabor were themselves interred *ad sanctos* near a previously established local cultic location. It was this knowledge of their translation that led Ambrose to be confident that there would be other martyrs buried near their new tombs. If there had been a previously established cult site at this location, then one has to wonder why it was necessary to bring their bodies to Milan. Or if their acquisition was, as McLynn claims, "precisely in order to supply Milan's deficiency of sanctified remains,"[26] then it seems highly unlikely that 60 years prior to Ambrose no-one remembered the graves of these illustrious martyrs. However, if these remains were actually translated in the 320s from Lodi after having been buried there since the death of the martyrs in 303, that would be an extraordinarily early date for such an endeavor. Despite these possible antecedents for Ambrose's own translation of martyr remains, his action was unprecedented in that after he moved them into a basilica he then dispersed pieces of them throughout the empire.

By 386 Ambrose had been embroiled in a protracted conflict with both the Emperor Valentinian II and the Empress Justina in Milan over the usage of church structures in Milan. They had introduced an Arian bishop into Milan and decreed that Ambrose should hand over a church structure for use by the Arians. He and his congregation barricaded themselves into the structure and Valentinian ultimately relented.[27]

Soon thereafter, Ambrose recounted, in a letter to his sister, a sermon that he gave upon the discovery of the bodies of the previously unknown martyrs Protasius and Gervais. Their discovery filled the void left by the absence of local martyrs, a void that apparently was felt not only by Ambrose but, at least according to Ambrose himself, also weighed heavily on the souls of his congregation: "For after I had dedicated the basilica, many, as it were, with one mouth began to address me, and said: 'Consecrate this as you did the Roman basilica.' And I answered: 'Certainly I will if I find any relics of martyrs.' And at once a kind of

---

25. Neil B. McLynn, *Ambrose of Milan: Church and Court in a Christian Capital* (Berkeley: University of California Press, 1994), 216. See also Gillian Mackie, *Early Christian Chapels in the West: Decoration, Function and Patronage* (Toronto: University of Toronto press, 2003), 126 n. 59, which makes passing reference of this tradition.

26. McLynn, *Ambrose*, 216.

27. For an overview of the Arian crisis in Milan during this period see Williams, *Ambrose*, 1995, especially Chapter 7; Krautheimer, *Three Christian Capitals*.

prophetic ardour seemed to enter my heart."[28] According to McLynn this popular call for martyr relics may have been an inconvenience for Ambrose. He had already prepared his basilica with the addition of his own final resting place reserved under the altar. To build a basilica with an aim toward ensuring one's own memory was not without precedence (e.g. Damasus's in Rome), yet the notion of pre-ordaining the burial location of prominence within that structure was revolutionary.[29] Consequently the call for relics, as Ambrose had used them in the consecration of the Roman Basilica, was problematic for Ambrose. It was more politically expedient for Ambrose to have had his own *martyrium* ready and waiting should he meet with a violent demise – which was always a possibility when you tangled with an emperor.

While the presence of his pre-constructed *martyrium* may have been a deterrent to his own possible martyrdom (lest an unruly popular uprising develop around that shrine), Ambrose's discovery of the martyrs (at the "request" of his congregation) would ultimately provide him with the means to reunify his own church in Milan, as well as to spread his influence throughout Europe and into North Africa. Unlike Damasus, who was content to let pilgrims make their way to Rome and revel in the grandeur of the martyr shrines there, Ambrose could not count on such a draw. However, through his eventual dispersal of the remains, and not simply secondary (or contact) relics, Ambrose was able to spread his influence nearly as far as Damasus had spread his own reputation.

Ambrose (or as he claimed, his congregation) felt that the lack of local martyrs was some sort of deficiency, keeping up with the Romans has always been hard. Once the martyrs had been discovered, both of them bloody, large skeletons, they were translated to the new basilica and laid to rest in the location that Ambrose had set up for his own body, under the altar. During the translation there was a miraculous healing of a blind man, which was momentous enough for Augustine (who was in attendance) to recount at least three times himself.[30]

Augustine was not the only one to recount the exhumation of these remains; Paulinus of Milan in his *Life of Ambrose* also relates a similar scene concerning the unearthing of these relics, long ago forgotten to have been martyrs at all. They had been buried, according to both Paulinus and Ambrose, anonymously yet *ad sanctos*, near the sepulchers of the

---

28. Ambrose, *Ep.* 22.1 (PL 16.1019B), trans. Romestin et al., *NPNF*[2] 10:436–7.
29. McLynn, *Ambrose*, 209.
30. Augustine, *Conf.* 9.7, *Civ.* 22.8.2, and *Serm.* 276.5. See also Paulinus of Milan, *Vit. Ambr.* 5 (PL 14.27A ff).

martyrs Felix and Nabor. When these remains were unearthed, miracles and exorcisms abounded.

The miracles also served to bolster Ambrose against his Arian opponents. Paulinus related that "by these good works of the martyrs the faith of the Catholic Church grew, at the same time the treachery of the Arians diminished."[31] As we shall see in the next chapter, the Arians were critical of the emerging martyr cult, especially as it was being used by Ambrose. It is entirely possible that their criticisms were almost exactly the same, for the same reasons even, as Augustine's criticism of the Donatists' usage of the cult surrounding local martyrs, or even Athanasius' almost complete rejection of the martyr cult. The ability to set the boundaries of who was a martyr, and what could be done at their shrine/grave, and where that shrine/grave could be located, were all means of delineating distinctions between groups when they are not necessarily immediately apparent.

If the gathering of remains and their early veneration was as important as the *Martyrdom of Ignatius* suggests, then how could the graves of Protasius and Gervais have gone without a cultic following, or at least have been without someone in the community remembering their location from the time of their death until the time of Ambrose's revelation concerning their location? If we do not grant that Ambrose actually found the intact bodies, dripping with blood and sweet-smelling, but simply dug up two unmarked graves and created the wide-ranging and important cult of Protasius and Gervais on his own, how then was this tolerated by his congregation? The answer lies somewhere between these two scenarios. Ambrose was drawing upon the tradition of the cult of the martyrs as described in Ignatius – one that had a long history within Christian circles, yet had evolved during the fourth century thanks primarily to the activities of Damasus and Constantine. The presence of local martyrs had become important, and hence the local congregation wanted their own locations of sanctity, their own martyrs. Ambrose drew upon that desire, that rhetoric, in formulating his own arguments. Ultimately it is unimportant for the current endeavor if the remains were actually those of Protasius and Gervais or even if Ambrose himself believed that they were. The importance of this action is the effect that it had upon his followers (who clearly *did* believe that the remains were authentic), and the direction that Ambrose went with these remains, which would become a precedent for several hundred years of Christian development.

---

31. Paulinus of Milan *Vit. Ambr.* 5.14 (PL 14.0032A), author's trans.

The bodies of Protasius and Gervais were not the only martyr relics that Ambrose miraculously discovered. Paulinus also discusses Ambrose building a church for the recently discovered Vitalis and Agricola, whose bodies had apparently been buried "amongst the Jews."[32] The body of Nazarius, who had been buried in a garden "outside the city," was translated to the Basilica of the Apostles, at the Roman gate of the city of Aquileia. Here too the blood of the martyr was still wet, and Paulinus observes that "then we were filled with a fragrance that outshone the sweetness of all of the spices."[33]

Ambrose is perhaps *the* central figure in the development of the distribution of relics, which would eventually become common with the cult of the saints. It was under his episcopal oversight that the cult of the saints grew into what it would become in the following centuries. His approach to the remains of the saints was significantly different from that of Damasus. Damasus saw the burial locations and inscriptions of the important dead as a perfect way in which to re-create an idealized and unified past, leading up to an idealized unified present with him at the head of this unified church. The remains were dynamic in their meaning but static in their locations. Ambrose of Milan was not to be thwarted by the fact that the important dead had been buried in one particular location, a location that (sadly) was not directly under the altar of his basilica. In prior church-building endeavors, done in relation to graves of saints or other important dead the church structure was molded around the saint's tomb. However in 386, after his congregation expressed their desire for relics of saints as other churches had, Ambrose received a vision in a dream, which told him of the exact location of the burial of Gervais and Protasius.

Power is always active and incorporates multiple forces, and it is not necessarily ever unidirectional. Power, or perhaps more precisely the ability to act upon others through the construction of truth and reality, must use tools that work effectively upon those that it is wished to influence. Some of Ambrose's authority and influence over his congregation came from the desire of his congregation for local martyrs to venerate: his usage of the remains of the saints was a means of solidifying his power

---

32. Paulinus of Milan *Vit. Ambr.* 8. This of course is further evidence for the idea discussed in Chapter One about the comingling of graves, or even the notion that at the time of their death, there was not a strong distinction between Jews and Christians in Milan. See Daniel Boyarin, *Dying for God: Martyrdom and the Making of Christianity and Judaism* (Stanford, CA: Stanford University Press, 1999), on the possibility of a false dichotomy surrounding these designations in the first two centuries.

33. Paulinus of Milan, *Vit. Ambr.* 8.32 (PL 14.0038C), author's trans.

within Milan, but also of projecting of his own (and by extension, Milan's) influence throughout Europe as he spread the relics from Milan.[34]

However, it should be noted that, at least according to Ambrose, the impetus for this discovery was not *his* desire for saints' remains within his church, but rather the popular demands of his congregation. He had already consecrated the Basilica Apostolorum (what he refers to in *Ep.* 22 as the "Roman basilica") with the relics of martyrs.[35] Afterwards he observed the power that the presence of these foreign martyrs had on his congregation. Those in power were using the cult of the saints as a tool for the establishment of social control, but one must also bear in mind that this was a tool that they were given by the larger Christian population. While it is possible that Ambrose's use of the remains of the saints was a complete Ambrosian creation (and I am not unsympathetic to this stance), it is also important to note that his novel uses of the martyr's relics would not have been tolerated, or embraced, if there had not been some desire for this sort of commemoration among his congregation. Without a receptive audience – one which was willing to accept the novel language of relic dissemination – Ambrose's actions would not have been effective. McLynn is surprisingly uncritical of Ambrose's intentions with regard to this essentially unprecedented discovery and translation. He argues: "The fourth-century cult of the martyrs was not a pantomime staged for the vulgar but a channeling of powerful energies too intractable for the bishop to have controlled at will, and too pervasive for him to have thought to try."[36] This argument places far too much credence upon the the cult of the martyrs as propelled by random tidal forces, pulling Ambrose from the safe shores of his (deliberate, calculated) plan of enshrining himself in his basilica, out to the unsteady seas of the cult. Indeed, it is precisely the "pervasive" and "powerful energies" of the cult of the martyrs that made it the perfect tool for Ambrose to use to satisfy his congregation, unify the church in Milan,

---

34. My understanding of power in this case stems from my understanding of Foucault's usage of power; see Michel Foucault, "Afterword: The Subject and Power," in H. C. Dreyfus and Paul Rabinow, *Michel Foucault: Beyond Structuralism and Hermeneutics* (2nd ed.: Chicago: University of Chicago Press), 208–26, as well as the interviews he gave in *Power/Knowledge: Selected Interviews and Other Writings, 1972–1977* (ed. Colin Gordon: New York: Pantheon Books, 1980). For an overview of Foucault and power see Isaak Dore, "Foucault on Power," *UMKC Law Review* 78 (2009–10): 737–48.

35. The *Martyrologium Hieronymianum* describes those remains as that of the Apostles John, Andrew, and Thomas. This would mean that Andrew had been moved from Constantinople to Milan in 386. See Allan Doig, *Liturgy and Architecture from the Early Church to the Middle Ages* (Aldershot, UK: Ashgate, 2008), 58.

36. McLynn, *Ambrose*, 215.

counter his Arian opponents (who derided the cult) and re-establish his own power, and spread his influence throughout the West.

Specifically within Milan and the Arian conflict, Paulinus criticizes the Arians for not admitting properly the miraculous nature of the relics discovered by Ambrose:

> [A] great number of Arians who sided with [Empress] Justina ridiculed such grace of God as the Lord Jesus denied to confer upon His Catholic Church by the merits of the martyrs. And they claimed that the venerable man Ambrose had by means of money prepared men to state falsely that they were troubled by unclean spirits and to say that they were tortured by him just as by the martyrs.[37]

Here Paulinus may have been recounting actual events wherein a group of those loyal to Arius and his theology mocked the miracles that Ambrose claimed had taken place, accusing him of bribing men to claim that they had been healed. It may also have been polemical on the part of Paulinus, as another way to demonize his opponents. The important thing was that Paulinus saw the acceptance, as miraculous, of the events that took place around the remains of the martyrs as a sign of one's faith. Failure to accept these events as miraculous meant that one would be labeled as "other," and the other in this case was "Arian." In the text he also essentially accused the Arians of being like the "Jews"; that is to say, not sufficiently Christian. Here we have a litmus test for Paulinus: if you are truly Christian you will properly revere the relics of the saints, as presented to you by their mediator, the bishop of Milan.

If Ambrose had been content to discover, exhume, and rebury the remains of the martyrs, his importance to the creation of a universal Christian cultural memory would not have been nearly as central as it was. Ambrose was perhaps more important than Damasus and Constantine here, because he extended the power of the saints that he discovered – and consequently his own power – through the distribution of their remains. No-one prior to Ambrose had done this in the way that he did. Ambrose is known to have sent relic fragments to Paulinus, Severus, Gaudentius, Augustine,[38] and Victricius of Rouen. This spreading of the bloody seed of Christian memory throughout the empire was, according to Paulinus of Nola, inspired by Christ:

---

37. Paulinus of Milan, *Vit. Ambr.* 5.15 (PL 14.32b), trans. John A. Lacy in *Early Christian Biographies* (ed. Roy J. Deferrari: New York: Catholic University of America Press, 1952), 42.

38. Augustine briefly mentions the presence "here" of relics of Gervais and Protasius in *Serm.* 318. This sermon was most likely given in Hippo concerning the presence of the relics of Stephen, and as such may have been written ca. 425. Consequently it is entirely possible that the relics did not come from Ambrose, but rather from his successor in Milan, Simplicianus.

> Since the faith had initially not been spread through the whole world alike, many areas of the earth were without martyrs. This I think is why Christ has both inspired princes (in the first place when Constantine was Caesar) and acquainted His servants with His most generous decision to summon martyrs from their earlier homes and translate them to fresh lodgings on earth.[39]

Victricius of Rouen, in a sermon to commemorate the arrival of relics from Ambrose sometime after 395, also discusses the nature of the whole of the martyr as present in each tiny fragment:

> Before our eyes are blood and clay. [...] We demonstrate that the whole can be in the part. So we can no longer complain of smallness: for when we said that, as in the genus, nothing of sacred bodies perishes, we certainly reckoned that what is divine cannot be diminished, because it is wholly present in the whole. And wherever it is anything, it is whole. [...] Moreover, their healing power is no less in the parts than in the entirety.[40]

Through his control over the early trade in relics, Ambrose situated himself to become a sort of patron of relics and their power in the late fourth-century church. His actions appeared to be in flagrant disregard of an edict proclaimed by Maximus, Valentinian, and Theodosius delivered at Constantinople in February of 386, which declared that it was illegal to translate a body already buried, or to dismember it for distribution or sale.[41] There was a desire for martyrs' relics, and the church in Rome – home to the highest density of those relics – jealously guarded them as a way to maintain the importance of the Eternal City (even as the capital of the West had been moved to Milan, and Constantinople had replaced Rome as the capitol of the empire). By proclaiming that he had found these relics, and then generously sharing them with his fellow clergy, Ambrose cemented his personal role in the newly expanding sacred geography of Europe, as well as the prominence of Milan. He was the one to whom bishops turned when they needed to share in the sanctity (or political effectiveness) of the martyrs. Even if a city had martyr tombs (as in Hippo or Nola), the reception of relics from Ambrose may have become something akin to a status symbol, an official spiritual connection to the larger church. The reception of relics was a means of creating a

---

39. Paulinus of Nola, *Carm.* 19.317 (PL 61.0530B), trans. P. G. Walsh, *The Poems of St. Paulinus of Nola* (New York: Paulist Press, 1975), 142.

40. Victricius of Rouen, *De Laude Sanctorum,* 10.2 (PL 20.0452B), 10.15 (PL 20.0452C), 11.1 (PL 20.0453A). All extracts trans. in Gillian Clark "Victricius of Rouen: Praising the Saints," *Journal of Early Christian Studies* 7 (1999): 356–99. Gregory of Nazianzus also expresses this sentiment in *Or.* 4.

41. See Clark, "Translating Relics," 169. Could the Emperors have been concerned with the distribution of the sacred, and the consequential loss of prestige for Constantinople? It is possible that Ambrose received relics from Luke and Andrew from Constantinople at almost exactly the same time as this decree was issued.

degree of sacred homogeneity, which would have been an effective way for less powerful or charismatic bishops to ward off rival claims of power, or subvert local cults.

Paulinus of Nola inscribed his gratitude to Ambrose into the altar at his basilica at Fundi:

> Under the lighted altar, a royal slab of purple marble covers the bones of holy men. Here God's grace sets before you the power of the apostles by the great pledges contained in this meagre dust. Here lies father Andrew, the gloriously famed Luke, and Nazarius, a martyr glorious for the blood he shed; here are Protasius and his peer Gervais whom God made known after long ages to His servant Ambrose. One simple casket embraces here his holy band, and in its tiny bosom embraces names so great.[42]

Here Paulinus not only discussed whose relics were within the altar, but also where they came from. Ambrose, through his distribution of Protasius and Gervais, ensured his own stamp upon the ecclesiastical infrastructure. Ambrose was explicitly named in Paulinus's inscription, again both ensuring his own fame and prestige and also solidifying the importance of Milan. In essence, Ambrose was engaging in advertising, in building the "brand" of Milan as the home of Protasius and Gervais, through his distribution of their relics. If people were constantly made aware of these two previously unknown martyrs, they might have been inclined to make pilgrimages to Milan (instead of, or at least in addition to, Rome) which would have solidified the status of Milan as a (if not "the") focal city. Even if the altar described by Paulinus was not physically aimed at Milan, in a very real sense it pointed to Milan directly.

Peter Brown suggests that the willingness of the late fourth-century episcopate to participate in the cult of the saints through the construction of these elaborate basilicas in their honor had much to do with the growing wealth of the Church, and a need to spend that wealth in a seemly fashion.[43] I cannot argue against the reality of the Church's acquisition of wealth, and its effect on the magnitude of Christian construction endeavors. I do not, however, feel that this accounts for the entirety of the excitement and eagerness of the bishops. When Paulinus replied to his dear friend Severus that he could not give him any relics for the consecration of his basilica (see below p. 110), the basilica was at the time nearly complete

---

42. Paulinus of Nola, *Ep.* 32.18 (PL 61.0339a-b), trans. P. G. Walsh in vol. 2 of *Letters of St. Paulinus of Nola* (2 vols. New York: Newman Press, 1967), 151.

43. Peter Brown, *The Cult of the Saints: Its Rise and Function in Latin Christianity* (Chicago: University of Chicago Press, 1981), 39 ff. To be fair to Brown, this was not the only reason he proposes that the episcopate embraced the Cult of the Saints.

(if not consecrated), which means that it was being built with or without the relics; relics therefore were desirable but not necessary for Christian construction. This desirability must have followed Constantine's building endeavors, which had been focused around (especially in regard to basilica construction) the remains of the saints. Ambrose himself mirrors that association, with both the dedication of the "Roman" basilica as well as with the translation of the remains to the "Ambrosian." I submit that the Constantinian basilicas were especially effective due in large part to the incorporation of the remains of the saints, and it was this effectiveness that was the impetus for imitation.

The Roman Church had no interest in diluting its power. Paulinus, Prudentius, Damasus, and even Constantine (through the translations of important relics to Constantinople so that it would rival Rome) saw the spiritual power and consequential importance of Rome as stemming from its possession of a tremendous number of relics, most importantly those of Peter and Paul. At a time when Rome (and Milan for that matter) was working to create a Western Christianity with Latin as its primary language,[44] the Roman saints were important to Rome precisely because they were *in* Rome. In the shadow of this spiritual powerhouse, Milan could not claim any sort of primacy. While the "notorious invention of Sts. Gervais and Protasius by Ambrose in 386"[45] appeased Ambrose's own population in Milan, their fame would not spread much past the walls of the city without help.

Ambrose saw to it that the relics did not remain within Milan, tucked safely away under the altar in the resting spot that he had intended for himself. He did not jealously guard the power of his relics, as did the Roman Church, but rather through his generous distribution of those relics guaranteed a place for both himself and his city in the heart of Nola, Brescia, Hippo, Roan, and Aquitaine. We know from the writings of Augustine, Paulinus, and Victricius that these relics were not seen as abominations, but rather were welcomed and even sought out for the consecration of basilicas. Paulinus and Victricius both wrote that this was God's plan so as to spread the seed of Christianity as far and wide as possible. One has to wonder if it would have been possible for anyone other than Ambrose to have accomplished this paradigm shift in the approach to the translation of relics. He was the mentor to Augustine, one of the most dominant figures within Western Christianity at the time; he also commanded the respect of Paulinus of Nola, a fierce enthusiast for the

---

44. See Lafferty, "Translating Faith."
45. Cyril Mango "Constantine's Mausoleum and the Translation of Relics," *Byzantinische Zeitschrift* 83 (1990): 53.

cult of Felix in Nola. Would anyone else have been able to have sent out bits of martyrs' bodies and had the recipients see it as an act of generosity rather than a rather disturbing package to have received?

Despite the warm reception with which these relics were met, this practice of distribution was not widely employed. Ambrose was unique in his generation in his eagerness to spread his influence in what Peter Brown refers to as a Christian innovation on the idea of patronage.[46] Although Paulinus sent a sliver of the True Cross to Severus, he did not divide Felix or send on other relics at his friend's request. Cyril Mango may have overstated the revulsion that would have met the dismemberment of corpses in the Roman psyche;[47] it was, however, not something that other bishops (e.g. Paulinus, Damasus) were eager to replicate, either because of squeamishness or the desire to keep the cult center under their own control.

Ambrose's model may not have become the standard form of treatment of relics until the following centuries, yet his method did have something in common with those who wished to keep the bodies of the martyrs whole. Both groups sought to keep the remains of the saints under episcopal control. Through the incorporation of the remains of Protasius and Gervais into the basilica in Milan, and through the construction of other official church structures over the remains of the important dead, the episcopate nearly universally sought to bring the corpses of the important dead, and more importantly the cultic activity that surrounded those corpses, under the control of the official church structure. Ambrose's innovative dispersal of relics was possibly unique to him, yet he was not distributing them to the powerful wealthy widows, or other *individuals*. Ambrose was sending his relics to fellow bishops. These bishops would then have been able to control the use of the relics, and any cultic activity that surrounded them; they would not have become private talismans, but would have remained available to the whole of the Christian community for use in an approved of manner.[48] There would have been less and less private devotion (as well as feasting and drinking) at the smaller memorials and more communal veneration of the saints within the church structures, where the practices, and more importantly the message, could be tightly controlled. This aided the creation of cultural memory, precisely because it ensured that memory was

---

46. Brown, *Cult of the Saints*, 41ff.
47. Mango, "Constantine's Mausoleum."
48. See also Hippolyte Delehaye, *Les origines du culte des martyrs* (Bruxelles: Bureaux de la Société des Bollandistes, 1912), 65–6; Brown, *Cult of the Saints*; Michael Roberts, *Poetry and the Cult of the Martyrs: The* Liber Peristphanon *of Prudentius* (Urbana: University of Michigan Press, 1993), 15–17.

available to the entire community and allowed that memory to be more consistent. The fact that the episcopate retained control of these remains (and their cult) tells us who controlled the *form* that cultural memory took, but the cultural memory only *exists at all* precisely because the episcopate sought to ensure the communal nature of the martyrs' remains. For collective memory to exist it must be a "collective notion (not an individual belief) about the way things were in the past."[49]

Augustine of Hippo

> But then the only reason why the name Memorials or Monuments is given to those sepulchres of the dead which become specially distinguished, is that they recall to memory, and by putting in mind cause us to think of, them who by death are withdrawn from the eyes of the living, that they may not by forgetfulness be also withdrawn from men's hearts.[50]

Augustine's development of his understanding of the efficacy of the role of the tombs of the martyrs may well have coincided with his own understanding of the usefulness of the cult as a means of inspiring his congregation. His treatment of the martyr cult is one that is filled with ambiguity, but no real contradiction; rather, there was a progression in his thought over the latter half of the fourth century into the early fifth.[51] While at no point does he actually contradict his previous statements concerning the role of the martyr grave, or *ad sanctos* burial, he does seem to be ill at ease at times with some of the practices surrounding the cult of the saints.

In the last half of the fourth century, Paulinus of Nola, a strong proponent of the miraculous nature of the remains of martyrs, wrote to Augustine to ask his perspective on the efficacy of *ad sanctos* burials, prompting a cautionary response.[52] One must not think that the physical location in and of itself of burial near a saint can have any direct effect on the deceased, Augustine told his friend, but that it was "more to console the living than care for the dead."[53] However, Augustine then

---

49. Ruth M. Van Dyke and Susan Alcock, eds., *Archaeologies of Memory* (Malden, MA: Wiley-Blackwell, 2002), 2.
50. Augustine, *Cur.* 6 (PL 40.596), trans. H. Browne, *NPNF*² 3:542.
51. See Peter Brown, *Augustine of Hippo: A Biography* (2nd ed.: Berkeley: University of California Press, 2000); "Enjoying the Saints in Late Antiquity," *Early Medieval Europe* 9 (2000): 1–24; Serge Lancel, *Saint Augustine* (London: SCM Press, 2010), 320, for discussions of Augustine becoming more receptive, and eventually enthusiastically repeating, miracle stories associated with the martyrs' relics.
52. Augustine, *Cur.* (PL 40.0591).
53. Augustine, *Cur.* 2.4 (PL 40.0594), author's trans.

softens his criticism of *ad sanctos* burial, noting that it may be advantageous to the dead:

> I do not see how it helps the dead [...] except in this way: through remembrance of the site where they placed the bodies of their loved ones; they will pray on their behalf to those saints [by whom they are buried], who act like their patrons and assist them before the Lord.[54]

For Augustine, the remains of the saints themselves would not aid those buried near to them. It was more the simple fact that if you are buried in a place that people frequent, you are more apt to be remembered than if you were buried in a desolate field. This desire to be buried in a prominent place was reminiscent of the previous Roman desire to be buried along the important roads leading to Rome. It was not because the road itself contained any special power, but rather that it was there that they had the best chance of being remembered, and therefore of gaining immortality.

Augustine is not saying that memory alone is the benefit of *ad sanctos* burial. Rather, it is being remembered by the faithful and then the subsequent prayers given to the martyr that may influence the martyr so as to intercede on behalf of the departed, who then act like patrons for the deceased, in front of God.[55] There is merit in burying the dead, and as such there has to be merit in caring about the location of that burial, but as that merit benefits only the living it will have no effect on the departed.[56] Without the prayers and their subsequent intercession on behalf of the departed, there would be no advantageous effects from burial near the saints. Here Augustine's understanding of the importance of placement for the memory of the departed was decidedly in keeping with previous (and continued) Roman practice.

In addition to the popular, yet for Augustine theologically vacuous, notion that *ad sanctos* burial helped those interred near the martyr's tomb, Augustine had to confront the issue of people offering sacrifices *to* the martyr. In Book 10 of *The City of God*, Augustine indicates that it might be acceptable to worship, revere, or even address in prayer entities who are not God. Nonetheless, it is never acceptable to offer sacrifices to them:

> There are indeed many kinds of worship that have been appropriated from the service of God to be conferred upon men for their honour, an abuse that may come either from carrying humility too far or from the pestilential practice of flattery. Yet those who received such tribute were still considered only men.

---

54. Augustine, *Cur.* 4.6 (PL 40.0596), author's trans.
55. Augustine, *Cur.* 4.6 (PL 40.0596).
56. Augustine, *Cur.* 4.6 (PL 40.0596), repeated at 5.7.

> They are spoken of as men worthy of worship, or of reverence, or even, if we choose to bestow sill more honour, men worthy of being addressed in prayer. But whoever thought it right to offer sacrifice except to one who he knew or considered or pretended was God?[57]

He takes up this theme regarding the cult of the saints when he argues against Faustus the Manichean, who criticized the Christian practices associated with the relics (according to Augustine) – essentially saying that they were different in name only from previous non-Christian traditions: "The sacrifices you change into love feasts, the idols into martyrs, to whom you pray as they to do their idols. You appease the shades of the departed with wine and food."[58] Augustine responds that Christians do not sacrifice to martyrs, but only honor them

> both to excite us to imitate them, and to obtain a share in their merits, and the assistance of their prayers. But we build altars not to the martyrs, but to the God of the martyrs, although it is to the memory of the martyrs [...]. The offering is made to God, who gave the crown of Martyrdom, while it is memory of those thus crowned. The emotion is increased by the associations of the place.[59]

Augustine was concerned with commemorating the memory of the martyrs, and argues that it was through proximity to the remains that the living could feel a stronger connection with the divine. Furthermore, this strong emotion was a psychological consequence within the living, not an effect of the spiritual powers of the deceased.

Faustus also condemned Christians not only for worshiping the martyrs and offering sacrifices to them, but also for getting drunk at the tombs of those martyrs. Faustus could not see any significant difference between the actions of the Christians and those of their non-Christian gentile neighbors. In response to this Augustine had to effectively draw a boundary around the actions of Christians, distinguishing them from those of their neighbors. To do this he pushed for the importance of intentionality. Augustine does not argue that there might be some drunkenness at the tombs, but that even if that is the case, it is better than sacrificing *to* the martyrs; he argues that any misconduct at the shrines should be condemned, just as it should be if it was done in their own homes, "yet even in this, the guilt of intemperance is much less than that of impiety."[60]

In this passage Augustine acknowledged that drunkenness at the memorial meals for the dead was a practice that Christians would have

---

57. Augustine *Civ.* 10.4 (Wiesen LCL).
58. Augustine, *Faust.* 20.4 (PL 42.370).
59. Augustine, *Faust.* 20.21 (PL 42.385), trans. Richard Stothert, *NPNF*[1] 3:262.
60. Augustine, *Faust.* 20.23 (PL 42.388), author's trans.

to "bear for a time," and that it must be grudgingly accepted due to the greater good. Indeed, Augustine speaks from experience as he confesses in "On Obedience":

> When I went to vigils as a student in this city, I spent the night rubbing up beside women, along with other boys anxious to make an impression on the girls, and where, who knows, the opportunity might present itself to have a love-affair with them.[61]

It was not only the opponents of the cult of the martyrs who observed the nefarious acts that were committed at the martyr festivals. Here Augustine, himself a participant and defender of the martyr vigils, is frank in admitting that while he was in his early twenties, he would frequent these festivals where he would mingle (and rub against) women with lascivious intentions. It is important to note that he is recalling a time (the 370s) before he had converted to Christianity, but when he made a regular habit of attending these festivals. Martyr festivals were open to all: those who were baptized, those within the community who were not yet baptized, and those outside the community altogether. They blurred the distinctions between social groups which would have been more strictly enforced elsewhere, allowing an almost unprecedented mingling of disparate groups.

When he preached on the martyrs, Augustine attempted to counteract the influence of the Donatist "heresy," which had both a strong presence in Hippo and had eagerly embraced the cult of the martyrs.[62] Augustine employed the cult of the martyrs not as a means of discussing the joys of the crown of martyrdom, as many had before, but rather as a foil by which he could direct his congregation's attention toward matters of piety which he considered more important. Eventually, through his control of some of the relics of Stephen, he sought to counter the activities of more popular (and unruly) commemorations of local saints, which may have been embraced by his opponents. As in Rome under

---

61. Augustine, *Serm.* 395B5, trans. in Brown, *Augustine*, 456–7. Brown also notes that a Syrian holy man was reputed to have kept his virginity "even though he frequently went to feasts of the martyrs" (457). The presence of this laudatory behavior at the feasts of the martyrs bespeaks a general understanding (warranted or not) of the accessibility of sexual activity at these drunken festivals.

62. The most influential work on the Donatist church remains William H. C. Frend, *The Donatist Church: A Movement of Protest in Roman North Africa* (Oxford: Clarendon Press, 1952). For a general overview of Augustine's interaction with the Donatists see Edward L. Smither, "Persuasion or Coercion: Augustine on the State's Role in Dealing with Other Religions and Heresies" (Faculty Publications and Presentations 14, Liberty Baptist Theological Seminary and Graduate School, 2006). Available at: http://digitalcommons.liberty.edu/cgi/viewcontent.cgi?article=1013&context=lts_fac_pubs

Damasus, Augustine used his power to name authentic martyrs and their relics as a means of solidifying his control in Hippo, and to present the image of the church as one that was unified, universal, and Catholic. This image was in contradistinction with that of his opponents, which was local, without connection to the rest of Christianity (especially that associated with Rome and imperial powers), and Donatist.

Augustine exerted his authority to determine who could be considered a martyr and, more importantly, who could not. He proclaimed that it was impossible for the "heretics" (Donatists) to be martyrs, and explicitly says the dreaded Circumcellions were not.[63] In a letter arguing how the Catholics had been wronged by the Donatists, Augustine complained about the treatment that the Catholics received at the hands of the Circumcellions, and also that once they had died, their thuggery earned them the honor of martyrs: "What they do to us they do not blame on themselves; what they do to themselves, they blame on us. They live as brigands, they die as Circumcellions, they are honored as martyrs."[64] This was echoed in a sermon in which he criticized both those who (he claimed) threw themselves off cliffs in their desire to become a martyr and, even worse (in Augustine's eyes), those who collected the blood of those jumpers, who honored their tombs, and got drunk during their vigils.[65]

It was not only the drinking and self-martyrdom that Augustine railed against; he claimed that the Circumcellions also trafficked in "martyr" relics. In the early years of the fifth century, Augustine protested that the Donatists were selling supposed relics which might not even have been those of martyrs at all.[66] Augustine was more concerned about the sale of the objects and their dubious authenticity than he was the transferal of relics from one place to another. He was also probably annoyed that this was an aspect of his rivals, and therefore took the view that it should be criticized.

Augustine was aware of the popular devotion to martyrs (including those martyrs of his opponents), and rather than subvert it was trying to control who could be seen as having gained the crown of martyrdom. He was, unambiguously, establishing his own power to name, to determine

---

63. Augustine, *Serm.* 313E.7.
64. Augustine, *Ep.* 88.8 (PL 33.0307), trans. Sister Wilfrid Parsons, *St. Augustine: Letters*, vol. 2 *(83–130)* (New York: Fathers of the Church, 1953), 30.
65. Augustine, *Serm.* 313E.5; on self-inflicted martyrdom see Augustine, *Ep.* 185.3.12.
66. Augustine, *Mon.* 28 (PL 40.556).

who should be the proper recipient of the respect given to martyrs, rather than condemning the process as a whole.

After Augustine's conversion and subsequent rise in the episcopal ranks he attempted to limit the actions that could be performed at the martyr shrines. However, as we see in *Ep.* 29.9 he placed the blame for bad behavior on those who had previously been pagan (although here he does not admit that he, himself, had been one of those troublemakers in his youth).[67] Elsewhere he criticizes those who have converted to Christianity in name only, but still carry on at the festivals as if they were still pagan.[68] Augustine eventually wrote to Bishop Aurelius of Carthage for help with what he clearly saw as a problem of the Church in North Africa as a whole. The problem was principally that "drinking and partying are considered to be acceptable, that even on the most blessed days honoring the martyrs this behavior was tolerated."[69] Augustine's main concern was not necessarily the practices associated with the memorials of the saints, but general drunkenness. How, he wonders, can one prohibit an activity in the homes of men that is allowed in honor of the martyrs? Augustine cautions, however, that there might be other ways of dealing with these practices than through strict denunciation; he favored teaching proper behavior rather than simply forbidding that which was improper.[70] One of the concerns that Augustine presents is that there was inconsistency within the African church concerning these practices, and he wants Aurelius to issue clear advice.

Eating and drinking at the tombs of the saints was not only the purview of those with a desire for riotous partying. Augustine's own mother was once criticized for bringing wine and food with her when she visited the martyrs' shrines:

> When she came to the tomb of the saints the sexton prevented her from bringing porridge and bread and wine with her, as she had in Africa. As soon as she understood that the Bishop had forbidden this, she so piously and obediently obeyed that I marveled at how easily she put aside her own custom rather than complain about the present prohibition.[71]

Augustine quickly notes that his mother was no drunkard, but that she brought her pot of wine which was lukewarm and mixed with water.

---

67. He also blames "the Heretics" for bad behavior in *Ep.* 29.11.
68. Augustine, *Mor. Eccl.* 34 (PL 32.1326).
69. Augustine, *Ep.* 22.1.3 (PL 33.0091), author's trans.
70. Augustine, *Ep.* 22.5. One has to wonder if he was here responding to Ambrose's prohibitions in Milan.
71. Augustine, *Conf.* 6.2, author's trans.

It was none other than Ambrose who prohibited the consumption of wine at the martyr shrines, not for those such as Augustine's mother – of course – but to ensure that the anniversaries of the martyrdom, among the more unscrupulous, might not continue to be hotbeds of debauchery.

From this passage we see that the practice of bringing wine and foods to the tombs of the martyrs was an African custom, with which his mother was familiar. Drinking at the graveside was something that was becoming enough of a problem that Ambrose at this point sought to curtail it in Milan. Augustine discusses this event not so much to tell the reader about the events surrounding the shrines of the martyrs, which were quite possibly so well-known at the time of his writing that it would not have occurred to him that it might need discussion. Rather, he wished to contrast his pious and obedient mother with the other groups of less pious or less obedient Christians who were not so willing to give up their customs. Augustine does not discuss how long this custom had been practiced in Africa, but the assumption is that it was not something new to either Augustine or to his mother at the time of his tenure in Milan (ca. 384).

For Augustine, the cult of the saints was something, at least early in his career, that was to be tolerated, but also something that needed to be held in check. The beliefs of those who held it dear were to some extent quaint, drawing upon ethnic customs (as in the case of his own mother), but often for Augustine theologically questionable. However, toward the end of his life (explicitly in *City of God*) he was more open and willing to include the martyr cult into his own spiritual life and ultimately into his own church. Book 22 of *The City of God* recounts many miraculous occurrences, most of which relate to martyr relics in one way or another. Here Augustine recounted, with some degree of pride, the miraculous occurrences associated with Stephen in Hippo. The relics came to Hippo under Augustine's oversight, who asked people to share publically the miracles associated with these relics.[72] Augustine was interested in giving the community access to the martyrs' remains (under his control, of course). He also wanted everyone to know about the efficacy of these relics to cure ailments, and for this memory to be effective in bringing people to God it had to be collective among the Christian community.

---

72. Clark, "Translating Relics," 168, traces Stephen's circuitous route to Augustine. Despite John of Jerusalem taking them to Jerusalem, Lucian kept some bones and dust and then gave them to Avitus of Braga (on pilgrimage to the Holy Land as well as to debate Pelagianism). Avitus then gave some to Orosius (from Spain) who then gave some to Evodius of Uzalis, who then gave some to Augustine. See also Scott Bradbury, *Severus of Minorca* (New York: Oxford University Press, 1996), 16–24.

Iver Kaufman argues that for Augustine, his "*City* certainly supposes that Christians will search in time rather than in particular places, in history rather than exclusively at gravesites and shrines."[73] While this may be true, it is also equally true that even though the shrines of the saints presented some problems in terms of the practices associated with them, they were instrumental in the creation of the cultural memory of the Christian community in Hippo. Augustine was attempting to craft a memory that would survive attacks from multiple fronts: from those who also claimed to be Christians, but whose orthodoxy Augustine disputed, as well as from those who had migrated south after the disastrous events of 410 and who had not embraced Christianity. This memory was one that was informed by the misery of this earthly life.

For Augustine the miracles of the saints were important to more than those healed by them, primarily because they drew the attention of the believer (and non-believer alike) to the god of the martyrs. When he discussed, in a sermon, the discovery of the relics of Stephen, and finally the construction of the shrine for Stephen in Augustine's basilica in Hippo, he was quite explicit that the altar was not built *to* Stephen, but rather to God: "We have not erected an altar to Stephen, but with the relics of Stephen we have erected an altar to God."[74]

Augustine preached about the martyrs primarily on their feast days. Almost every time he did so he then used the martyrs as a means of instructing his congregation about how to live a more perfect Christian life. In *Serm.* 318, when discussing the discovery of Stephen's relics he turns the sermon not to the miraculous nature of that discovery, but rather to how life is fraught with temptation. The martyrs were the primary example of how one should deal with this.[75] Even if there was no threat of martyrdom for the residents of Hippo near the end of the fourth century, they were likely of a mind to listen to an "'occult' tempter" who urged the sick person to wear a charm so that they might live. Augustine argued that this was tantamount to the offer of the old pagan emperors who would also grant life to those who offered sacrifice to them. Be steadfast in your faith, he instructed his congregation, just as the martyrs had been in theirs.

---

73. Peter Iver Kaufman, "Augustine, Martyrs and Misery," *Church History* 63 (1994): 8.

74. Augustine, *Serm.* 318.1 (PL 38.1438), author's trans.

75. This is also interesting because it implies that some of the remains of Gervais and Protasius made their way to Hippo. This seems to be the only reference to the presence of these two saints in Hippo.

Serm. 323 was to be delivered after the reading of an account recounting how a young man had been healed from his tremors at the shrine of Stephen in Hippo.[76] Augustine took the opportunity not to preach so much on Stephen, but rather on the need for children to honor their parents. The young man was stricken with this curse after his mother had been beaten by his older brother. She then went to the baptistery and called upon God to curse that child. Sadly her curse was so effective that all of her children were afflicted, which ultimately led to her suicide.[77] To children, he cautioned that they should honor their parents, and he urged parents to remember their role as parents. Finally there was the admonition that "you must learn only to make requests to God which you are not afraid of being granted." In all of this Stephen was secondary, at best. The relics were simply the particular medium that God chose. This was the point that Augustine was trying to get across to his congregation. However, it would also appear that the mother sought out Stephen's relics because she believed that they were the effective agent.

Augustine's life and preaching exemplify some of the debates surrounding the cult of the saints at their graves which persisted through the end of the fourth century and into the fifth. In his youth, he participated in the festive atmosphere that surrounded the late-night vigils and comingling of the sexes at the graves of the martyrs. Later he tolerated the idea that there was some benefit to the practice of *ad sanctos* burial, but it was only through the prayers of the living whose memory was jogged by the presence of the grave, and not through physical proximity (absent the intercessory living agent to pray to the martyr on behalf of the deceased) to the grave. He also strongly defended the intercessory role of the martyr, who would mediate with the living God, while bemoaning the popular practices (especially of drinking) that took place at the tombs. Finally, he warmly embraced the relics of Stephen into Hippo, and became a strong supporter of that cult and of its miraculous aspects.

If we look at the development of Augustine's thought, it may appear to be inconsistent and perhaps irreconcilable. However, for Augustine, as with many other bishops near the end of the fourth century, the cult of the saints was the site on which the battle for the cultural memory and self-definition of Christianity was waged. I submit that when Augustine embraced the cult of Stephen, he was not so much embracing the cult of the saints, but was rather looking to use existing North African practices associated with the cult (including those of the Donatists) as a means of

---

76. We will deal with another aspect of this narrative in Chapter Five.
77. See also Augustine, *Serm.* 322 (PL 38.1444).

moving away from local divisions within Christianity. It was not unique to North Africans to focus on the cult of the *local* saint, but it was a practice that Augustine sought to counter in his own community. The local saints' cults had pre-existing and troublesome practices associated with them; the local saint maintained the boundaries of one Christian group against another (most explicitly the notion that there were Donatist martyrs and Catholic martyrs). Augustine saw the cult of Stephen as a means of breaking down these local boundaries and he sought to use their predispositions toward the cult of the saints as a way to focus his countrymen's energies on a saint that embraced a Catholic, or universal, Christianity.

Augustine demonstrated a preference for universal (or trans-local) saints over and against the ones found locally, even when there were no relics of that saint within his city. However, he was not always successful in this, no matter how significant the chosen universal saint was, and the relics of local saints in Hippo remained the most important for his congregation, often to his consternation. In *Serm.* 298, on the feast day of Peter and Paul, Augustine lamented the small turn out of the faithful, contrasting it to the much larger crowds at the festivals of local saints. These local saints he calls "lambs," as distinct from the festival of the "rams" who should be much more honored.[78] Augustine sought to entice and seduce his congregation through a medium that they traditionally embraced, and focus their energy soberly toward the church of the empire and away from the church of the particular locality.

Paulinus of Nola

Unlike many of his episcopal peers, Paulinus of Nola unabashedly embraced, encouraged, and promoted the cult of the saints, especially that of Nola's local hero, Felix.[79] In contrast to Augustine's ambivalence regarding the place of the martyr in Christian practice (as noted above), Paulinus was decidedly unambiguous and consistent in his endorsement of the cult of the saints. Prior to his arrival at Nola and his tenure as the bishop thereof, Paulinus had a fondness for a third-century saint, Felix of Nola. Once Paulinus rose to the episcopate, he became the central force for the revival of his cult. Through his use of the martyr cult, the reach of Paulinus extended far beyond the confines of his relatively small urban center. The annual festival of Felix's "birthday"

---

78. Augustine, *Serm.* 289.1.1 (PL 38.1365).
79. Paulinus knew of Felix as a confessor (that is to say someone who was willing and scheduled to suffer martyrdom, but who does not actually do so) but often refers to him as a martyr, and in every other sense treats him as a martyr.

was an event that drew crowds of pilgrims from Rome, some 224 km northwest of Nola.

As regards the direction of popular practice in the Church in the following centuries, it can be argued that Paulinus was second only to his esteemed friend Ambrose when it comes to the cult of the saints and the creation of a Christian memory at the graves of the saints. Indeed, through his nearly complete reinvention of the cult of Felix in Nola,[80] and his assistance to other Italian bishops in the construction of saints' shrines, he may even rival Ambrose as the most influential bishop of the fourth and early fifth centuries.

As noted above, Paulinus had a reputation for poetic eloquence, based on the poems that he composed annually for the "birthday" of Felix as well as his inscriptions over the remains of the saints in Nola. Paulinus's longtime friend Severus contacted Paulinus asking him for help in writing inscriptions for his own church. The letter that Paulinus penned in response to this request demonstrates how the two bishops were continuing the tradition of Damasus and were clearly interested in establishing text in stone over the remains of martyrs. It is also a testament to the importance of the cult of Felix to Paulinus, and the congregation at Nola.

There are two letters from Paulinus to Severus which help us understand the importance of relics in both of their churches. *Ep.* 31, dated to 403, was written in response to Severus's request for "some blessed object from the sacred relics of the saints, with which to adorn your family church in a manner worthy of your faith and service."[81] Paulinus expresses his regret that he cannot fulfill the request from his close friend, but is relieved that there is a possibility of a relic from Silvia, "who had promised him some of the relics of many Eastern Martyrs." Paulinus, as he had no relics or ashes (that he was willing) to share, was able to spare a tiny fragment of the True Cross, which he believed would also enhance Severus's collection of relics and aid in the consecration of the basilica.[82]

In *Ep.* 32, Paulinus presents a collection of verses that Severus had asked him to write to commemorate the saint's relics that were going to be found in Severus's new basilica, which would be in close imitation of Paulinus's own church structure. The inscriptions that Paulinus

---

80. See Catherine Conybeare, *Paulinus Noster: Self and Symbols in the Letters of Paulinus of Nola* (New York: Oxford University Press, 2000), 3ff.
81. Paulinus of Nola, *Ep.* 31.1 (PL 61.0325B), trans. Walsh, *Letters*, vol. 2, 125.
82. Paulinus of Nola, *Ep.* 31.1 (PL 61.0325B).

suggests in *Ep.* 32 differ significantly from those that Damasus established in Rome: there is no discourse on the unity of the church, indicating that this was not a concern for either Paulinus or Severus, and that whereas Damasus had to secure his own position and authority through the inscriptions over the relics of the martyrs, Paulinus did not feel that this was necessary. He did not offer potential inscriptions to his friend which would promote Severus either. While some of the inscriptions that Paulinus offers to Severus include a brief mention that Severus built the structure, the inscriptions over the relics do not exhibit the self-referential nature that we saw with the Damasian inscriptions.

One exception to this tendency of avoiding explicit references to himself or Severus was a poem written as a prayer to Clarus (who was interred beneath an altar); rather than being an expository text discussing his life, the prayer sought protection for himself and Severus:

> In your kindness receive these prayers of sinners who ask you to be mindful of Paulinus and Therasia. Love these persons entrusted to you by the mediation of Severus, though when you were here in the flesh you were unaware of their merits [...]. So embrace Severus and Paulinus together as brothers indivisible. Love us and join with us in this union. God summoned us together, Martin loved us together. So, Clarus, you must likewise protect us together.[83]

It is unknown which poem Severus chose from those provided by Paulinus, if any, but simply the fact that Paulinus would have seen this as an appropriate inscription to have been placed near the altar indicates that at least *Paulinus* would have approved. It also demonstrates the influential role that Paulinus himself had, in the eyes of a contemporary (and close friend), in fostering "appropriate" memorials at the graves of the saints. Paulinus was explicitly calling upon Clarus to care for his soul, to remember him, much as Damasus was calling upon the reader of his inscriptions (although more often implicitly) to remember him as they were remembering the martyr. The important difference here was that Paulinus was demonstrating the desire for a saint to remember him (explicitly), which would have (as per Damasus, implicitly) been enacted by the reader of the text.

Once Paulinus has finished offering these verses to Severus he recounts the poems that he has placed in the basilica in Nola, as well as another basilica he had constructed in Fundi, where Paulinus once held property and visited frequently. It is not only the words that are inscribed on the tombs of the martyrs, but the structures themselves which break with

---

83. Paulinus of Nola, *Ep.* 32 (PL 61.333D–334A), trans. Walsh, *Letters*, vol. 2, 141.

tradition and focus on what Paulinus considers to be the most important cultic feature: "The outlook of the basilica is not, after the usual fashion, towards the East, but faces the basilica of blessed Lord Felix, looking out upon his tomb."[84] Felix has taken the place of Jerusalem as the primary point of orientation of this basilica, announcing to any and all who observe the outlook of the building that Felix was the point around which their shared culture was focused. Where previously the church structure looked to Jerusalem for salvation from the returning Jesus, it now looked to Felix. He was even given, by Paulinus, the honorific "Lord" which was traditionally (even in this letter) reserved for Jesus.[85] The altar contained a sliver of the True Cross, presumably the one that Paulinus fragmented further to send a piece to Severus with his previous letter (*Ep.* 31). The inscription before this altar repeated the refrain that "the whole power of the cross lies in this small segment."[86] Here, as he had suggested that Severus do, the cross is buried in the altar with the ashes of martyrs.

As he further described the basilica he noted that the twin colonnades contained four chapels, each for private meditation and for the funeral monuments of the clergy "and their friends, so that they may rest in eternal peace." One has to wonder if this letter was influenced by the letter that Paulinus received from Augustine, entitled *On the Care of the Dead*. Note that Paulinus did not observe that these essentially *ad sanctos* burial locations would aid in the salvation of the priests and their friends, but rather that burial near the saint would ensure their peace. There was no discussion at all of how burial *ad sanctos* might relate to their salvation, which would suggest that this may well have been written after his correspondence with Augustine, as prior to that discourse, Paulinus appeared to have been uncertain about the efficacy of *ad sanctos* burial – otherwise he would not have written to Augustine for a second opinion on the matter.

Inscriptions that reference Paulinus as the bishop of Nola who constructed both the new and old churches imply that Paulinus had little to do with the church's construction and possibly only had his own inscriptions added subsequently (he does claim them as his own earlier[87]). However, the basilica at Fundi seems to have been entirely Paulinus's own creation. It was the basilica that he had long desired to build; as noted

---

84. Paulinus of Nola, *Ep.* 32.13 (PL 61.337A), trans. Walsh, *Letters*, vol. 2, 147.
85. For a discussion of the church structures in Nola see R. C. Goldschmidt, *Paulinus' Churches at Nola* (Amsterdam: Noord-Hollandsche Uitg. Maatschappij, 1940).
86. Paulinus of Nola, *Ep.* 32.11 (PL 61.0336B), trans. Walsh, *Letters*, vol. 2, 146.
87. Paulinus of Nola, *Ep.* 32.15 (PL 61.0336).

above, he was fond of Fundi due to his previous possession of property (an estate) there.[88] The basilica was not quite consecrated when he wrote this letter, but would eventually "be consecrated by sacred ashes from the blessed remains of apostles and martyrs."[89]

Paulinus's annual poems celebrating Felix's birthday provide a glimpse into how he presented the festival celebrating the day, framing the event in which the original audience of the poem were themselves participating. Paulinus also recounted how huge crowds would throng to the tomb:

> from the mouth of the Porta Capena she [Rome] pour[ed] fourth thousands, dispatching them in a thick swarm over the hundred and twenty miles to the walls of friendly Nola. The Appian way [was] invisible for long distances through the thick-massed crowds.[90]

Under his tutelage the cult of Felix broadened its appeal from that of a local saint to one which drew pilgrims from all over. Rome itself, home to uncounted martyrs and their shrines, disgorged massive crowds to make the not insignificant trip to Nola for the celebration of the "birthday" of its patron saint. The memory of Felix had a gravitational pull that extended beyond the surrounding countryside, allowing Paulinus, through his promotion of the cult of Felix, to craft the cultural memory not only of his local congregation but also to influence that of Rome. The pilgrims would have taken their experience in Nola back with them to Rome, where it would (of necessity) have influenced their experiences with martyr's shrines at home.

Paulinus's annual poems celebrating the "birthday" of Felix reveal an author who fully embraced the cult of the saints as it had developed under his sponsorship. For Paulinus, the corpse of the martyr was *the* central way that a city gained sanctity. Rome, for Paulinus, was first in sanctity and power *only* because of the presence of the relics of Peter and Paul. Rome itself had no privileged place in his mind beyond the presence of its relics. Nola too, as exemplified by the crowds which could not be contained by the basilica on Felix's feast day, claimed importance through the presence of Felix.[91]

By the time that *Carm.* 27 was written (January 403), Paulinus's church was undergoing renovations enhancing it with various types of embellishment. One of these was lodgings, the uppermost of which

---

88. Paulinus of Nola, *Ep.* 32.17 (PL 61.0336).
89. Paulinus of Nola, *Ep.* 32.17 (PL 61.0338C), trans. Walsh, *Letters*, vol. 2, 150.
90. Paulinus of Nola, *Carm.*14.65–70 (PL 61.0466B), trans. Walsh, *Poems*, 79.
91. Paulinus of Nola, *Carm.* 27 (PL 61.0619).

> look[ed] from their windows above on the inviolate altars, beneath which the saints have their recessed abodes. For the ashes even of apostles have been set beneath that table of heaven, and consecrated amongst other holy offerings they emit a fragrance pleasing to Christ from their living dust.[92]

The list of those interred in the altars is most impressive: the apostles Andrew and Thomas, and also John the Baptist and Luke; and the martyrs Agricola, Vitalis, Proculus, Euphemia, and Nazarius, many of whom had been sent by Ambrose. *Carm* 27 signals the impressiveness of the collection that Paulinus had amassed for the city of Nola, but it was still the presence of the entire corpse of Felix and not the bits and pieces of these other illustrious figures in Christian history that brought the crowds to Nola for Felix's festival.

Drinking during festivals was a widespread practice that most of his contemporaries denounced, but Paulinus was considerably more tolerant: the festival and its less savory aspects, he argued, opened the hearts and minds of the illiterate masses to Felix, and through Felix to God. In *Carm*. 27 he recounts:

> Now the greater number among the crowds here are country folk not without belief but unskilled in reading. For years they have been used to following profane cults in which their god was their belly, and at last they have turned as converts to Christ out of admiration for the undisputed achievements of the saints performed in Christ's name. Notice in what numbers they assemble from all the country districts, and how they roam around, their unsophisticated minds beguiled in devotion [...]. See how they in great numbers keep vigil and prolong their joy throughout the night, dispelling sleep with joy and darkness with torchlight. I only wish they would channel this joy in sober prayer, and introduce their wine cups within the holy thresholds [...]. I none the less believe that such merriment arising from modest feasting is pardonable because their minds beguiled by such guilt are uninitiated [...] and their sins arise from devotion, for they wrongly believe that saints are delighted to have their tombs doused with reeking wine.[93]

Rather than simply bemoan this practice, or ban wine and punish the offender, Paulinus sought to educate and distract the crowds with paintings and inscriptions within the church so that they will be awed by the church structure, and, especially, the example of Felix. This will lead them to drink less and forget the desire for too much wine. So they spend their time admiring the building, which means that not much time would remain for indulging in food and drink.[94] One aspect of the

---

92. Paulinus of Nola, *Carm*. 27.396–405 (PL 61.0675A-B), trans. Walsh, *Poems*, 288.
93. Paulinus of Nola, *Carm*. 27.547–67 (PL 61.0660C–0661A), trans. Walsh, *Poems*, 290.
94. Paulinus of Nola, *Carm*. 27.570ff (PL 61.066).

popular cult that Paulinus depicts here, as he argues against it, is the offering of libations to the dead. Wine was directly offered to the grave of the important dead: "doused with reeking wine."

Paulinus appears to have been alone among his peers in the leniency with which he regarded the consumption of wine at the birthday celebration of Felix. He was comfortable with the consumption of wine during the "modest feasting," as it allowed him to educate their rustic minds. This indulgence, or active encouragement, of previously non-Christian gentile practices surrounding cult centers goes further: in *Carm.* 20 he incorporates images of animal sacrifice, and clearly describes the ritualistic slaughter of two pigs and a cow (of which two had been offered to Felix at their birth). These animals were then cooked and distributed to the poor who had gathered at the shrine to Felix for his annual feast.[95] It was this willing, perhaps eager, incorporation of aspects of the cultic activities of his Nolan neighbors that made the cult of Felix so very popular. This was something that Paulinus seemed to be quite aware of, and perhaps this is why he defends himself against detractors in the opening verses of *Carmen* 20.5:

> Good masters often minister dutifully to their dear charges. They protect subordinate slaves with fatherly love, and show kindness by nurturing with closer care those who with the eyes of love they see are less resourceful or deficient in strength […]. This is my allotted situation under Felix's patronage.[96]

Superficially this passage discusses how Paulinus has been helpful to those who wish to offer their vows to Felix; however, it also defends his willingness to allow practices at the tomb of Felix that had been harshly criticized elsewhere. While Augustine describes his mother's practices as a local phenomenon, they clearly were not. Augustine's mother would have felt right at home at the tomb of Felix, watered-down lukewarm wine and all – even away from her own countrymen.

Paulinus's willingness to indulge practices that others had openly criticized allowed him to welcome huge crowds into the Church. These were decisions that Paulinus could not have taken lightly, as they went against the desires of other, extremely influential, bishops. Perhaps he did not have to worry about the impression that his compatriots would be considered parochial – as did Augustine – due to the proximity of Nola to Rome. He also may not have needed to concern himself as much as did the episcopate in Rome about maintaining practical purity. In any

---

95. Dennis Trout, "Christianizing the Nolan Countryside: Animal Sacrifices at the Tomb of St. Felix," *Journal of Early Christian Studies* 3 (1995): 281–98.

96. Paulinus of Nola, *Carm.* 20.5–10 (PL 61.0551.A), trans. Walsh, *Poems*, 157.

event, Paulinus's allowances permitted the cult of Felix to grow, and his own authority did not suffer because of this. However, unlike Damasus, Ambrose, or Athanasius, the evidence does not support the idea that Paulinus was acting out of a desire for personal influence and prestige. Paulinus was not engaged in any particular struggle within the congregation of Nola, and he did not have to use the cult of the martyrs as a means of expressing his authority over an audience that may have been directly opposed to him. Instead, he was able to work with traditions which were not threatening to him, and through that he leveraged the cult of Felix to impressive popularity.

Sulpicius Severus

What little is known about Sulpicius Severus comes primarily from his correspondence with Paulinus. However, we do know that he was of noble heritage and had received a good education, but that he had ultimately given it all up after his wife died at a young age. While it is true that he did not embrace the cult of the martyrs with quite the enthusiasm that we have seen with the other figures in this chapter, he was interested in its development in his congregation, despite the ambivalence that his predecessor, Martin of Tours, had toward the cult. We see from his correspondence with Paulinus that Sulpicius incorporated relics into his basilica and wanted to honor them with verse

In Severus we also see some caution regarding the popular cult of the saints. In his *Life of Martin* we encounter evidence of a push-back against an over exuberance of the (vernacular) cult of the saints. According to his account, Martin attempted to ensure that the cult of the martyrs did not completely escape episcopal control, and he was concerned about an altar over the remains of an unknown martyr. Martin attempted to verify any popular practices associated with the veneration of martyrs. In one instance, after careful investigation he prayed over the sepulture asking God for guidance as to the character of the individual honored as a martyr:

> Next turning to the left-hand side, he sees standing very near a shade of a mean and cruel appearance. Martin commands him to tell his name and character. Upon this, he declares his name, and confesses his guilt. He says that he had been a robber, and that he was beheaded on account of his crimes; that he had been honored simply by an error of the multitude [...]. Then Martin made known what he had seen, and ordered the altar which had been there to be removed, and thus he delivered the people from the error of that superstition.[97]

---

97. Sulpicius Severus, *Mart.* 11 (PL 20.0166D–0167A), trans. Alexander Roberts,

Here we see Martin, through his prayers, enacted a sort of necromancy, whereby he was able to conjure the spirit of the robber who was buried within the sepulture. This confirmed Martin's suspicion that the altar was not properly placed by a martyr's tomb, but only through the "false opinion of humans." Previously, Martin had been pleased that there was some religious veneration taking place, and so stayed away until such a time as he could verify whose sepulture was being honored as that of a martyr. Severus does not tell us what the impetus was for his decision to go and see this shrine for himself. One could well imagine that the religious veneration that was taking place there had ceased to be of the sort that he found proper, or that it was moving in a direction that Martin could no longer control. Through the summoning of a spirit that no-one else could see, he effectively nullified a cult center that was out of his control.

Apa Shenoute

Apa Shenoute (d. 465), like many Christian leaders in North Africa and his European counterparts, had an ambivalent relationship with the uses of the remains of the martyrs. He was primarily concerned with what was, and what was not, appropriate to do at the tombs of the deceased. He faced similar riotous problems with the anniversaries of the martyrs' death. Shenoute lists the shameful practices that he had seen at the shrines of the saints:

> But to sing, to eat, to drink, to laugh and especially to fornicate and to kill people because of drunkenness and debauchery and fighting in total ignorance is lawless [*lacuna*]. Some within are singing Psalms, reading and performing the sacrament, while others outside have made the sound of the horns and flutes fill the whole place with anger against those who do these things.[98]

Shenoute penned two distinct texts that deal with the use of martyr bodies and the practices associated with their memorials: *Since it Behooves Christians* and *Those Who Work Evil*. Discussions of these texts by David Frankfurter consistently presents Shenoute as an ardent opponent of the martyr cult, but this is not completely supported by the material.[99] In his

---

*NPNF*² 11:9. This chapter is the only time that Severus explicitly mentions martyrs in this work.
    98. Shenoute, *Since it Behooves Christians* (*Œuvres* I: 199–200), unpublished trans. Brakke.
    99. David Frankfurter, *Religion in Roman Egypt: Assimilation and Resistance* (Princeton, NJ: Princeton University Press, 2000), 193; "Beyond Magic and Superstition,"

chapter "Beyond Magic and Superstition," Frankfurter quotes from the latter part of *Those Who Work Evil*:

> Those who adore [martyrs] in some shrine built in their name worship demons, not God. Those who trust that healings come to them, or goods, in a place that they built over some skeletons without knowing whose they are, are no different from those who worshiped the calves that Jeroboam set up in Samaria. [...]
>
> Who among those who fear God will not say "Woe to those who say 'I saw a light in the shrine that they built over some bones of a skeleton in the church, and I was eased of my illness after I slept there'"?[100]

What is worse is that those who introduce bones into a church "do not understand what is proper to do in a church." In another work Frankfurter discusses the idea of spirit possession and necromancy at the tombs of the saints.[101]

There was clearly a strong distrust of the cult of the saints in Shenoute's corpus, especially *Those Who Work Evil*, yet to characterize it as solely a diatribe against the martyr cult is a misrepresentation. To read Frankfurter's interpretation of the text would lead one to believe that Shenoute was critical of all those who worshiped at the shrines of the martyrs, and that everyone there looked to them for necromantic inspiration, which was not the case. *Those Who Work Evil* focused on the practices associated with the relic cult and the "discovery" of the relics, not on the martyr cult as a whole.

Ultimately, Shenoute was attempting to control the practices at the shrines, to limit what could be performed there, in much the same way that we saw with Augustine and Ambrose. The shrine was good when it is used "properly," but it is not always used this way. The tension continued well into the fifth century between those who wanted to continue the festive atmosphere which surrounded the martyrs' vigils, and those who condemned it. In *Since it Behooves Christians* Shenoute asks his readers: "But if what is bitter beyond all bitterness is mixed with what is sweet, will you drink it, oh man?" This begins a discourse on the activities that he sees as polluting the shrines of the saints. He does not dismiss the shrines out of hand, but rather is critical of the bitterness that is mixed

---

in *Late Ancient Christianity*. Vol. 2 of *A People's History of Christianity* (ed. Virginia Burrus: Minneapolis, MN: Fortress Press, 2005), 257; *Pilgrimage and Holy Space in Late Antique Egypt* (Illustrated ed.: Leiden: Brill, 1998).

100. Shenoute, *Those Who Work Evil* (*Œuvres* I: 219), trans. in Frankfurter, "Beyond Magic," 263.

101. David Frankfurter, "Where the Spirits Dwell: Possession, Christianization, and Saints' Shrines in Late Antiquity," *Harvard Theological Review* 103 (2010): 27–46.

with the sweetness of the true meaning of the shrine. He continues: "To go to the places of the martyrs to pray, to read, to sing Psalms, to purify yourself, to bring the offering in the fear of Christ is good; it is the pattern of the Church; it is the cannon of God's house."[102] It is good to go to the tombs of the martyrs, and there is no problem with treating them in roughly the same fashion that you would a church, even going so far as to "bring the offering."

Of course the problems that both Augustine and Jerome were forced to defend against, namely behavior unsuited to these sacred locations, was also a problem for Shenoute in Egypt. Shenoute does not seem to be defending the martyr cult against those who would be rid of the whole project, or who ridicule Christianity because of it; rather, he is saying that it is a good thing, but one needs to be reserved and careful in one's behavior, which is entirely consistent with his approach to life in general (physical as well as spiritual – if they could be divided for him).[103]

One can clearly see how Shenoute envisioned proper behavior within the shrines: the pious taking the Eucharist over the tomb of the martyr, dedicating their attention to God. The peaceful reverence of the pious Christians was too often disturbed by the drunken ignorant masses outside. These crowds came to the shrine to drink and commemorate the deceased through a festival, complete with horns and flutes. Most likely as with the events that Augustine described earlier, the social boundaries were dissolved, men and women mingled and secreted off into the night. Shenoute may well have been dabbling in hyperbole when he described killing as a common part of the vigil; however, it is not completely outside the realm of possibility that fights might have emerged from the intoxicated crowds, possibly engaging in gambling over horse races: "you have made them [the burial locations] places for competition among your animals,"[104] which could have led to death.

For the most part, Shenoute's anger was primarily directed at the priests who allowed such things to happen at the tombs of the martyrs, reminding them that the "place of the martyr is the house of Christ," and then quoting Jesus: "My house shall be called the house of prayer, but you have made it a den of thieves."[105] It is hard to reconcile Frank-

---

102. Shenoute, *Since it Behooves Christians* (*Œuvres* I: 199), trans. David Brakke.
103. Caroline T. Schroeder, *Monastic Bodies: Discipline and Salvation in Shenoute of Atripe* (Illustrated ed.: Philadephia: University of Pennsylvania Press, 2007).
104. Shenoute, *Since it Behooves Christians* (*Œuvres* I: 201).
105. Shenoute, *Since it Behooves Christians* (*Œuvres* I: 200). Shenoute quoted Jesus's cleansing of the temple here (Mt: 21.13, Mk: 11.17, Lk: 19.46).

furter's image of Shenoute being an ardent opponent of the cult of the martyrs, with the one who here compares the tomb of the martyr to the "house of Christ" and the temple in Jerusalem. Even later (in *Those Who Work Evil*), when he accuses those who bring bones into a church of not knowing what is proper to do in a church, he is *not* saying that no bones are proper for a church, but rather that bones of unknown origin are improper. The bones of martyrs are (according to the passage above) the house of Christ by their very nature as martyr relics. It was important to treat the tombs of the martyrs like a church, and not a marketplace (or even worse than a marketplace): "The things that are not done in the marketplaces to those who sell their wares have been done to those who sell their things in the places of the martyrs."[106]

In *Since it Behooves Christians* he had the martyrs speak for themselves, as if they were alive to see the practices of those who were defiling their tombs. The tombs were places that purify the individual, but too often according to Shenoute they were soiled by the activities of those who frequented them. While the accusations of murder were provocative, Shenoute's primary complaint centered on the potential for fornication. He singled out those who protested that they were unmarried, and could not then have been committing adultery, and he went on at length about their finding inconspicuous corners for their inappropriate deeds.[107] Martyr shrines were places where both men and women could go and mingle in a way that was improper elsewhere, and, as a result, apparently darkened corners were found for other reasons than prayer. While these practices, along with the sacrificing of goats and other animals, clearly offend Shenoute, the refrain that Shenoute comes back to again and again in *Since it Behooves Christians* is that these behaviors offended the martyr, who had the power to intercede on behalf of humanity with God. The logical conclusion is that if this offended the martyrs, the behaviors should not be done, and could even acquire the enmity of the martyr and the martyr's god.[108] Theologically, this understanding of the intercessory role of the martyr is one that is completely in accordance with Shenoute's European counterparts.

Shenoute's ire was not aimed at those who feasted at the martyr's tomb, but rather those who claimed to have visions of martyrs proclaiming that they were buried in a particular location and that they should

---

106. Shenoute, *Since it Behooves Christians* (*Œuvres* I: 201).
107. Shenoute, *Since it Behooves Christians* (*Œuvres* I: 203–4).
108. Shenoute, *Since it Behooves Christians* (*Œuvres* I: 205–6).

be exhumed and placed in a church.[109] Shenoute targeted not only his fellow Egyptians but also, possibly, Ambrose, who famously engaged in exactly this sort of behavior. Shenoute even claimed that this behavior only served human ambition and pride: the desire to possess the bones of martyrs within one's church. This ambition, he proclaimed, would be our death.[110]

Shenoute had three problems with those who claimed to have had a vision of the saint telling them where their remains were buried. First, as noted above, there was no way to tell whose bones one was digging up – this even included the possibility of claiming that the bones of a dog were those of a saint, with the scandalous possibility of building a church around those venerable canine remains.[111] However, despite Frankfurter's quotation claiming that those who put bones in churches did not know what is proper to do in a church, Shenoute was not as clear in his prohibition of relics in churches. He was against putting the bones of common Christians, or worse – dogs or non-Christians – into the church, but he was quick to use the disclaimer that no-one knows *whose* bones people claim to have found.[112]

Shenoute had the healthy skepticism of one who did not believe everything that he heard. However, it is not clear that he would have been completely against the remains of one who was clearly and indisputably known to have been a martyr being present in the church. He pointed out that nearly all of the activities that could take place in the church building could take place at the tombs of the martyrs, and he even called the martyrs' tombs "houses of Christ" where the Eucharist could be performed piously. Shenoute said he admired and praised a priest in areas to the south, who, when men came to him claiming to have found the remains of a martyr, replied that either they were incorrect about whose remains they had found, or that they thought the priest would allow the remains of a common man into his church.[113] Note that it was not that he would not allow them to bring bones into the church, but that it was only problematic if they were those of a "common man."

---

109. Shenoute, *Those Who Work Evil* (*Œuvres* I: 212–13).
110. Shenoute, *Those Who Work Evil* (*Œuvres* I: 213).
111. Shenoute, *Those Who Work Evil* (*Œuvres* I: 208).
112. Incidentally, I know of no instances where the bone of anything other than a human has been found in a reliquary. However, given the prominence of the fears in the fourth and fifth centuries that this was happening, and the popularity of the cult, it is not outside of the realm of possibility.
113. Shenoute, *Those Who Work Evil* (*Œuvres* I: 218–19).

This leaves open the possibility that if the remains were something other than *"un homme simple"* they might have had a place in the church.

Second, Shenoute cited the wishes of the venerable brothers themselves, who, he said, had made it clear that they did not wish to have their bones venerated.[114] If it was their wish that no-one know their burial locations, who are you, Shenoute wondered, to deny them their wishes to remain anonymous in death? Shenoute's third concern over the reverence paid to bone fragments of unknown origins, was that they were being lit by candles, and riches were being heaped upon them in the attempt to honor a martyr who may not have desired such honors. This was money wasted when it could have gone to widows and orphans.[115] It was not necessarily that there was anything wrong with lighting lamps or using oil, it was just that the money would have been better spent taking care of the poor (a practice for which that Shenoute was known).

While Shenoute has been cited as an example of an opponent of the martyr cult, a brief survey of his writings suggests that, in his disapproval, he was decidedly different from the opponents that Augustine and Jerome found themselves defending the martyr cult against. He was in favor of reverence being paid to the saints, even at the martyr's tomb. Yet he saw clearly – and condemned – the abuses of the sites themselves. He was also concerned that there was considerable potential for the fabrication of martyr relics.

One aspect that Shenoute did not address was the power of the bones themselves. As we have seen, Augustine, Ambrose, and Paulinus, et al., all argued that there were miracles associated with the remains of the martyrs. This was a subject on which Shenoute was remarkably silent, and he made no mention of the tell-tale signs of a martyr's corpse: perfect preservation, a sweet smell, and liquid blood, which were all demonstrative of the saints who had gained dominance over putrification itself.[116] However, as Armand Veilleux reminds us in his preface to a modern reprint of Besa's *Life of Shenoute,* Shenoute's spirituality lacks any mystical dimension, and has even been described as "Christ-less."[117] The miracles

---

114. Shenoute, *Those Who Work Evil* (Œuvres I: 213). One clear record of the desire of a holy man not to have his bones venerated comes from Athanasius's *Life of Anthony*, where Anthony expressed the desire to be buried in secret so that his body would not be exhumed and carried around on a stretcher, as he claimed was the practice of the Egyptians.

115. Shenoute, *Those Who Work Evil* (Œuvres I: 218–19).

116. See also Bynum, *Resurrection*, for a discussion on the fear of putrification in the emergent church, and its subsequent influence on the development of Christian theology.

117. Armand Veilleux, "Preface: Shenoute or the Pitfalls of Monasticism," in *The*

that others associated with martyrs' relics may have been an aspect of spirituality that was outside the interest that Shenoute paid to anything, not just in relation to the reputed power of the relics.

Shenoute was attempting an action that was quite different from his European counterparts. He was not using the relics of the saints as a means of solidifying his control in the face of opponents. Nor was he creating new martyr shrines or incorporating newly found martyrs within church structures. Ambrose's discovery of relics, and those who claimed to have done likewise in Egypt, were running the risk of polluting churches with the incorporation of relics that were not verifiable, which for Shenoute was unacceptable. He was attempting to control the actions of his countrymen at the shrines of the saints, and lambasting those priests who, like Paulinus in Nola, were tolerant of debauchery at the martyrs' tombs. In the same way as many of the Western bishops he was struggling to enforce his image of appropriate behavior in the face of other Christians who did not always agree about what should be done at these shrines. The specific locations of the martyrs' tombs required sobriety and decorum: they should not be treated like marketplaces; they should be set apart from the rest of the world in much the same way as a church. As we have seen with his European counterparts – especially Augustine and Ambrose – Shenoute's discourse did not attempt to keep people from worshiping at martyr shrines; he just wanted them to worship at the shrines appropriately. He was also calling upon the memory of the suffering of the martyr as a tool to get the rowdiness of the martyr shrines brought under control. The shrines were the concrete representations of the memory of the martyr and as such Shenoute deftly reminds his audience of the martyr's sufferings to beat back their base behavior.

Conclusion

The innovations made by Constantine and Damasus were meaningful only because they drew upon pre-Christian practices associated with the care of the dead combined with the importance of the figure of the martyr within Christianity. Consequently, the power struggles associated with the martyr cult were far from fully ironed out when subsequent Christian leaders sought to impose their own image of the church upon their congregations. Once again the martyr cult became a tool that they used

---

Life of Shenoute by Besa (trans. David N. Bell: Kalamazoo, MI: Cistercian Publications, 1994), v.

as they sought to control the Christian message and the practices of their congregations.

Ambrose was not the first to translate the corpses of martyrs into church structures separate from their initial burial locations, yet he was instrumental in the establishment of relic distribution as a recognized Christian practice. Through his generous contributions of relics he controlled in Milan, Ambrose ensured that his own reputation and that of Milan extended far beyond the borders of his city. In doing so he also continued the process of transforming the local martyr into a translocal, universal, figure. He opposed the importance of Rome, which closely guarded its important saints, with his own munificence, which may have had more importance, ultimately, in the development of the unifying of Christendom through the universal martyr cult.

Whereas Ambrose sought to spread the saints from Milan to willing recipients, Augustine was initially dubious about the importance or even the efficacy of the martyr cult. This hesitation was primarily due to the importance of the martyr cult with his Donatist neighbors, Augustine downplayed its significance. However, once he was in possession of Stephen's relics his attitude toward the martyr cult shifted considerably. Augustine saw Stephen as a biblical martyr with universal appeal, one that united the Church as a whole, rather than dividing it based on local practices. Consequently he could accept the practices associated with Stephen's cult while rejecting those of local martyrs, especially those honored by the Donatists.

Both Augustine and Ambrose (among others) confronted the pre-Christian practices associated with the care of the dead, principally feasting at the graves of the departed, especially those of the important dead. To this end they sought to curb the enthusiasm of their congregations, urging temperance during the all-night vigils where men and women comingled suggestively. These calls for abstinence were not necessarily observed immediately; the number of times that they were repeated indicated that they frequently fell on deaf ears. Yet this was an important aspect of their attempts at controlling the martyr cult. If one could not control the activities which surrounded the cult, it was especially difficult to control the message that the cult transmitted.

Paulinus of Nola differed from his contemporaries in several significant ways. In Nola there was no significant struggle for power. Neither the Arians (who scoffed at the martyr cult in Milan) nor the Donatists (who warmly embraced it in North Africa) were vying for the hearts and minds of the population of Nola. As a result, Paulinus was able to let his own enthusiasm for the cult of Felix shine unconcealed, without political interference. Unlike Ambrose and Augustine, he did not disallow drinking at the martyrs' festivals, arguing that it was better to encourage the veneration of the saint, and that once that was accomplished the congregation's love of God would naturally encourage temperance. Perhaps this more lenient atmosphere in Nola led to the feast associated with Felix gaining tremendous popularity. Paulinus reported that legions of the faithful from Rome annually made the pilgrimage to Nola, to honor Felix's birthday.

At the end of the fourth century or early in the fifth, Shenoute expressed hesitancy toward the unbridled martyr cult that has led some commentators to claim that he opposed it altogether. However, Shenoute was not opposed to the martyr cult, or even the introduction of relics into church structures. What he did oppose was the rampant, unchecked spread of the martyr cult, which could lead only to people digging up random corpses and presenting them as martyr relics. It was acceptable to incorporate the bones of saints into a church, but only those whose derivation was known. Shenoute also objected to the carnival atmosphere which he claimed was common at the martyr festivals. The form of enthusiastic piety that was found in the popular martyr cult did not fit well with Shenoute's own extreme abstemiousness. Consequently, the fact that he did not prohibit the veneration of the saints, or even attempt to limit it (other than calling for a less riotous observance, and greater care over whose relics were venerated), confirmed how important the cult of the saints had become by the early fifth century.

All of the men discussed in this chapter sought to control the martyr cult in one way or another, to greater and lesser degrees of efficacy. Their usage of the martyr cult served to project their image of Christianity, as well as their own personal place within the Church.

Chapter Four: To Reject

Not Everyone Loves a Corpse

Late in the fourth century (381), the Christian emperors Gratian, Valentinian, and Theodosius issued an edict banning from Rome the introduction of new bodies of apostles and martyrs. They also subjected anyone dislocating the bodies in a tomb to previously existing Roman law which formerly had been aimed only at those who disturbed (through destruction or re-use) a tomb structure itself. These emperors were not only disturbed by the introduction of human remains into the city of Rome: they were also concerned with the sale and/or movement of relics from one place to another.[1] Even with the concentrated efforts of Christian (and imperial) leaders to create a cultural memory situated squarely on the shoulders of the tombs of the important dead, the presence of these laws denotes a continued suspicion of the breakdown of the boundaries which separated the living and the dead within the walls of the Roman city.

Cyril Mango uses these laws to demonstrate that the translation of relics was repugnant to the Roman population, and that it was shocking how quickly the practice developed in the latter half of the century. While I cannot but agree that the spread of the practice is noteworthy, I also think that Mango has overstated the case for this aversion. It would appear that Mango lets his own distaste for the practice get in the way of accurately understanding the motivations for the decree.[2] Constantius II was concerned enough about the tombs of the dead to add the aspect regarding the disturbing of remains of the dead – to a legal understanding regarding the destruction of the *tomb structure* – precisely because people *were* removing the bodies, although by 386 the disturbance and

---

1. *Codex Theodosianus* (*TC*) 240.9.17.6 and 240.9.17.7. See Gillian Mackie, *Early Christian Chapels in the West: Decoration, Function and Patronage* (Toronto: University of Toronto press, 2003), 264 nn. 1 and 2; Cyril Mango "Constantine's Mausoleum and the Translation of Relics," *Byzantinische Zeitschrift* 83 (1990): 51. For previous legislation, see *TC* 240.9.17.1–4 (Constantius II proclaimed in Milan in 351); Julian first seems concerned about the dead in 363 (see *TC* 240.9.17.5), yet here it is about the insult that would be dealt to the dead if their tomb were to be disturbed, and not the movement of the tomb itself.

2. He begins the article thus: "Among the practices of the Early Church that inspire in us feelings of embarrassment, not to say revulsion, is that of the translations of the saints' relics" (Mango, "Constantine's Mausoleum," 51).

dismemberment of the remains of the important dead was only in its infancy. Contrary to the point that Mango attempts to make, one can observe that the practice of corpse exhumation and distribution was *not* repugnant to the entire population. The practice of disinterment and possibly the circulation of relics was practiced widely enough that it was necessary to legislate against it.

Christianity in the fourth century underwent seismic shifts in its understanding of the relationship between the living and the remains of the martyrs. The previously universally established practices concerning the familial care of the dead broadened into the church taking over the role of burying both the Christian indigent, as well as concern for the burial of, and care for, the important dead: martyrs and church leaders. In this care there existed tensions between those who wanted to continue their normative behaviors associated with the commemoration of the departed (feasting, drinking, etc.) and those who desired more somber and subdued celebrations of the death of the martyrs. Both groups (boisterous and restrained) accepted the martyr cult as an important part of what it meant to be a Christian. They disagreed over the form that it should take, but not over its centrality to Christian identity and self-identity. Bishops like Augustine, Ambrose, Paulinus, Basil, and Gregory of Nyssa sought to use the popularity of the martyr cult as a way of directing the lives of their congregations, while at the same time defending their own authority against the claims of their rivals. Despite the fact that their preferences would ultimately become normative by the fifth and sixth centuries, their desires were not universally accepted by their contemporaries. The aim of this chapter is to examine the ways in which the martyr cult was rejected in the fourth century, and especially as regards practices associated with martyr graves. Our concern here is not with those who simply dismissed Augustine's calls for sobriety, or Shenoute's complaints about the introduction of the remains of unknown individuals into churches (the fact that appeals for decorum had to be repeated again and again demonstrates that this rejection was real). Instead, this chapter surveys how some Christians and non-Christians rejected the cult of the martyr altogether, including the whole spectrum of behavior associated with the care of the martyr's remains.

Julian "The Apostate"

In the middle of the fourth century, the most notable opponent of the cult of the saints was the Emperor Julian, often given the title "the Apostate."[3]

---

3. Julian reigned as Emperor from 361 to 363, after having first been Caesar of the West starting in 355.

Julian rejected his Christian heritage, and he sought to reverse the Christianization of the empire that had been initiated by Constantine. In 362–363 Julian put in place several measures that appear to have been aimed at hindering the practices associated with the martyr cult.

For Julian the cult of the dead was a rhetorical device that he used to bolster his argument that Rome should return to its Hellenistic religious roots. The association between Christians and the graves of their important dead had become, especially by the 360s, a clearly distinct aspect of Christian worship and an element of Christian self-presentation; and as Juana Torres observes: "Julian attacked the veneration of relics in his works not so much as a personal obsession, as it might appear, but because it was a characteristic trait of Christians in his time. His ultimate goal was to discredit everything connected with their cults in favour of the ideals of Hellenism."[4]

In the *Misopogon* Julian expressed his disgust for the Christian practice of praying at tombs, recalling this was something that he had been forced to "put up with."[5] Julian described those who prayed at the tombs as "old crones," and his use of gendered language here may have been an additional means of demeaning his Christian opponents. Candida Moss observes, concerning a dream sequence in the *Passion of Perpetua and Felicitas* in which Perpetua is transformed bodily into a male, that this is "a performance of masculinity that exemplifie[d] Christian discourse in which Christian and male became coterminous in the martyr."[6] In a reversal of the notion that through martyrdom women could become male (and consequently legitimate), Julian implied that those who prayed at tombs were becoming feminized and consequently illegitimate, or, at the very least, non-masculine. Conversely, there may well have been an impression that those most interested in the care of the martyrs were, in fact, women; certainly, in narratives concerning martyrs' remains, women play a disproportionately prominent role.[7]

---

4. Juana Torres, "Emperor Julian and the Veneration of Relics," *Antiquité Tardive* 17 (2009): 210.

5. Julian, *Mis.* 344A.

6. Candida Moss, *Ancient Christian Martyrdom: Diverse Practices, Theologies, and Traditions* (New Haven, CT: Yale University Press, 2012), 140, concerning *Passio* 10.12.

7. For a discussion of the presentation of women in the literature surrounding the martyr cult see Nicola Denzey, *The Bone Gatherers: The Lost Worlds of Early Christian Women* (Boston: Beacon, 2007); Kate Cooper, "The Martyr, the Matrona, and the Bishop: The Matron Lucina and the Politics of the Martyr Cult in Fifth- and Sixth-Century Rome," *Early Medieval Europe* 8 (1999): 297–317. Neither work addresses Julian's criticism directly.

Julian was raised a Christian, and according to at least one biographer, he had a mastery of their texts and used that knowledge to argue against the veneration of the saints at their tombs from within the Christian tradition.[8] However, Julian was not only critical of Christianity philosophically, but as it was being practiced, which he argued was not in accordance with the gospels. In his diatribe *Against the Galilaeans* he argues (correctly) that the reverence paid at the graves of the saints was not something that could be traced back to Jesus. He also criticized Christians for their failure to observe that graves were unclean (citing Jesus) and consequently one could not invoke God at them. Ultimately he noted that within ancient Judaism sleeping in tombs for the sake of visions or dreams was a form of witchcraft.[9] As this would have been completely unacceptable within Judaism, it should, by extension, also be rejected by Christians as well. His criticism here was not only aimed at his Christian contemporaries; he also leveled his accusations against the apostles for performing this same sort of divination after Jesus had died. Julian was not opposed to the practice of divination in itself (he himself was wont to visit Delphi to consult the oracle); rather, he was pointing out the hypocrisy of Christians who were not following the teachings of Jesus. His engagement with the question of what should be normative behavior for good Christians is especially interesting, in that he is engaged in that conversation from outside of the fold of Christianity. Nearly all other non-Christian opponents of the martyr cult based their criticism on traditional Roman mores, while Julian's attack came from within the textual tradition that Christians claimed as their own.

It should be borne in mind that the Romans themselves had a long history of elaborate burials, the locations of which were visited with a certain degree of frequency. Often these tombs contained physical structures for eating and drinking, where the living would interact with the shades of the dead. However, there remained for the most part a distinction between the "religious" practices associated with the official cult and the practices of individuals and families for their dead. Graves in the context of Julian's priests were not part of civic religious life, but rather part of the familial expressions of grief and remembrance, none of which had anything to do with the gods, but clearly had what we (the modern observer) consider to be a religious context: rituals designed to appease the spirits of the dead.

In general the care of the dead was seen as a function of the family; Christians were the exception here. It was believed that when the dead

---

8. Eunapius of Sardis, *VS* 473–4.
9. Julian, *Gal.* 335C (LCL 157).

were improperly cared for, chaos and destruction could ensue, but it was *not* seen as the responsibility of the official priests to care for the dead. Julian himself makes this distinction in his letter to Arsacius,[10] where he laments that the charitable actions of the Christians has advanced their cause. Julian explicitly mentions the care for the graves of the dead (which, as we also saw in Chapter One, Christians considered a great act of piety), as well as their sobriety and care of strangers. The remainder of the letter goes on to describe the reforms within the civic priesthood that Julian sought to make, based primarily on the model of charity that he observed within the Christian community. The one obvious absence from this reworking of Christian behavior, however, is that at no point does he dictate that the priests should have anything to do with the burial of the dead. This remained a private function of the family. Julian even restricted burial further when he decreed that funerals should be carried out only at night.[11] As part of his justification for this decree he explained later in a letter that he had observed that there are no good omens on days with funerals.[12]

Julian was also annoyed with the presence of martyr graves near his own religious sites. Rufinus of Aquileia wrote that Julian had the body of the martyr Babylas moved as its presence made the oracle in Daphne mute to his questions.

> Then he ordered the Galileans, for thus he called our people, to come and remove the martyr's tomb. The whole church therefore came together, mothers and husbands, virgins and youths, and with immense rejoicing pulled along the martyr's coffin in a long procession singing psalms with loud cries and exultation [...].[13]

Whether the oracle was silent because it was displeased by the presence of Babylas's grave, or if there was some inherent power in the martyr's tomb that overpowered the oracle's ability to perform effectively, was a matter of perspective. Clearly for Julian it was the pollution of the corpse, while for the Christians, including his brother Gallus, who moved it to that location in the first place, it was the power of the martyr's remains. Shortly afterwards, the temple was destroyed by fire, which according to Sozomen was an act of God demonstrating his displeasure at the removal

---

10. Julian, *Ep.* 84 (LCL 157, 67–71).
11. Julian, *Ep.* 56 (LCL 157, 191–7); see also Torres, "Emperor Julian."
12. Julian, *Ep.* 136 (LCL 157), ca. 363.
13. Rufinus of Aquileia, *Hist.* 35 (PL 21.503B), trans. Philip R. Amidon, *The Church History of Rufinus of Aquileia, Books 10 and 11* (Oxford: Oxford University Press, 1997), 40; Glanville Downey, *A History of Antioch in Syria* (Princeton, NJ: Princeton University Press, 1961), 364, 387–8, dates this occurrence to 351–4 under Caesar Gallus (see also p. 86 above).

of Babylas.[14] Julian, however, charged that the displeasure and fire came from a much more earthly source: the Christians.[15] According to Sozomen, after (or in response to?) the fire, Julian ordered the governor of Caria to destroy all martyr shrines complete with an altar and a roof which were close to the temple of Apollo Didymus in Miletus.[16]

Babylas's tomb was not the only shrine that suffered under the reign of Julian. Rufinus recounts the events that lead to the destruction of the tomb of John the Baptist: "[T]hey frenziedly attacked the tomb of John the Baptist with murderous hands and set about scattering the bones, gathering them again, burning them, mixing the holy ashes with dust, and scattering them throughout the fields and countryside."[17] The ashes were collected by a group of monks from the monastery of Philip, who had made a pilgrimage to John's sepulture to pray. After mixing with the crowd they managed to collect all of the ashes "as far as they could in the circumstances." Once the ashes were in hand these clandestine monks made their escape, and took the relics to Philip who – believing it was beyond his ability to care for them – sent them off to Athanasius. Despite, as we will see below, Athanasius's own antipathy toward relic veneration as used by his opponents, according to this tale he received the remains and hid them within a hole in the wall of the sacristy. Athanasius perhaps did this, to keep them from falling into the hands of his opponents,[18] but it is also possible that Rufinus himself had them deposited in Alexandria in order to bolster a later claim by the Alexandrian church to those same relics.

In this instance, it was not a decree from Julian that caused the desecration of the tomb, which it was still against Roman law to disturb, but rather the fervor of the general pagan population. Despite Julian's apparent disgust with the veneration paid at the tombs of the martyrs, it is noteworthy that he did not make it an imperial agenda to confiscate or desecrate these graves or shrines. He even pointed out that a group of people in Emesa (near Antioch) who had overturned Christian tombs and attacked those who were praying there had exceeded his wishes with their cleansing of the holy places.[19] Julian made it clear that he was not interested in violence against the Christians, but that he could not

---

14. Sozomen, *HE* 5.20 (PG 67.844).
15. Julian, *Mis.* 361 (LCL 29).
16. Sozomen, *HE* 5.20 (PG 67.844).
17. Rufinus of Aquileia, *Hist.* 11.28 (PL 21.00536A-B), trans. Amidon, *Church History*, 85.
18. Rufinus of Aquileia, *Hist.* 11.28 (PL 21.00536A-B).
19. Julian, *Mis.* 361 (LCL 29). The violence that was perpetrated in this instance of the destruction of tombs was more than simply the destruction of the structures (which was illegal under Roman law); it was the destruction of memory.

be blamed for the bad behavior of individuals who got caught up in the moment. The fact that these events, only one of which was explicitly ordered by Julian, were the only instances that both he and his opponents recounted, denotes that they were the exception rather than the rule under his reign. Gregory of Nazianzus even complained that Julian was careful not to grant the Christian community martyrs.[20]

The only credible exception to this lack of new martyrs ordered directly by Julian was a tradition which was briefly discussed by Sozomen, where a statue of Jesus was removed by Julian and dragged around the city and destroyed by Julian's supporters. After the destruction of the statue the Christians recovered its fragments, and the description of this process is nearly indistinguishable to accounts of the recovery of ashes or pieces of martyrs after execution in hagiographic texts. The remains of the statue were then placed in a church, and from them a previously unknown plant grew, which could miraculously cure any disorder.[21] Here, then, we have a tale that is nearly identical to martyr narratives: from the mutilation of the body, to the gathering of the remains and subsequent interment in a church, followed by miraculous healing for the faithful. Even if Julian was not content to give Christians the opportunity to become martyrs, the Christians themselves created something nearly identical.

Julian was not only critical of martyr veneration as a defilement; he also observed that it divided Christians from each other. Julian correctly accused Christians of slaughtering each other over differences in style of worship,[22] at least some of which concerned the corpses of the important dead. For evidence, one need only look to the persecution of Donatists in North Africa:[23] this included a controversy over Lucilla's kissing the bone of a martyr in 311 during the pivotal period for the schism between the Meletians and the Catholics.[24] Athanasius's complaints about the "Egyptians" putting martyrs on stretchers and carrying them from place to place is another example of conflict (see below p. 135).

In his attempt to re-establish traditional Roman religious practices, Julian used the practices associated with the martyr cult against his Christian opponents to argue that not only is Christianity false, but that one of its most recognizable and popular aspects isn't even consistent

---

20. "He begrudged the honor of martyrdom to our combatants" (*Oratio* 4.58, PG 35.0581).
21. Sozomen, *HE* 5.21 (PG 67.844).
22. Julian, *Gal.* 206A (LCL 157).
23. Maureen A. Tilley, *Donatist Martyr Stories: The Church in Conflict in Roman North Africa* (Liverpool: Liverpool University Press, 1996).
24. William H. C. Frend, *The Donatist Church: A Movement of Protest in Roman North Africa* (Oxford: Clarendon Press, 1952), 18.

with the religion's foundational teachings. The fact that he singled out the Christian the martyr cult (along with teaching) as a primary activity to suppress demonstrates that for Julian, the practices performed at the graves of the martyrs was one of the most important signifiers of the Christianity of the mid-fourth century.

Other Non-Christian Opponents

Julian was far from being the only non-Christian gentile who was disturbed by the practices associated with the martyr cult. Others were critical due to the perception (whether correct or not) that Christians were violating the taboo surrounding the incorporation of corpses within the city limits. Others dismissed the crowds at the martyrs' shrines as belonging to the simple and unwashed masses, while others again distrusted what appeared to be clandestine meetings that perhaps even included underground assemblies in the catacombs.

An account by Marcus Diaconus in his biography *The Life of Porphyry of Gaza*[25] is a good example of the first of the concerns. The strength of the corpse taboo in Gaza was such that a group of non-Christians (within the text described as "they of the idol-madness") believed that the Christian deacon Cornelius and two other Christians were bringing a corpse into the city, when in fact they were bringing in an injured a Christian named Barochas who had been beaten and left for dead by some of the inhabitants of a nearby village. However, believing that Barochas was dead and that consequently his presence was defiling the city, they attacked the Christians. In the confusion of the attack Cornelius and some others once again rescued Barochas and hid with him in the church for the night. However, a new crowd gathered the next day again accusing the Christians of polluting the city and demanding that the presumed corpse be removed. At this point Barochas (who was very much not dead) rose up and, grabbing a piece of wood, set about attacking the bystanders and caused them to flee.

In this case there was no corpse pollution, although the non-Christian inhabitants of Gaza had been very quick to believe that Christians would be bringing a corpse into the city. Their actions reflected a common perception of Christians, as well as opposition to the Christian association between the living and the dead and a deep-seated fear of the degradation of the long-established boundaries between the living and the dead. Here, despite the shocking conclusion in which the supposed corpse rose

---

25. Marcus Diaconus, *Vita Porphyrii Gazensis*. Trans. G. F. Hill, *Mark the Deacon: The Life of Porphyry, Bishop of Gaza* (Oxford: Clarendon Press, 1913), 23ff.

up and began beating those who complained about the presence of that "corpse" within the city with a piece of wood, we can appreciate just how anxious the non-Christian population was over the perceived violation of this taboo.

Not every instance of conflict over the Christian relationship with the remains of their dead needed to be settled with blows. In 390, the pagan Maximus of Madaura wrote a letter to Augustine, in which he was dismissively critical of the honor paid to the martyrs at their graves:

> The tombs of these men (it is a folly almost beneath our notice) are visited by crowds of simpletons, who forsake our temples and despise the memory of their ancestors, so that the prediction of the indignant bard is notably fulfilled: "Rome shall, in the temples of the gods, swear by the shades of men."[26]

Here Maximus appeared to be looking to Augustine for a sympathetic audience when he criticized the "folly" of those "simpletons" who revered and worshiped at the tombs of the martyrs. Maximus was also critical of the Christians for meeting in "secret places," possibly the darkened crypts of the shrines of the saints, such as that described by Prudentius which surrounded the tomb of Hippolytus. Augustine, in his reply to Maximus, did not take up this particular argument about the "folly" of the martyr cult, but was scathing of Maximus nonetheless. One wonders, had Augustine replied to this letter 25 years later, if he would have passed by the opportunity to extol the virtues of the martyr cult more fully.

The fourth-century Greek historian and Sophist Eunapius of Sardis likewise was disgusted with the practice of integrating the remains of martyrs into temples in Egypt:

> For they collected the bones and skulls of criminals who had been put to death for numerous crimes [... and] made them out to be gods, haunted their sepulchers, and thought that they became better by defiling themselves at their graves. "Martyrs" the dead were called, and "ministers" of a sort, and "ambassadors" with the gods to carry men's prayers.[27]

As with the remarks by Maximus, Eunapius here seemed to be both shocked and incredulous that these events were actually transpiring. The practice of collecting the bones of those executed for criminal activity was so absurd, to these late antique non-Christians, that it defied credulity more than it elicited feelings of offense.

---

26. Included as *Ep.* 16 in Augustine's corpus; Maximus to Augustine (PL 33.0082), trans. J. G. Cunningham, *NPNF*[1] 1:233.

27. Eunapius of Sardis, *VS* (Wright LCL 134). See Peter Brown, *The Cult of the Saints: Its Rise and Function in Latin Christianity* (Chicago: University of Chicago Press, 1981), 7; *Society and the Holy in Late Antiquity* (Berkeley: University of California Press, 1982), 177; also Julian, *Mis.* 344A.

Christian Opposition to the Martyr Cult

We have discussed opposition from Christians who were critical of the martyr cult primarily due to the actions of those who went to the festivals for less than pious purposes in the preceding chapters. These criticisms were aimed principally at the fact that scandalous deeds were carried out in dimly lit corners of the shrine where women and men mingled during all-night vigils,[28] rather than disagreement over the role of the important dead, or out of revulsion from the integration of the remains of the dead into religious piety. Concern over debauchery, however, was not the only way in which Christians rejected the role of the martyrs' remains.

Athanasius of Alexandria

Wandering errant bodies, could only lead to wandering errant minds.[29]

Athanasius of Alexandria (296–373) was a dominant force in his city for much of the fourth century, and was the bishop of the great Egyptian city sporadically between 328 and his death in 373. His episcopate, however, was not without significant controversy: he was nearly constantly engaged in disagreement and political wrangling with the "Arians," while also struggling for control of the city with the Meletians, a "heretical" group who eventually joined forces with the Arians precisely because they both opposed Athanasius. As we will see below, in the *Life of Anthony* and in the *Festal Letters* of 369 and 370,[30] Athanasius was extremely critical of what he claimed to be Meletian practices surrounding the bodies of the martyrs. However, considering the exceptionally long duration of his conflict, it is notable that he only deals with the issues of burial and martyr remains in three texts.

In some ways his tactics were similar to those of Damasus in Rome, such as his use of controlled violence of thugs to intimidate his

---

28. I believe that these events did happen: the ubiquity of accounts gives them credence, as does the complete absence of Christian apologists denying them. When Christians did address these accounts they simply stated that they were not done by true Christians, or argued that it was still better to have the martyr festival despite these less savory aspects, but they did not deny that they occurred. Finally, we have a figure no less prominent than Augustine himself admit to seeking out encounters with women during martyr festivals in his pre-Christian days (see p. 103 above). However, this does not mean that they were a constant presence, or that they were not used for rhetorical effect by the detractors of the martyr cult.

29. David Brakke, "'Outside the Places, Within the Truth' Athanasius of Alexandria and the Localization of the Holy," in *Pilgrimage and Holy Space in Late Antique Egypt* (ed. David Frankfurter: Leiden: Brill, 1998), 466.

30. Athanasius, *Ep. Fest.* 41 and 42.

opponents, but in others he was exactly the opposite of Damasus: in particular, he was critical of martyr bodies as the locus of the sacred within the community.[31] This may well have been because he was not in control of those bodies in the way that Damasus was, and was in conflict with those who did claim control over them. However, from his *Life of Anthony* it appears that Athanasius was not unsympathetic to the visceral appeal of the cult of the saints: he described the sheepskin that he had been given by Anthony (essentially a contact relic) as one of his favorite possessions. But as he was unable to harness the remains of the saints, he had in effect to undermine the arguments that were serving his Western brethren so well in their own efforts to construct the cultural memory of the emergent church. In both cases the episcopate sought to influence their flock against their opponents through the use of the remains of the martyrs, either through embracing them (as in the case of Damasus and others) or by denying them.

Athanasius recorded his *Life of Anthony* at the request of "foreign monks" some time in 356 and 357, and in doing so he composed the first Christian biography of someone who had achieved sainthood without suffering martyrdom. Anthony was an ascetic who served as an exemplar of Egyptian monasticism in the fourth century, and a prominent theme in the biography is Anthony's demonic temptations. From Athanasius's account we learn that it was not uncommon for ascetics to pray in tombs (of martyrs or otherwise), and it is a location where Anthony himself prays and is confronted by Satan.

Towards the end of his account, Athanasius noted that despite the desire of the faithful to have Anthony with them during his last days, Anthony did not grant their wish. Athanasius explains that this was due to the practice of "the Egyptians," who would wrap the bodies of martyrs in linen and who believed that they honored their departed by keeping the dead in their homes. Anthony did not want to receive this treatment.[32] One should observe that Athanasius here describes a Christian practice surrounding the remains of Christian martyrs, although he clearly distances himself and his community (the "Orthodox" community) from this behavior by ascribing it to "the Egyptians." This echoes the New Testament (especially the Gospel of John) when it uses "the Jews" as a generic term for those who opposed the early Jesus movement. Boundaries were

---

31. For a discussion Athanasius's use of violence to disrupt civic proceedings as a means of solidifying his power see Richard E. Rubenstein, *When Jesus Became God: The Struggle to Define Christianity During the Last Days of Rome* (San Diego: Harcourt, 1999), 107.

32. Athanasius, *v. Anton.* 90 (PG 26.837).

drawn between those inside the community, who buried the dead, and those outside, who did not. Those others are the ones who do this, or oppose that, and who are clearly not our co-religionists. Markus observes in *The End of Ancient Christianity* that during periods of peace the monastic ideal was replacing the role of the martyr in Christian thought. As such Athanasius used someone of equal stature to the martyrs to disabuse his followers of the martyr cult.[33]

Anthony was ultimately buried in a secret location so that his body would not be disturbed by the faithful, or made into relics. However, those who buried him were given a sheepskin that had been worn by Anthony. Athanasius describes those contact relics in terms that were not unlike those used by Paulinus concerning primary relics of the martyrs: that looking upon the sheepskins was the same as looking upon Anthony.

This sets the stage for the first of the two *Festal Letters* that will be examined here. *Ep.* 41 was written for Easter in 369, and is concerned with the Meletians and the Arians. The Meletians were not, as Athanasius proclaimed in this *Festal Letter*, the inheritors of Arianism – as noted above,[34] it was not until some time after they became a distinct group that they began to be associated with the Arians, and it is possible that they embraced Arianism not because of its theology, but because of a shared hatred of Athanasius. Rather, they were strict regarding the readmission of the *lapsi* (or those who had become apostates during Diocletian's persecutions at the beginning of the fourth century) into the Church.[35] Despite claiming the title the "Church of the Martyrs" they were best known for the name of their founder Melitus.[36] The Meletians claimed that they were the true descendants of the Church, having endured the persecutions of Decius and Diocletian while staying true to Christian doctrines. We know little of the practices of the "Church of the Martyrs," although from Epiphanius it would seem that the Meletians were theologically nearly indistinct from their "Catholic" adversaries.

In *Ep. Fest.* 41 of 369 Athanasius discussed a practice that he considered to have been abhorrent, and which was related to the cult of the martyrs.

---

33. Athanasius, *v. Anton.* 90 (PG 26.837).
34. See page 135.
35. See R. D. Williams, "Changing Attitudes to Virgil: A Study in the History of Taste from Dryden to Tennyson," in *Virgil* (ed. D. R. Dudley: London: Routledge and Kegan Paul), 119–38, for a detailed discussion on the sources for this understanding. Williams seems to be alone in his dismissal of Epiphanius's account that the schism was based on the issue of the *lapsi*. He chooses Sozomen's rendition of the events, which has the schism quite possibly taking place prior to the persecution.
36. Epiphanius, *Panarion* 2.47–80, trans. Frank Williams, *The Panarion of Epiphanius of Salamis: Books II and III: De Fide* (Leiden: Brill, 1994), 318.

He also injected this same revulsion into the mouth of Anthony, who, as we have seen, desired to be buried in secret rather than suffer this fate. According to Athanasius's account, the Meletians were exhuming the remains of martyrs and placing them on portable stretchers. Once they were on these mobile devices and no longer trapped in their sepulchers, the Meletians were able to take them anywhere they wanted, thereby creating mobile locations of sanctity. David Brakke suggests this practice was introduced because the Meletians no longer controlled the church structures and consequently no longer had access to the remains of the saints in structures that were constructed around their graves. For the Meletians it may have been the only way that they could have participated in an aspect of their religious practice once they no longer controlled the church structures. Unearthing the bodies of martyrs may also have helped the Meletians to maintain their title of "Church of the Martyrs."

Athanasius countered the alleged Meletian practice by arguing that bodies should be buried underground, and with a series of scriptural examples that speak of patriarchs being buried in tombs. However, in his ire (or apparent anger for the sake of his rhetoric) he argues not against reverence being paid to the saints, but rather the specific ways in which this reverence was expressed by the Meletians. Athanasius also complained that the Meletians might be selling relics, and in one digression in which he exerted his authority to name and to proclaim who is and who is not a martyr he accused his opponents of not actually even having the bodies of martyrs.[37]

Athanasius then went on to provide a series of scriptural examples that spoke of patriarchs being buried in tombs. Ultimately he asked the Meletians from whence they received the idea that it was good to exhume the bodies of the martyrs.[38] Here Athanasius appeared to be very upset (or at least is for the sake of his rhetoric) about the practices of the Meletians regarding the remains of the saints, not necessarily because of the reverence that was being paid to the saints, but rather because of the form that reverence took, including the possibility that they were selling the relics.[39] Athanasius did not argue, at least in this letter, that there was no value in paying homage to the martyrs; but he *was* critical of the transportation of the corpse of the martyr around on a stretcher or piece of wood, asking from where the Meletians got the idea of exhuming bodies. From his argument that the Meletians did not have the remains of

---

37. Brakke, "Outside the Places," 477–8.
38. Brakke, "Outside the Places," 477.
39. Brakke, "Outside the Places," 477–8.

any martyrs in their city, Athanasius tacitly admitted that there is importance in the possession of remains, but his view was that these remains *must* remain buried. They cannot be movable, for the threat of movement means that the sanctity that they held would no longer be in the possession of the episcopate.[40]

Despite this ambiguity concerning their theology, the Meletians were clearly focused on the relics of the martyrs to such an extent that they may have exhumed their corpses and focused their worship around these relics.[41] The Meletians would ultimately claim for themselves that they were the true descendants of the Church which had suffered the persecutions, and had stayed true to the doctrines. They were separate from the others who wanted to let those who had abandoned their faith during the Diocletian persecutions back into the church universal. It was not until sometime later that they began to be associated with the Arians. It is possible that they embraced Arianism not because of the theology, but because of a shared hatred of Athanasius. However, even from an early period they closely associated themselves with the suffering and persecution that took place during the Decian persecutions. Epiphanius reports that they called themselves the "Church of the Martyrs."[42] From Athanasius's letter, one can clearly see how they might claim such a title, if they were traveling from location to location with the portable sanctity of the remains of the saints. Ample evidence suggests that the behavior Athanasius desired was not the normative behavior of the majority of Egyptian Christians during his lifetime (or even after, as we have seen with Shenoute).[43] Athanasius does present us with evidence that there were practices in Egypt that he lamented (or at least something very close),[44] although he may have

---

40. For a discussion about Athanasius's sometime over-reliance upon rhetoric and the way that can get in the way of even his theology see G. Christopher Stead, "Rhetorical Method in Athanasius," *Vigiliae Christianae* 30 (1976): 121–37.

41. See Rowan Williams, "Arius and the Meletian Schism," *Journal of Theological Studies*, NS, 37 (1987): 35–52, for a detailed discussion on the sources for this understanding. Williams seems to be alone in his dismissal of Epiphanius's account that the schism was based on the issue of the lapsi. He chooses Sozomen's rendition of the events, which quite possibly has the schism take place prior to the persecution.

42. Epiphanius, *Panarion* 68.3 (PG 42.186).

43. For a discussion on how he most likely misrepresented Anthony in his *Vita* by presenting him as much more subservient to the bishop and to scripture than is conveyed by Anthony's letters (which are more in line with the Nag Hammadi Codex I) see Lance Jenott and Elaine Pagels, "Anthony's Letters and the Nag Hammadi Codex I: Sources of Religious Conflict in Fourth-Century Egypt," *Journal of Early Christian Studies* 18 (2010): 557–89.

44. Supporting material for Athanasius's claim that Anthony did not want his burial location to be public because of fear of exhumation and translation comes

presented his accounts in a certain way as an effective means of establishing his power by painting his opponents in a negative light. Either way, the treatment of the dead was important to his congregation, as demonstrated by his belief in the grave's effectiveness in the creation of the cultural memory of what it meant to be a Christian in Alexandria.

In his *Ep. Fest.* 42, from 370, Athanasius once again turned his attention to those who would inappropriately use the memories of the martyrs, and their shrines. In this instance the problem was not that the remains were being carried around, but rather they were being used for the exorcism of demons and for divination (bordering upon necromancy). Athanasius quickly reminded them that they were not healed by the martyr, but rather by Jesus – the Savior.[45] The misconception (as it was deemed by the episcopate) that it was the martyr her/himself who was responsible for the chasing out of demons would continue to plague the cult of the saints. Here Athanasius instructed the reader that the martyr shrine has no power without the savior for whom the martyr died.

For Athanasius it would not have been quite so bad if these ignorant fools were just going to the shrines to exorcise demons, and they simply misunderstood whence the power to exorcise came. But they also asked the demons, once they have been cast out, about the future: "These people give glory to them [the demons] and ask them about what will happen."[46] They also brought condemnation "upon themselves by thinking that the demons are the prophets of the martyrs."[47] For Athanasius, this use of the martyr's shrine was "not a Christian act."[48] Those who practiced this necromantic divination, according to Athanasius, should be shunned.

John Wortley rightly questions how fully we could trust Athanasius in his commentary concerning the Meletians, given his opposition to them.[49] This accusation that they placed martyrs on stretchers is attested

---

from Jerome, who wrote ca. 390 that Hilarion likewise wanted to be buried quickly before anyone could venerate his remains. His wishes were carried out; however, his good friend Hesychius could not bear this. Hesychius convinced the locals who were guarding the grave in a garden (perhaps they wanted the local holy man to remain a local holy man, desiring the honor of his grave) and pretended he wanted to live in the garden. Over the next 10 months "at great peril to his life" he personally exhumed the corpse and stole it away to Majuma, where it was interred in a monastery (Jerome, *vit. Hil.* 100.44–6 [PL 23]).

45. Brakke, "Outside the Places," 479.
46. Brakke, "Outside the Places," 479.
47. Brakke, "Outside the Places," 479.
48. Brakke, "Outside the Places," 479.
49. John Wortley, "The Origins of Christian Veneration of Body-Parts," *Revue de l'histoire des religions* 1 (2006): 24.

nowhere else, although Wortley does accept that prior Roman commentary on the practices of Egyptians concerning placing the mummified remains of the important dead within private homes means that it is reasonable to suppose that some of the important dead within Christianity in Egypt would also have received the same treatment. However, I am not here interested in the veracity of the actual practices so much as the fact that the practices (real or imaginary) were used as examples of what "proper" behavior was to the bishops who were arguing against them. One would not use an example of the behavior of others if no-one cared about the implied behavior (e.g. Athanasius does not discuss the eating habits of the Arians). This usage of the treatment of the remains of the martyr was a trope through which Athanasius could argue against his adversaries, and it consequently allowed the speaker to persuade or influence (to exert the power to create) the cultural memory of that community.

It may well have been the case that this idea of unearthing the remains of the important dead was something that may have been considered so repugnant to the Egyptian Christian population that it could have been a strawman created by Athanasius, as this practice is unattested to elsewhere. It may also have served Athanasius's purpose to have Anthony express his desire to be buried in secret, as a reaction against this practice. This would have been true especially if Athanasius was unable to claim the remains of such an esteemed figure of the Egyptian Church, if there had been a call by members of his community to visit Anthony's tomb.

Athanasius was confronted with a decidedly different set of circumstances than his European contemporaries. He was never fully in control of the geographic space of the Church in Alexandria. He was also beset by an opponent that had previously (and perhaps more justly) laid claim to being the true descendants of the martyrs: the Meletians. He also had to deal with a practice which involved movable shrines, which limited his ability to control the development of both the martyr cult as well as the access to Christian sacred space. To this end he argued against the cult of the martyrs, most effectively by putting a local hero, Anthony, on literary display. While on display Anthony spoke for Athanasius against the practice of moving corpses, and pleaded for an anonymous burial. Despite his best efforts, his usage of the literary remains of the dead did little to diminish the importance of the martyr cult in Egypt, as seen with Shenoute in the previous chapter.

Vigilantius

Augustine was not alone in being forced to answer the accusations of debauchery at the graves of the saints. While Augustine was answering a Meletian opponent, other supporters of the cult of the saints had to confront Christians who denied that this was an appropriate form of worship for Christians. Early in the fifth century Jerome was exceedingly aggravated by the claims made by Vigilantius regarding the activities surrounding the martyr cult. Vigilantius, a presbyter, was no outsider to those who favored the cult of the martyrs. He was known to Severus, Paulinus, and Jerome, having acted as a messenger for all three.[50] However, as we can tell from Jerome's response to a text that is no longer extant, Vigilantius was adamantly opposed to the practices surrounding the cult of the saints, and he condemned the vigils and reverence paid to martyrs at their tombs. Consequently, Jerome could not "turn a deaf ear to the wrongs inflicted on apostles and martyrs."[51] Vigilantius derided the practice of contact relics:

> What need is there for you not only to pay such honor, not to say adoration, to the thing, whatever it may be, which you carry about in a little vessel and worship? [...] Why do you kiss and adore a bit of powder wrapped up in cloth? [...] Under the cloak of religion we see what is all but a heathen ceremony introduced into the churches [...].[52]

To this Jerome responded that Vigilantius was a "madman," observing, as did Augustine, that there was no adoration paid to the martyrs, but rather to God through the martyrs. He was likewise disgusted that Vigilantius would refer to the relics of the martyrs, and contact relics,[53] as "bits of powder wrapped in cloth." Jerome then went on to ask rhetorically if a long list of emperors and bishops had been sacrilegious when they translated relics.

Jerome's rebuttal of Vigilantius, while written with a good deal of rage, lays out a clear understanding of the theological reasons behind the belief in the efficacy of the martyrs. Based on Mt. 22:33 he noted that "the God of Abraham, the God of Isaac, the God of Jacob: he is not the God of the

---

50. Jerome, *Ep.* 58.11. See also Paulinus of Nola, *Ep.* 5. Dennis Trout, *Paulinus of Nola: Life, Letters, and Poems* (Berkeley: University of California Press, 1999), 220 n. 132, cites relevant modern scholarship.
51. Jerome, *Vigil.* 1 (PL 23.0339), trans. W. H. Fremantle et al., *NPNF*[2] 6:417.
52. Jerome, *Vigil.* 4 (PL 23.0342), trans. Fremantle et al., *NPNF*[2] 6:418.
53. These are also sometimes referred to as secondary relics (*brandea* or *sanctuaria*). That is to say, they are items that have come into contact with primary relics, remains of sacred humans, such as oil that was passed through a tomb and taken home with a pilgrim in a special flask, or strips of cloth that were lowered into the tomb. In the term "contact relic" I also include items that were owned by the individual or that came into contact with the individual prior to their death. These items may include Anthony's sheepskin discussed above, or the chains that bound Paul in Rome. The lucky faithful could take home some iron shavings of the chains. For a discussion specifically on secondary relics see David L. Eastman, *Paul the Martyr: The Cult of the Apostle in the Latin West* (Atlanta, GA: Society of Biblical Literature, 2011), 7–8.

dead, but of the living. If then they are alive, they are not, to use your expression, kept in honorable confinement."[54] He added that they follow the Lamb, and as such "if the lamb is present everywhere, the same must be believed respecting those who are with the Lamb."[55]

Jerome did acknowledge that there is a striking similarity between the practices of pagan idol worship and that which is done out of respect for the martyrs: "And because we formerly worshipped idols, does it follow that we ought not now to worship God lest we seem to pay like honor to Him and to idols? In one case respect was paid to idols, and therefore the ceremony is to be abhorred; in the other the martyrs are venerated, and the same ceremony is therefore to be allowed."[56] Like other pagan festivals, Vigilantius accused the vigils held in the honor of the martyrs to have been hotbeds of sin. This is a claim that Jerome does not exactly deny:

> We must not, however, impute to pious men the faults and errors of youths and worthless women such as are often detected at night. It is true that, even at the Easter vigils, something of the kind usually comes to light [...] and so should we not watch at Easter-tide for fear that adulterers may satisfy their long pent-up desires, or that the wife may find an opportunity for sinning without having the key turned against her by her husband. The occasions which seldom recur are those which are most eagerly longed for.[57]

Clearly the vigils practiced in honor of the martyrs were occasions that were not always used for what Jerome would consider pious purposes. Yet these things also happened at Easter, and it would be absurd in Jerome's eyes to forgo celebrating Easter simply because of the actions of a few bad apples. Likewise it would also be foolish to stop honoring the martyrs because of a few indiscretions.

Conclusion

As the martyr cult in the fourth and early fifth centuries faced opposition both from those inside and outside of Christian circles, it was far from a foregone conclusion that it would become as crucially important as it did in subsequent centuries. In every case that we have examined

---

54. Jerome, *Vigil.* 5 (PL 23.343–4), trans. Fremantle et al., *NPNF*[2] 6:419.
55. Jerome, *Vigil.* 6 (PL 23.344), trans. Fremantle et al., *NPNF*[2] 6:419. This is an interesting argument, as it would seem to counter the point that he is trying to make. If the martyrs were everywhere present with Jesus, then there would be no need for secondary or contact relics.
56. Jerome, *Vigil.* 7 (PL 23.344), trans. Fremantle et al., *NPNF*[2] 6:420.
57. Jerome, *Vigil.* 9 (PL 23.346–8), trans. Fremantle et al., *NPNF*[2] 6:421.

in this chapter, issues of power and control permeated the discussion surrounding the veneration of the saints in the presence of their bodies. Athanasius of Alexandria was concerned about who controlled the locations which housed those remains, and when his opponents simply took the remains from place to place (as he claimed they did) he became apoplectic. Through his biography of Anthony he sought to claim Anthony's authority to dissuade the veneration of the relics.

During the fourth century the cult of the martyrs, and specifically their tombs around which the cult centered, were a site of conflict. This conflict sought to delineate and determine several sets of boundaries. In the case of Julian it sought to reinforce what was acceptable behavior within Roman society; most notably, the Christian practices associated with the graves of the important dead were to be avoided. Perhaps for Julian it may have been acceptable if Christians felt the need to persist in being Christian, so long as they ended their graveside practices. His attempt at control is more subtle than that of his third- and early fourth-century predecessors, in that he does not simply seize the cemeteries, and execute those who opposed him, but rather he sought to demonstrate the folly of the martyr cult by using texts and traditions that Christians themselves viewed as authoritative. If, as Foucault observes, power does not act upon the "other" but rather acts upon the other's actions then the means of persuasion that is used must be one that can be accepted by the other. Power can create new representations of reality, but only if there is an inclination to accept that depiction. Julian's attempt to use his vast knowledge of scripture demonstrated his understanding that he needed to present his objection to arguably one of the most obvious aspects of Christian practice in a way that would be accepted willingly by his audience. Many other non-Christian opponents to the martyr cult were not so subtle in their approach. These ranged from physical confrontations with a Christian group whom they perceived to be breaking the corpse taboo, to simple incredulity and mockery.

The intra-Christian confrontations concerning the veneration of the martyrs' remains were similar to Julian's critique. They were subtle and attempted to delineate boundaries of what was and what was not acceptable Christian behavior, and who was and was not a proper martyr. In the case of Vigilantius there was a desire to shape the boundary of Christianity well away from Roman "idolatry," whereas with Athanasius the issues concerning the role of the martyr cult had more to do with his own power and authority within the Alexandrian community than they necessarily had to do with distancing himself from non-Christian practices.

Despite the widespread appeal of the cult of the saints during this period, the saints that were venerated were predominantly local heroes. With the exception of Constantinople, which had no local martyrs, the various locations from Rome, to Milan, to Nyssa, to Alexandria all strived to commemorate their local saints, to promote their own sites. The result of this was a fragmented Christian memory of the martyrs throughout the empire. In the next chapter we will look at how the rise of pilgrimage within Christianity smoothed over those differences, and allowed for the creation of trans-local cultural memory at various pilgrimage sites: the tombs of the martyrs.

Chapter Five: To Accept
Unification Through Travel

The yearning for the martyrs has disposed all of this inequality.[1]

In the mid- to late fourth century Christians began to travel to various specific locations important to their spiritual lives. Initially these locations were those associated with the life of Jesus, or other biblical narratives. The earliest recorded Christian pilgrimage was performed by Melito of Sardis in the middle of the second century, who traveled to the Holy Land was in order to accurately ascertain the authenticity of the books of the Hebrew Scriptures.[2] According to Melito's account, as recorded by Eusebius, there was no desire to visit any particular place, but only to gather information about the scriptures. In the later fourth century, pilgrims also began to visit shrines associated with the remains of the martyrs for reasons other than personal edification. Their travel was due to an increasing belief that the locations of the martyrs' remains could bring them into more intimate contact with those who acted as intermediaries between themselves and God than would be the case if they did not travel to the shrine. Christian pilgrimage, like the interest in the important dead, was not unique to Christianity. Sacred travel had significant antecedents in the Roman world among both the Jewish population and non-Christian gentiles.

Jewish pilgrimage often focused on those who lived outside of Jerusalem visiting the temple in Jerusalem. According to Exodus (23:17) there was a requirement to visit Jerusalem three times per year, and Josephus attests to this Jewish practice of pilgrimage to Jerusalem in the Common Era[3] as does the Gospel of Luke (2:41–43), which observes that Jesus and his parents traveled to Jerusalem every year for Passover. Early Christians pushed back against place-based holiness. Authors in the New Testament

---

1. John Chrysostom, *Hom. Mart.* 31 (PG 50.661–6), trans. in Wendy Meyer and Paul Allen, *John Chrysostom* (New York: Routledge, 2000), 76.
2. Eusebius, *H.e.* 4.26.14; see also Edward David Hunt, "Were there Christian Pilgrims before Constantine?," in *Pilgrimage Explored* (ed. J. Stopford: Woodbridge, UK: York Medieval Press, 1999): 25–40.
3. Josephus, *Ant.* 4.203.

argued that worship should be done in spirit rather than at a particular place.[4] This denial of sacred space was echoed by Christian writers in the second and third centuries, who were interested in demonstrating the distance between themselves and Roman religions as well as Judaism; they noted that they required neither altar nor temple, as worship was performed in the spirit. Tertullian argued that salvation was not promised to any one land when he argued against the primacy of Jerusalem, and Augustine cautioned Paulinus of Nola not to believe that there was anything special about burying a body in one place over another.[5] Even Jerome and Vigilantius would have agreed that "the Lamb is present everywhere," and consequently there would not have been any *need* to worship Jesus in any *particular* location.[6] God was not to be found in a temple, Roman or Jewish.

Despite the professed desire to worship in spirit rather than in place, we have early evidence of individuals in Rome (presumably Christians) who visited the *triclia* on the Appian Way dedicated to Peter and Paul.[7] Graffiti found at the site definitively dates the active veneration of these two important martyrs to before 260 and possibly as early as 225.[8] The inscriptions left by visitors to the location make reference to meals dedicated to Peter and Paul, and frequently ask for the martyred apostles to remember those who dedicated those meals. Two examples of these inscriptions will suffice here: "Peter and Paul, Tomius Coelius made (this) refrigerium"[9] and "Peter and Paul, come to the aid of Primitivos, a sinner."[10] In the first inscription, Tomius Coelius noted that he performed a commemorative meal for Peter and Paul, and wanted that fact to be remembered. In the second, Primitivos, after labeling himself a sinner, explicitly sought the aid of Peter and Paul.

It is unlikely that these inscriptions were made by what we might think of as pilgrims who traveled great distances (as would later pilgrims) to

---

4. E.g. Acts 7:47–49 and 17:24, Jn 4:21, and Jesus's criticism of the Pharisees who (according to Mt. 23:27–28) built and beautified tombs for the prophets.
5. Tertullian, *Res. De.* 26 (PL 2); Augustine *Cur.* (PL 40).
6. Jerome, *Vigil.* 6 (PL 23.344).
7. Excavated under S. Sebastiano. Graydon F Snyder, *Ante Pacem: Archaeological Evidence of Church Life Before Constantine* (Revised ed.: Macon, GA: Mercer University Press, 2003), 251ff, discusses what he considers to be the 13 most useful of the 222 inscriptions discovered at this site. See also Eastman, *Paul the Martyr*, 72ff.
8. Eastman, *Paul the Martyr*, 73.
9. "Petro et Paulo, Tomius Coelius, refrigeriusm Feci" (Tav. II), trans. in Snyder, *Ante Pacem*, 252.
10. "Petre et Paule sub venite Prim[itivo], peccatori" (Tav. VII, #9), trans. in Snyder, *Ante Pacem*, 253.

visit the cultic site of Peter and Paul. However it does disprove Joan Taylor's broad observation that "there is no evidence at all that Jewish-Christians, or any other kind of Christians, venerated sites as sacred before the beginning of the fourth century."[11] These visitors probably originated from the local Roman population endeavoring to travel outside the walls of the city to this one specific location to beseech the apostles for their aid and intervention. The physical space that surrounded the believed location of the remains of the twin pillars of Roman Christianity was seen as having a level of intimacy with Peter and Paul that was impossible to attain elsewhere. This is a form of pilgrimage that was present in the Roman Empire among its non-Christian population: Romans commonly traveled to various cult locations seeking healing or other forms of divine aid. Also, as I discussed in Chapter One, the obligation to travel to the graves of one's family members was nearly universal.

Despite this early attestation of Christians in and around Rome visiting the shrine of Peter and Paul, typically, when pilgrimage is examined in the context of the church in the late fourth century, the discussion is focused around the desire of the faithful to travel to the "places where Christ was physically present."[12] This is such a preoccupation of modern scholarship that often when people discuss Gregory of Nyssa's cautioning against visiting Jerusalem they take it to refer to a cautioning against pilgrimage of any sort.[13] This, of course, is far from what Gregory argued in his letter on the subject;[14] he was concerned not with theological issues surrounding the problematic idea that any one location could be more sacred than another,[15] but rather argued that pilgrimage to Palestine is unnecessary, and, more importantly, dangerous. Not only might there be physical temptations through the interaction of men and women who must of necessity travel together (apparently, women were unable to mount a horse on their own), but Jerusalem itself was home to various unsavory activities including rascality, adultery, theft, idolatry, poisoning, quarrelling, and murder.

---

11. Joan E. Taylor, *Christians and the Holy Places: The Myth of Jewish-Christian Origins* (Illustrated ed.: New York: Oxford University Press, 1993), 295.

12. Paulinus of Nola, *Ep.* 49.14 (PL 61), trans. P. G. Walsh in vol. 2 of *Letters of St. Paulinus of Nola* (2 vols. New York: Newman Press, 1967), 273.

13. For a discussion of various interpretations of Gregory of Nyssa's stance on pilgrimage in this work see Wes Williams, *Pilgrimage and Narrative in the French Renaissance: The Undiscovered Country* (New York: Oxford University Press, 1998), 94ff.

14. Gregory of Nyssa, *Ep.* 2 (PG 46), also known as "On Pilgrimages."

15. As was Origen in *Contra Celsum* 7.44; Although Gregory does rhetorically ask if the Holy Spirit might be concentrated in Jerusalem, but would then be unable to extend elsewhere.

It is easy to come away from this letter, as have many scholars, with the impression that Gregory is against pilgrimage in its entirety. This is simply not the case. Gregory was in favor of pilgrimage; he remarked after visiting the Holy Land himself that the local spaces are far holier than those in other territories and he even invited other bishops to partake in travel for sacred purposes, and traveled to the martyr festivals in other cities. For Gregory and his brother Basil, however, the focus of sacred travel should not have been Jerusalem, but the shrine of the martyr.[16] These local spaces were far holier than those in foreign lands. Christian pilgrimage may have been initially focused on Palestine, but increasingly toward the end of the fourth century it was aimed toward the matrix of sacred locations centered on the remains of the important Christian dead. These locations were promoted by the local bishops as a means of increasing the prestige of the city and, conveniently, the episcopal seat that went with it.

This chapter will explore the way that Christian pilgrimage, as it became focused around the tombs of the saints, created a degree of uniformity in veneration that had escaped the more deliberate intentions of the episcopate as described in earlier chapters. Christianity, especially in the East as well as North Africa, was focused around the *local* martyrs and veneration at their *local* shrines. Despite the work of the various bishops that I discussed in Chapter Three, there was still a significant degree of localization surrounding the martyr cult toward the end of the fourth century. The pilgrim, through his or her desire to visit sacred locations of far-off lands, or the shrines and festivals of neighboring cities, eased those local differences. In most of the pilgrim narratives that I discuss in this chapter there are instances of the pilgrim being instructed in how to venerate the various martyrs at their shrines – instructions that the pilgrim then relates to his or her readers, implying that those instructions should be replicated in their own practice. The pilgrims would then entreat their readers to join them in the veneration of these martyrs, and would also have frequently taken contact relics home with them from their travels.[17]

---

16. See Gregory of Nyssa, *Ep.* 122 on invitations sent to bishops to attend martyr festivals in Cappadocia. In general on Gregory of Nyssa and Basil's attitude to the martyr cult and pilgrimage see Brouria Bitton-Ashkelony, *Encountering the Sacred: The Debate on Christian Pilgrimage in Late Antiquity* (Berkeley: University of California Press, 2005), 34 ff on the number of pilgrimages both bishops made to various saints' festivals.

17. Pilgrim flasks often contained oils that had been passed through the tombs of the martyrs, and were believed to have the same efficacy as the relics within the tomb.

Pilgrimage and the subsequent iteration of the pilgrims' accounts then were responsible for taking what were once specifically local cultic activities and spreading them throughout Christendom, thereby creating a uniformity of cultural memory and identity that was centered on those sacred sites: the tombs of the martyrs.

Through the process of pilgrimage, local and widely divergent practice regarding the commemoration of the important dead became an empire-wide phenomenon, and pilgrims were ultimately responsible for the breakdown of local divisions between cultic shrines and practices. They created a degree of uniformity through their devotions to the martyrs that may have ultimately been impossible through the decrees and protests of the episcopate. Pilgrims crossed geographical boundaries to experience what Peter Brown refers to as the *preaesentia* of the relics.[18]

To each shrine pilgrims visited they brought their own expectations of what practices were appropriate, and then would have had those expectations altered by the practices that were acceptable at that location. Each visit to a shrine drew upon the previous encounters at martyr shrines, and at the same time foreshadowed subsequent experiences. Each repetition altered both the understanding of the pilgrim as well as the experiences of those who controlled the shrine. I submit that this repetition and alteration was the formation of a language of Christian pilgrimage.

Christian pilgrims developed their own language of pilgrimage, not only in the way that they wrote about their travels, but also through the way that they interacted with and at the martyr's shrines. Not every experience used the same individual "words" from this new language; however, they all eventually drew upon a common lexicon, a lexicon that was shaped as much by the lay pilgrim as it was by episcopal control. This would ultimately become the *lingua franca* which differing Christian communities from vastly divergent regions of the Mediterranean world would use to communicate with each other when they visited the archives of Christian cultural memory: again, the shrines of the martyrs.

One brief example of this repetition and alteration will suffice here. When she visited the shrines in Milan, Augustine's mother thought that it was perfectly acceptable to bring with her watered-down wine, as she

---

18. Peter Brown, *The Cult of the Saints: Its Rise and Function in Latin Christianity* (Chicago: University of Chicago Press, 1981), 93. Although it may also be appropriate to use Walter Benjamin's notion of the "aura" of an item, in this case that of the martyr's corpse. See Walter Benjamin, "The Work of Art in the Age of Mechanical Reproduction" [1936], in *Illuminations: Essays and Reflections* (by Walter Benjamin, ed. Hannah Arendt and trans. Harry Zohn: New York: Schocken, 1968), 217–52.

had been accustomed to in North Africa. However, when she arrived at the martyr's tomb, jar in hand, she discovered that Ambrose had prohibited that practice.[19] Being a pious woman, she submitted to Ambrose's decree and desisted. If she had returned to her home in North Africa, she would have brought back the practice of abstinence at the tombs of the martyrs, although unfortunately she instead died *en route*. Other pilgrims would have left similar traces of his or her own practices behind at (and picked some up from) the tombs that they visited. They would then have been responsible for both spreading the intentionality of the actors described in the preceding chapters, while at the same time subverting those same men in other areas of the empire.

The number of early Christian pilgrim autobiographical narratives is quite small. Five pilgrims will be examined in this chapter. The anonymous Bordeaux Pilgrim and the travel narrative of Egeria written some 20 years later are the earliest autobiographical pilgrimage narratives, and afford a view into the development of the importance of the martyr cult. I will also examine a narrative that is included in a sermon by Augustine which was read aloud to Augustine's congregation by a certain Paul. This account briefly describes the travels that Paul and his sister undertook as they searched for miraculous healing at various shrines to the protomartyr, Stephen.[20] Jerome's description of Paula's travels from Rome to Bethlehem is not autobiographical, although it includes note of the locations that she visited, and in one instance the shocking sights that she witnessed at the tombs of the saints.[21]

In addition to these four, I have included Prudentius among the ranks of late fourth-century pilgrims. Prudentius is best known for his devotional poetry, and is not often considered to have been a pilgrim in the same sense that the others mentioned above were, because he did not visit the Holy Land. However, Prudentius did travel significantly within Europe and several of his hymns to the martyrs express his own desire to visit these sacred locations. Even if Prudentius had other reasons for his travels (which he chose not to share with his readers), he was clearly

---

19. Augustine, *Conf.* 6.2 (LCL 26).
20. Augustine, *Serm.* 324 (PL 39).
21. Jerome, *Ep.* 108 (PL 23). Jerome did pen a letter with Paula inviting, indeed urging, Paula's friends to make a pilgrimage to Jerusalem (*Ep.* 46), and he also discussed Jerusalem when he wrote to Paulinus of Nola urging him *not* to make such a pilgrimage (*Ep.* 58). From these sources we can get a glimpse of how he viewed pilgrimage: ambiguously. Or perhaps, Jerome viewed pilgrimage as something that was suitable for women, but not for serious men like Paulinus.

interested in and devoted to the shrines of the saints. He took his place among those (native and foreign-born) at their altars. His attention to detail allows the modern reader to see not only how one individual pilgrim received the shrines, but also how other Christians worshiped at these sites.

There are also accounts of others who made pilgrimages: Eusebius noted that Constantine traveled to a martyr shrine in the hopes of receiving healing prior to his death, and Basil observed that people from Tarsus and Seleucia traveled back and forth from their respective towns, in order to revere Paul and Thecla respectively.[22] Gaudentius also was on a pilgrimage prior to his being raised to the rank of bishop in Brescia, and was forced to return from Jerusalem by other Western bishops including Ambrose.[23] While his desire may have been to visit the Holy Land, he returned from his journey with relics of John the Baptist and some ashes of the Forty Martyrs.

Pilgrimage as Unifier

For men of which nations do not send pilgrims to the holy places?[24]

The pilgrims themselves, in their new capacity *as* pilgrims, were the actors who helped to spread an empire-wide Christian cultural memory surrounding the tombs of the important dead. They entered into a new category within Christianity that had previously been largely absent. Through their pilgrimage they would now identify with other pilgrims, and share a common identity with this trans-local group over and above their own local circumstances. Victor Turner observes the following regarding the social situation of pilgrims:

> [I]nitiand and pilgrim cease to be members of a perduring *system* of social relations (family, lineage, village, neighbourhood, town, state) and become members of a transient class of initiands and pilgrims, moving *per agros*, through fields or lands [...]. Their relations with others are, at any rate at first, no longer those of interconnectedness but of similarity: no longer do they occupy social positions in a hierarchical or segmentary structure of localised status roles: now they are assigned to a class of anonymous novices or plainly and uniformly garbed pilgrims, all torn or self-torn from their familiar systemic environment.[25]

---

22. Eusebius, *v. C.*, Basil *v. Thecl.* 4.29; see also Bitton-Ashkelony, *Encountering the Sacred*, 34–5.
23. Gaudentius of Brescia, *Serm.* 16 (PL 20.0955).
24. Jerome, *Ep.* 108.3 (PL 22.0879), author's trans.
25. Victor Turner, *Process, Performance and Pilgrimage: A Comparative Symbology* (New Delhi: Naurang Rai, 1979), 122.

Turner's attempt at a systematic and comprehensive approach to pilgrimage has been the object of a considerable amount of criticism.[26] I do not intend to speak for the applicability of this theory for the entirety of pilgrimage studies. Indeed, Jas Elsner and Ian Rutherford have observed that the terms "pilgrim" and "pilgrimage" themselves can be problematic, as they often require a pro (or retro)jection of a Christian understanding of the idea onto non-Christian cultures.[27] However, for the practice that developed toward the end of the fourth century and early into the fifth century this description is quite accurate, especially within Christian circles.

Turner continues that in "Christian modes of liminality there are notions that initiands and pilgrims are simultaneously undergoing the death of social structure and regeneration in *communitas*, social antistructure."[28] This social anti-structure allowed pilgrims to travel, experience, and subtly alter the practices associated with the tombs of the saints. As pilgrims, set apart from their previous communities, they now interacted with other pilgrims who were also part of the same *communitas*. Men mingled with women, poor mingled with rich, urban and rural boundaries did not matter. In their status as pilgrims, they were responsible for creating the cult of the saints as a uniform phenomenon in a way that bishops and emperors had been unable to do earlier in the century, and, consequently, they established, or further cemented, the martyr's tomb as the site of Christian cultural memory. This is not to say that they turned every shrine, or church that contained relics, into a homogeneous carbon copy of every other shrine. Rather, pilgrims, as I demonstrate below, learned the appropriate actions and practices at the various shrines they visited, and communicated these to other members of their local communities who could not travel with them, and to people at the subsequent shrines that they visited. The early pilgrims did not want exactly the same experience at each shrine, other than the ability (perhaps) to glorify the god of each of the martyrs. However, they did want to have an experience that

---

26. John Eade and Michael J. Sallnow, "Introduction," in *Contesting the Sacred: The Anthropology of Christian Pilgrimage* (2nd edition, eds. John Eade and Michael J. Sallonw: Chicago: University of Illinois, 2000), 1–5.

27. Jaś Elsner and Ian Rutherford, "Introduction," in *Pilgrimage in Graeco-Roman and Early Christianity: Seeing the Gods* (eds. Jaś Elsner and Ian Rutherford: New York: Oxford, 2005), 2–3.

28. Turner, *Process*, 126. For a discussion of the problems with the idea that people can just step outside of their culturaly determined roles (especially those surrounding gender) when they enter into pilgrimage see Darlene M. Juschka, "Whose Turn is it to Cook? Communitas and Pilgrimage Questioned," *Mosaic* 36 (2003) 189–204.

was recognizable as an experience of a shrine, given reasonable variations appropriate to the localities that they visited. They accomplished this creation of a discernible experience through their community of pilgrims, refreshing and altering that memory every time they visited the shrine of a saint. The cultural memory spread as the community that shared it became larger and more geographically disparate.

The early Christian pilgrimages that I discuss below have been seen as either a radically new phenomenon, or a continuation of previous Greco-Roman practices. Elsner and Rutherford caution scholars of early Christian pilgrimage that:

> [I]n the move from numerous polytheisms to Christianity – a context that combined profound change with certain fundamental continuities in religion – the denial of the term pilgrimage (over-) emphasizes difference (and hence change), while its employment (over-) emphasizes similarity and hence continuity.[29]

Each stance is tied up with other more contemporary debates surrounding the practices of the church at this period. Despite their previous cautioning against drawing sharp boundaries between Christian practice and previous Roman practice, Elsner and Rutherford eventually do observe that the practice of Christian *relic* pilgrimage was "a radical Christian innovation by comparison with antique activity."[30] They argue that it was not that the idea of pilgrimage was radically new, but rather that the long distances traveled to the remains of the important dead was something that had no clear Roman antecedents. I submit that, in the light of the discussion in Chapter One about the church taking over several key features concerning the care and commemoration of the dead, Christian pilgrimage to the shrines of the important dead continued practices that had been carried out previously, only on a much smaller scale.

In the early decades of the fourth century, there was a significant rise in the importance of elaborate church structures, thanks to the efforts of Constantine, his successors, and subsequent bishops. The structures in Rome, Constantinople, and Jerusalem were resplendent and excited wonder in all who observed them.[31] The rise in impressive buildings and the importance placed upon them has caused many to observe that place-based holiness (which is ultimately necessary for the advent of

---

29. Elsner and Rutherford, "Introduction," 2–3. See 7 nn. 26 and 27 for an exhaustive list of scholars who have seen Christian pilgrimage as either radically new or essentially a continuation of previous pagan practice.
30. Elsner and Rutherford, "Introduction," 29.
31. Sozomen (*HE* 2.26) explicitly observes this regarding those in Jerusalem.

pilgrimage) was itself a development of the fourth century. In his essay concerning the creation of a Christian holy space, R. A. Markus observes: "What began in the 320s and 330s was something quite new."[32] In making a broad statement like this, he does not acknowledge that nothing like the building projects enacted under Constantine could have been possible prior to the presence of a Christian emperor and the wealth that nearly instantly infused the church. Of course, there were no previous Christian buildings and structures like those that Constantine funded. Simply because the buildings became more impressive, and more visible, did not mean that there was no veneration of the graves, both of the common Christian dead (by their immediate family) and of the important Christian dead (by the community which claimed that particular Christian, and by extension used the familial trope to tie themselves together around the graves of the dead). François Decret draws the distinction between the cult of the dead and the cult of the martyrs: the cult of the dead was a family practice; the cult of the martyrs was a church practice. He only needs to add one further step in his analysis: i.e., that the church was the new family.[33]

Not every Christian author in the fourth century believed that there was anything to be gained from the idea of place-based sanctity. Eusebius argued against it, although shortly thereafter Cyril of Jerusalem seemed especially fond of the idea of Jerusalem having a special status as the location of biblical events.[34] Athanasius argued against giving church structures significance on account of the relics that they may have contained. Moreover, as discussed above, Augustine's views on the importance of the place of the relics seems to have shifted significantly in the last few years of his life. I argue here that these disagreements had less to do with theological arguments than they did with the politics of power and control. Those who controlled locations that might be considered holy – either through their association with biblical events or through the control of the bodies of the important dead – stressed their prestige within the larger Christian population (even before the advent of wide-scale pilgrimages); while those who did not control such places were much less inclined to view them as important. If you argued that there was no importance of place,

---

32. Markus, "How on Earth Could Places Become Holy?" *Journal of Early Christian Studies* 2 (1994): 260.
33. François Decret, *Early Christianity in North Africa* (trans. Edward Smither). Eugene, OR: Cascade, 2009 [1996], 95.
34. See Jan Willem Drijvers, *Cyril of Jerusalem: Bishop and City* (Leiden: Brill, 2004), 154.

156 *Death's Dominion*

then it did not matter that you did not control that place. If you argued that there was an importance in the fact that Rome held the remains of Peter and Paul then it was good to be the bishop of Rome.

One aspect that neither Brown nor Markus discusses is the way in which the act of pilgrimage subverted a general Christian movement toward public practice (martyr cult and otherwise) while at the same time increasing the universality of the Christianization of space. Pilgrimage is an inherently individual form of devotion, especially pilgrimages that cross great distances. Pilgrims would only do so, alone or in small groups, if there were a significantly noteworthy *telos*. Yet despite the solitary path of the pilgrim, the act of pilgrimage was one that created solidarity and cross-cultural identity between those lonely individuals. Philo of Alexandria had noted in the first century that pilgrimage, for Jews, "was a social rite that united the people and created in them a sense of duty."[35] Likewise Philo's contemporary (and estranged) compatriot Josephus observed that pilgrimage fostered "mutual affection" among Jews, "for it is good that they should not be ignorant of one another, since they are members of the same race and share the same pursuits."[36]

Brown's *Cult of the Saints* does consider the rise of an elite group of pilgrims, but discusses its importance in the light of the transmission (and associated authenticity) of relics, which brought about concord within the Church.[37] According to Brown, this established itself in the place of structures of patronage, as well as the *preaesentia* that was part of the ceremonial reception that accompanied an imperial visit. The translation of relics did more than cement power structures through patronage; it also created varied foci for pilgrimage, both short- and long-distance. These foci were important places for Christians, both pilgrims and locals, to interact with each other, further cementing the Catholic nature of the Church.

Early Pilgrim Narratives, the Bordeaux Pilgrim, and Paula

In 326, Constantine's mother, Helen, traveled to Jerusalem, where she discovered what was believed to be True Cross and established a basilica covering a site identified as the location of Golgotha and Jesus's tomb.[38]

---

35. Philo of Alexandria, *Spec.* 1.66–70, trans. in Robert Louis Wilken, *The Land Called Holy: Palestine in Christian History and Thought* (New Haven, CT: Yale University Press, 1994), 36.
36. Josephus, *Antiquities* 4.206, trans. in Wilken, *Land Called Holy*, 105.
37. Brown, *Cult of the Saints*, 96–9.
38. On Helen's work see Edward David Hunt, *Holy Land Pilgrimage in the Later*

With Helen's work at preserving, or rediscovering, important Christian sites in the Holy Land, there was a sharp rise in Christians who likewise were interested in visiting these sites for themselves, in a way that was non-existent in the pre-Constantinian period.

The first pilgrim narrative appeared in the middle decades of the fourth century, possibly as early as 330. In the *Itinerarium Burdigalense,* the anonymous traveler, known as "the Bordeaux Pilgrim," described his journey to the Holy Land. The first section, which describes his journey, has few details, although the author's account of the area in and around Jerusalem is quite detailed. Aside from Jesus's own tomb, graves and tombs appear only four times in his itinerary, and not one of them belongs to a Christian. Instead, these were the tombs of important figures from the Hebrew Scriptures: those of Joseph, Isaiah, and Hezekiah (whose monuments were of "wondrous beauty"), and a single tomb (which appears to have been underground or in a cave) near Bethlehem (and the Church of the Nativity) that contained the remains of Ezekiel, Asaph, Job, Jesse, David, and Solomon. At no point was the pilgrim interested in locations of martyrdom or the graves of the martyrs.

In the 50 years between the Bordeaux Pilgrim and Egeria, there was a significant shift in both the geography of the Holy Land and the interest expressed by the pilgrims themselves. The Bordeaux Pilgrim mentioned none of the structures that Egeria observed over the graves of the martyrs; either they had not then been built, or they simply were not important enough for the Bordeaux Pilgrim to note. Either way, the differences between the accounts clearly demonstrate that the gravesites of the important dead had become the locus of the holy for Christianity during this 50-year period.

Paula, who later became well known through her oversight of a monastery and convent in Bethlehem, along with her support of Jerome, also made the arduous journey from Rome to the Holy Land. After her death, Jerome wrote a letter to console Eustochium, her daughter, in which he provided a very specific account of Paula's travels from Rome to Bethlehem.[39] These travels predated her time in Bethlehem by 20 years,[40] which means that they took place sometime around 384–385, possibly preceding

---

Roman Empire: AD 312–460 (New York: Oxford University Press, 1984); Kenneth G. Holum, "Hadrian and Saint Helena: Imperial Travel and the Origins of Christian Pilgrimage," in *The Blessings of Pilgrimage* (ed. Robert Ousterhout, Chicago: University of Illinois Press, 1990), 66–81.

39. Jerome, *Ep.* 108, written in 404.
40. Jerome, *Ep.*108.35 (PL 22.889).

158   *Death's Dominion*

Egeria by about ten years. It is unclear if Jerome penned this letter with the intention of being descriptive or proscriptive; did he simply intend to let Paula's daughter know about her mother's life? It would be odd if Paula's own daughter was ignorant of her mother's travels and importance. It is possible that Jerome saw the letter as an opportunity to present Paula as the model Christian woman, and her pilgrimage as something to be replicated (especially by women – elsewhere, he suggested to Paulinus of Nola that he might have better things to do).

The majority of the places that Jerome described Paula as having visited focused around scriptural events. The few tombs that Paula did visit were primarily Jewish and exclusively those related to the Hebrew Bible and New Testament. She visited Rachel's tomb,[41] and the city of Hebron, which is also called the city of "The Four Men" who were believed to be buried there (Abraham, Isaac, Jacob, and either Adam or Caleb), and she saw the tomb of Lazarus (it is unclear whether this was the one he left after being raised from the dead by Jesus or the one in which he was later entombed, although from the focus on biblical events one should assume the former). In Samaria, Paula visited the tombs of the Twelve Patriarchs and of Elisha and Obadiah, as well as that of John the Baptist. This last tomb was the most notable:

> Here she was filled with terror by the marvels she beheld; for she saw demons screaming under different tortures before the tombs of the saints, and men howling like wolves, baying like dogs, roaring like lions, hissing like serpents and bellowing like bulls. They twisted their heads and bent them back until they touched the ground; women too were suspended head downward and their clothes did not fall off.[42]

This excitement caused Paula to pity the poor souls and to pray that Jesus would have mercy on them, before she continued on her journey. Of the tombs that she visited, this was the only one wherein extraordinary events were recorded to have taken place. We have here evidence of the importance not just of John's tomb, but that of Christian tombs, especially of those Christians who died a violent death and therefore manifested more power than the tombs of the patriarchs. This may well be a problematic description of John the Baptist as "Christian"; however, as he was one

41. Jerome, *Ep.*108.10 (PL 22.889).
42. Jerome, *Ep.*108.13 (PL 22.889), trans. Fremantle et al., *NPNF*[2] 6:201. The reference to the tomb of John the Baptist is unclear, as, according to Rufinus, that tomb had been desecrated during the reign of Julian and the relics moved to Alexandria for safekeeping under the watchful eyes of Athanasius. What tomb, then, did Paula see in 385?

of the first to declare the special relationship of Jesus with God, and as his bones were considered relics, akin to those of the martyrs, it appears that in the eyes of those visiting his tomb he is within the fold of Christianity to a degree that the heroes from the Hebrew Scriptures were not.

After Paula arrived in Bethlehem, she herself became a marvel of the Holy Land that others would meet on their own pilgrimages.[43] This is an important observation by Jerome, as he notes that Paula was a consistent source of contact for pilgrims visiting Bethlehem from Europe. Paula would have been instrumental in shaping the experience of their pilgrimage, the experience that they took home with them. She would have pointed them in the direction of one shrine or another. This would have ensured the popularity and prominence of whichever locations she chose to promote, both among the pilgrims themselves and among those with whom the pilgrims discussed their travels (both during their pilgrimage and once they returned home).

Egeria

Paula was not the only woman who traveled east on a pilgrimage. Egeria set off on her solitary pilgrimage to the Holy Land most likely sometime in the late fourth century,[44] and her account reveals the importance of the location of the sacred in the life of a fourth-century Christian woman – one who underwent hardship in order to physically visit the sites of this holiness. Burial locations were a significant percentage of the locations that Egeria visited. She also provided early evidence of thriving groups of pilgrims. These pilgrims often went to the newly constructed Christian churches located over the graves of important figures in the Jewish Scriptures. Most often, these graves had previously been unknown, with their presence being made known through dreams, in much the same way as Ambrose "discovered" martyr remains in Milan. These Jewish figures also took on some of the characteristics of the

---

43. Jerome, *Ep.*108.3 (PL 22.890).
44. I use the term "newly" with some trepidation. However, as Christians had been arguing against the notion that Jerusalem had any special sanctity, and that it was possible to worship God more effectively in one location than another, it was only during the (late) fourth century that Christians began to see this area as the "Holy Land." On Egeria and the problems of dating the narrative, see George E. Gingras's introduction to his translation of the *Itinerarium Egeriae*. He concludes that it was written no earlier than 394 and no later than 404. All translations for Egeria, unless otherwise noted, are taken from this text. George E. Gingras, *Egeria: Diary of a Pilgrimage* (New York: Newman), 1970: 12–14.

important Christian dead *vis-à-vis* the locations of the remains in the structure commemorating them. They were physically central, either in the place of the pulpit (as in the case of the memorial tomb of Moses on the top of Mount Nebo,[45] or under the altar, as she takes time to describe in detail regarding Job's tomb:

> When they had completely uncovered the stone, they found carved on top of it "Job." In honor of Job, at that time and in that place, was built the church which you see, but in such a way that the stone with the body was not moved to another spot, but was placed where the body was found, so that the body would lie beneath the altar. [46]

Here Egeria described the centrality of the remains of the dead as the focus of the church building. The presence of Job's remains here was unusual or perhaps unique – I know of no other example where the dead under the altar was *not* Christian. Egeria related that this was a location that many other pilgrim monks had told her about, demonstrating both that it was noteworthy and that there were enough other pilgrims at this point for there to be a discussion of the sites of interest. It was possible that Egeria would not have visited this site had there not been a network of pilgrims sharing information concerning what shrines should not be missed. Inevitably, this networking ensured the fame of some shrines at the expense of others.

Of course, the majority of the gravesites Egeria visited were those of the important Christian dead, housing anything from fragments of relics to the entire corpse. At the *martyria* in Heroopolis she observed that it contained a "great many cells," while at the *martyrium* of the apostle Thomas, she specifically pointed out that it contained his entire body, which seemed to have been an important point for her. She does not tell us if that was because the entire body contained more sanctity or power, or if it was simply that by this time it was odd to have the whole body of an important figure from the early period of the church all together in one place. Her visit was most likely nearly 30 years after Ambrose famously began sending out bits of martyrs, rather than simply their ashes or contact relics.[47] That this site was a well-known pilgrimage location (perhaps due to the inclusion of the whole body) is also demonstrated by her

---

45. Egeria, *Itinerarium Egeriae* 12.1.

46. Egeria, *Itinerarium Egeriae* 16.6, trans. Gingras, *Egeria*, 75. One also has to note that this seems to be a distinctly different Job's tomb from the one visited by the anonymous Bordeaux Pilgrim earlier in the century.

47. One also has to wonder if Thomas's whole corpse was located here, whose remains were being honored at the other locations that claimed to have relics of Thomas?

observation that no-one who takes a pilgrimage to Jerusalem missed the chance to go to Edessa where Thomas was interred.

Egeria provided a very brief description of the church located at the tomb, which was "large and beautiful, built in the new way, just right in fact to be a house of God"[48] and containing many other *martyria*. Egeria also visited several other sites of interest, including the *martyrium* of Thecla, who was the only female martyr mentioned specifically in her travels. It is possible that she visited other shrines that included the graves of women martyrs, but this is conjecture as they did not receive special attention or were discussed in passages of the travels that are no longer extant. Egeria seemed to have strong feelings surrounding the *martyrium* of Thecla, as she spent some time discussing her stint there. It is impossible to know if these strong feelings were because Thecla was a woman, or if her martyrdom was a popular tale in European Christianity.[49]

One disappointing aspect of Egeria's account was that she did not spend significant time discussing how she felt about the way in which the martyr graves were presented, with the exception of the "new style" of the church built around Thomas's grave, nor did she discuss how she felt about being in the presence of the remains of the important dead. However, it is clear from her account that these were important locations that she and many other Christian pilgrims felt the need to visit.

The interest of Egeria and the other pilgrims she encountered in the tombs of the martyrs was apparently a novel addition to late fourth-century pilgrimage. The Bordeaux Pilgrim did not visit these places, and Paula's interest in them is significantly less intense than Egeria's. Gaudentius's motivations in visiting the Holy Land in 387 are unclear; however, one thing that we do know is that he returned from that journey with relics. If we look at the activities surrounding the development of the cult of the martyrs in Europe, we can see that several important events took place in the brief time between Paula's pilgrimage and that of Egeria. The translocal martyr relics began to blossom; Ambrose received relics, and then happily sent out the relics of those martyrs that he discovered. There was a growing rise in the European imagination concerning the importance of the relics of the martyrs, as locations of special sanctity for all Christians, not simply the local community. Basil and Gregory of Nyssa (who were

---

48. Egeria, *Itinerarium Egeriae* 19.3, trans. Gingras, *Egeria*, 77.
49. Tertullian makes reference to it in *Bapt.* 17, as well as Hippolytus in his *Com. Dan.* 3.29. Jeremy W. Barrier, *The Acts of Paul and Thecla: A Critical Introduction and Commentary* (Tübingen: Mohr Siebeck, 2009), 15. For a description of the cult of Thecla see Stephen J. Davis, *The Cult of Saint Thecla: A Tradition of Women's Piety in Late Antiquity* (Oxford: Oxford University Press, 2001).

not unique in this practice) traveled to other cities on their local saint's festivals, and likewise invited other bishops to visit Caesarea on similar occasions.[50] With this episcopal practice, I submit, the local martyr's fame would also have spread. In the West, Felix was a confessor (and treated as a martyr) local to Nola; however, through the dedication and promotion that Paulinus lavished on his cult Felix's festival drew in people from far beyond the surrounding countryside. Likewise, once Christian pilgrimage began, those pilgrims would have conveyed their experiences (Paula may have shared her harrowing time at John the Baptist's tomb with those who stayed with her in Jerusalem), which would only have made the fame of that tomb spread. As I discuss below, Prudentius not only wrote poems concerning his experiences at the tombs of the martyrs, but also claims to have gone home singing their praises, all of which would have been an enticement for other travelers to seek out the tombs of the martyrs.

Consequently, when pilgrims began to visit the Holy Land they desired to visit not only the already familiar biblical locations, but also the locations of the martyr's tombs. Once the desire to visit tombs had been initiated, it would not have been difficult for entrepreneurial bishops, with whom Shenoute would have been disgusted, to remember (or invent) long-forgotten sepulchers to other important dead.

Healing Pilgrimage

The pilgrims that we have discussed thus far traveled out of a sense of personal piety or curiosity. There was another set of pilgrims who made their travels for a significantly different and more individually pressing reason: healing at the martyr's tombs. Graffiti evidence of thanksgiving for services rendered at the shrine of Peter and Paul in Rome at the Appian Way is attested as far back as the first decades of the third century; we also know – because he addressed those who were looking for Peter and Paul with his inscription – that Damasus was aware of people making pilgrimages to that particular location. However, it is unclear from whence those who etched the walls originated.

Constantine, prior to his death in 337, traveled to receive healing at specific locations, and it would be hard to describe his practice as

---

50. For a discussion of Basil's and his brother Gregory of Nyssa's frequent pilgrimages to local saint's festivals see Bitton-Ashkelony, *Encountering the Sacred*, 33. As well as the occasionally petulant letters Basil sent to those who complained about not getting invited, or did not come when they were invited. See also Yves Courtonne, *Un Temoin du IVe Siecle oriental: Saint Basile en son temps d'apres as correspondence* (Paris: Les Belles Lettres, 1973), 356–9.

anything other than a pilgrimage. One cannot imagine, however, that he entered in to the *communitas* described by Turner. First he visited hot baths immediately after he felt ill. After that proved ineffective, he traveled to the city of his mother, where he prayed in the church dedicated to the martyrs there.[51] Unfortunately for Constantine, these prayers and supplications did not provide the desired relief from his illness. However, the very fact that Constantine traveled to visit the remains of martyrs with the hope of receiving healing demonstrated an early Christian pilgrimage which looked for physical healing, in much the same way that had been common in previous non-Christian gentile practices.

Most miraculous healings associated with the remains of the martyrs came spontaneously, such as the healing of a blind man who had the good fortune to be standing nearby when Ambrose translated the relics of Protasius and Gervais.[52] Some accounts speak of local congregations being the beneficiaries of miraculous healings. There were, like Constantine, pilgrims who traveled to shrines solely to pray to the martyr to intercede on their behalf and ease their physical suffering. A pair of such pilgrims eventually made their way to the new shrine of Stephen situated in Hippo, and their story was recounted by Augustine in *Sermons* 320–4.[53] On Easter day in 426 Augustine began what would be a four-part sermon aimed at demonstrating the miraculous cures performed by the martyr Stephen, whose relics had recently been discovered. Some of the dust from those remains was eventually sent to Hippo, where Augustine constructed a martyr shrine. The aim of the sermon was to show his congregation a certain man who had been healed by the relics of Stephen, and to let him read his account (Augustine was in the practice of preparing short pieces which described miracles) out loud, thus demonstrating his health. On Easter Tuesday, the pilgrim, Paul, read aloud the account of the tragedies that had beset him and his sister after being cursed by their mother. The spell caused them, and all of their siblings, to tremble uncontrollably. In order to be cured the siblings went looking for remedies at the shrines of various martyrs. While visiting another shrine of Stephen in the Italian city of Ancona, where many miracles had been performed, Paul had a vision. In this vision Augustine appeared to him

---

51. Eusebius, *v. C.* 4.61.
52. Ambrose, *Ep.* 22.2 (PL 16).
53. The account is also repeated in *Civ.* 22: 8, 22. It is in the *City of God* that Augustine names the brother and sister: Paul and Palladia. In his retelling of the tale in *City of God* Augustine leaves out the claim made by Paul that Augustine appeared to him in visions several times.

and told him to make his way to Hippo and that he would be healed in three months.

> On Easter Sunday, as others who were present could see, while I was holding the railings as I prayed with loud weeping, I suddenly fell down. I did lose consciousness, and did not know where I had been. After a little while I got up, and experienced none of that trembling in my body.[54]

In the midst of Augustine's sermon following the reading of the account, Augustine was interrupted by crowds shouting that Palladia had also been cured.

We know from both the account of Paul's healing, as well as the remaining sermon,[55] that these siblings had been traveling for quite some time, from shrine to shrine, hoping to be cured. Augustine reminded his audience that they could have been cured at Ancona, or in the African city of Uzalis, both of which had shrines to Stephen. According to Augustine they were not healed at either of these other shrines so that they could be healed in Hippo, which would strengthen the church there. Their healing was a gift to the city of Hippo as much as it was to Paul and Palladia.

Here is an account of two pilgrims who traveled from city to city, from martyr shrine to martyr shrine, looking for a cure for their disease. There was no reason to think that they did not travel further afield than these three named cities in their quest for health. They would have taken their experiences with them concerning what was appropriate to do at the martyr shrines, as well as their expectations of what to expect from the shrines. It was not noteworthy for Augustine in 426 (nearly a century after Constantine's own search for healing at a martyr shrine) that there would be roving pilgrims going from shrine to shrine, hoping to be healed.

Prudentius

Prudentius was decidedly a creature of the latter half of the fourth century, in the same vein as Paulinus of Nola. Both men had successful and lucrative careers that they abandoned when they became Christians and subsequently devoted themselves to God and the veneration of the martyrs. Prudentius was born in 348, in Spain, and had served as a governmental official under Theodosius. Most of his poetry seems to have been

---

54. Augustine, *Serm.* 322 (PL 38.1444), trans. Edmund Hill and John E. Rotelle, *Sermons 306-340A On the Saints* (The Complete Works of Saint Augustine III/9. New York: New City Press, 1994), 160.
55. Augustine, *Serm.* 324 (PL 38.1456).

written after 390.[56] Like Damasus some 50 years previously, Prudentius incorporated the tales of Christian martyrs into traditional Latin poetic forms.

Little else is known about the life of Prudentius other than his devotion to the cult of the martyrs, as evidenced by his collection of poems, *Liber Peristephanon*. Unlike other poetic devotees of the cult such as Paulinus, Prudentius was not himself in control of a cult center.[57] I have listed him among the ranks of late fourth-century pilgrims as he recounted his travels and veneration at the tombs of the martyrs. However, the sophistication of his accounts was far beyond the simple travel narratives of Egeria or the Bordeaux Pilgrim. *Peristephanon* (typically translated as *Crowns of Martyrdom*) is a collection of 14 poems that he wrote in devotion to various martyrs. Three of these were explicitly pilgrimage-related poems: 9, 11, and 12. In addition to the pilgrimage narratives, Prudentius provides us with a firsthand perspective on the behaviors of those visiting these shrines for their own personal piety. These poems contain details about the site of the shrine of the martyrs, as well as tales of the occasions when the martyrs won their "crowns of martyrdom."

Jill Ross observes regarding his writing that: "Death and writing become one in the transformation of the bodies of the martyrs into texts inscribed with bloody letters."[58] This creates, she argues, "a specifically Christian conception of writing."[59] While her argument is interesting, it seems a bit hasty to place the genesis of such writing in the hands of Prudentius alone, when other previous Christians were engaged in similar endeavors. Writers like Eusebius were engaged with the hagiography of the martyr's passion, while authors such as Paulinus and Damasus were engaged in the utilization of Latin poetic styles in order to make their inscriptions speak to a wider audience.

The *Liber Peristephanon* was widely known and referenced for several hundred years after Prudentius's death.[60] Consequently, Prudentius had a central role in the production of the cult of the saints in subsequent generations of Christians. For the sake of the current work, I see Prudentius

---

56. Michael Roberts, *Poetry and the Cult of the Martyrs: The* Liber Peristephanon *of Prudentius* (Urbana: University of Michigan Press, 1993), 3 n. 7 for a discussion of the dating of his poems. While there is some dispute regarding the 390 date (and that some poems may have predated this) the exact dates are unimportant for the discussion at hand.

57. For a more detailed discussion of his life see Roberts, *Poetry and the Cult*.

58. Jill Ross, "Dynamic Writing and Martyrs' Bodies in Prudentius' Peristephanon," *Journal of Early Christian Studies* 3 (1995): 325.

59. Ross, "Dynamic Writing," 328.

60. See Roberts, *Poetry and the Cult*, 8 n. 21.

as perhaps the perfect accumulation of the cult of the martyrs in the fourth century, and the perfect observer of several significant cult centers. He was the receiver of Hippolytus's tomb, a tomb whose history stretched back 150 years. In *Pe.* 11, on his experience at this shrine, Prudentius allows us to see how the actions of two bishops of Rome were received at a time when the tombs had become a prominent cult center. Prudentius was clearly enraptured with the lives of the martyrs that he wrote about, and was not interested in the initiation of any new aspects of the cult of the saints, so far as we can tell. Yet his very interest in these shrines and subsequent poems concerning them helped spread the fame of those martyrs that he wrote about, and consequently helped to create a modicum of homogeneity within Christian observation. While there were literary embellishments here and there (primarily with the hagiography), there is no reason to doubt his descriptions of the forms of worship that he encountered at the shrines and then recounted, especially in the pilgrimage poems.

Poems 9 and 12 both have Prudentius *being explicitly instructed* about the object of veneration (the martyr[s]) as well as the manner in which he was to pray. In the first of these, Prudentius visits the shrine of Cassian in the Forum Cornelii (located in northern Italy). After seeing a painting depicting the death of the martyr by the martyr's students (who killed him with their styli), Prudentius was told by the *aedituus* of the shrine the events of Cassian's martyrdom. At the end of the poem, that same *aedituus* instructed Prudentius how to pray and what to pray for: "Declare now any upright and worthy wish you have, any hope, any desire that burns in your heart."[61] After his prayer, Prudentius observed thankfully: "I was heard. I visited Rome and found all things issue happily. I returned home and now proclaim the praise of Cassian."[62] Not only was Prudentius influenced by the practices that he encountered at the shrine, but he also carried those practices and even the reverence for Cassian home with him. Through his poetry he encouraged others to likewise venerate the foreign martyr.

In much the same fashion *Pe.* 12 begins with Prudentius asking a Roman man what all of the excitement was about that he was witnessing in Rome. The reply, with a polite lack if incredulity, was that this was the day honoring the deaths of Peter and Paul, who according to this account were killed on the same day, one year apart. Prudentius – or, rather, his anonymous narrator – goes on to describe the nature of their martyrdom,

---

61. Prudentius, *Pe.* 9.95 (Thomson LCL).
62. Prudentius, *Pe.* 10.5–6 (Thomson LCL).

as well as the impressive monuments constructed for them on either side of the Tiber. Within the poem itself, the narrator lays a very protective claim around Peter and Paul as the "two dowers of the faith, the gift of the Father supreme, which He has given to the toga to revere."[63] They were given by God specifically for the city of Rome to venerate, which echoed the inscription set up in the previous century by Damasus. However, the poem ended with the narrator entreating Prudentius: "It is enough for you to have learned all this at Rome; when you return home, remember to keep this day of two festivals as you see it here."[64] Prudentius was explicitly commanded to take the practices and the memory of the festival with him as he traveled home. This would have reiterated and re-created the cultic behavior in the West, and ultimately wherever (and whenever) his poems were read.

Pe. 11 is unique among the poems in that it begins with an address more appropriate for a letter than a work of poetry. Prudentius framed the poem as a correspondence with the Spanish bishop of Calahorra, Valerian, who asked for the names of the martyrs of Rome and the inscriptions cut on their tombs. Here we see Prudentius acting as a virtual tour guide to an important bishop in his homeland. Despite this clear objective, Prudentius claimed to be overwhelmed by the task, and instead focused the narrative on Hippolytus, whose name he just "happened" to find inscribed on a tomb. He wrote that: "[i]n surveying these memorials and hunting over them for any letters telling of the deeds of old, that might escape the eye, I found that Hippolytus."[65]

The description that follows this makes it hard to believe that Prudentius just happened to spy this one inscription; yet, the idea that this was one of many in Rome is not unbelievable. Prudentius professes that he focused on Hippolytus in his depiction to Valerian due to the overwhelming number of martyrs to be found in Rome, many of whom are commemorated without name, their tombs only recording the number of martyrs buried therein: "I remember finding that the remains of sixty persons were buried there under one massive stone, whose names Christ alone knows, since He has added them to the company of his friends."[66] Prudentius then, focusing his attention on Hippolytus, recorded a history that was clearly dependent on the Damasian inscription discussed in Chapter Three. Prudentius, based upon his reception of the inscription left by Damasus, uncritically associated Hippolytus with the Novitian

---

63. Prudentius, *Pe.* 12.55–6 (Thomson LCL).
64. Prudentius, *Pe.* 12.64–5 (Thomson LCL).
65. Prudentius, *Pe.* 11.17–19 (Thomson LCL).
66. Prudentius, *Pe.* 11.13–16 (Thomson LCL).

schism. According to this narrative Hippolytus then recanted his previous position and sought, above all else, unity and wholeness within the Catholic Church as he went to his death.

The account of Hippolytus's martyrdom that followed was an interesting amalgamation of differing traditions, possibly including the martyrdom of a Hippolytus of Portus, as well as the dismembering of Hippolytus of Greek mythology (who was torn apart by wild horses).[67] Prudentius combined these three traditions in his account of the martyrdom at the shores of the Tiber. In the midst of the death of less notable Christians, Hippolytus was presented to the judge: "While he was loudly giving these orders, an elderly man enveloped in bonds was suddenly presented before the high judgment-seat, and the young men who crowded round were crying out that he was the head of the hosts which worshiped Christ."[68] Here we have a proclamation that Hippolytus was a leader of the Church, perhaps even a bishop of Rome, not a tradition that is found within the Damasian inscription. Nevertheless, this is consistent with Hippolytus's historical role as a leader within the church, if not an outright schismatic, as claimed by Damasus. Due to Hippolytus's prominence within the Christian community, the judge sought a special form of punishment: being torn in two, and dragged behind wild horses "who had never known the bridle." It is possible that there was a painting representing this scene at the cult center, as described by Prudentius, or that this was a comingling of sacred histories, mixing the Greek hero with the same name as that of our own protagonist. Either way, Michael Roberts comments that the death of Hippolytus is fitting for the figure that is presented as a member of a schismatic sect by both Damasus and Prudentius. As Hippolytus had previously sought to tear the body of the church in two, so too did his corporeal body suffer the same fate at the hands of Prudentius: "The manner of martyrdom absolves Hippolytus of the crime he had formerly committed against the Church." [69] When the judge proclaimed, after hearing his name for the first time, "Hippolytus let him be,"[70] the allusion was likely to the classical imagery: if he was called Hippolytus, then he should die in the same manner as the classical Hippolytus.

As we see after the gory account regarding the dismemberment of Hippolytus, the faithful gather together all of the fresh martyr pieces:

---

67. Footnote "a" by Thomson in the Loeb Classical Library edition of Prudentius, *Pe.*, 304–5.
68. Prudentius, *Pe.* 11.70–80 (Thomson LCL).
69. Roberts, *Poetry and the Cult*, 146.
70. Prudentius, *Pe.* 11.87 (Thomson LCL).

stunned with grief, they were searching with their eyes as they went, and gathering the mangled flesh in their bosoms. One clasps the snowy head, cherishing the venerable white hair on this loving breast, while another picks up the shoulders, the severed hands, arms, elbows, knees, bare fragments of legs.[71]

Prudentius here aligned himself with the Roman understanding of the saints' remains: that they should be complete.[72] Prudentius went on to describe the location in which they interred Hippolytus, once all of his various pieces were re-united. They laid him in a long cave, which was illuminated by shafts running up to the daylight: "Still through the holes pierced in the vault many a gleam of light makes its way down to the hollow interior of the disemboweled mount."[73]

At the tomb of Hippolytus, Prudentius was not simply an observer, but came as a pilgrim to ask for Hippolytus's help:

> Whenever I bowed in prayer here, a sick man diseased in soul and body both, I gained help. My glad return, my chance to embrace you, reverend priest, my writing these words, I know that I owe to Hippolytus, to whom Christ our God has given power to grant one's request.[74]

Prudentius also recounted that from dawn till dusk countless other pilgrims made their way to the altar to pay their respects. Some of these pilgrims came from Rome, but many others (like Prudentius himself) traveled over great distances. While there may have been significant differences between these people, "[t]he love of their religion masses Latins and strangers together in one general body."[75] As Roberts observes: "The company assembled in the basilica for the saint's festival embodies the new Christian *civitas*, brought together from various cities and stations in life, united by their common devotion to the saint."[76] As we noted at the beginning of the chapter, this is precisely what Turner described with regard to the social changes that occurred when people engaged in pilgrimage. They became united into a new community, a community of pilgrims, which defied local stratification.

The masses that gathered from day to day pale in comparison with the multitudes that amassed on the saint's festival, the Ides of August:

> The majestic city disgorges her Romans in a stream; with equal ardour patricians and plebian host are jumbled together shoulder to shoulder, for the faith banishes distinctions of birth; and equally from Alba's gates the white-robed

---

71. Prudentius, *Pe.* 11.135–40 (Thomson LCL).
72. Roberts, *Poetry and the Cult*, 16.
73. Prudentius, *Pe.* 11.160 (Thomson LCL).
74. Prudentius, *Pe.* 11.179 (Thomson LCL).
75. Prudentius, *Pe.* 11.191–2 (Thomson LCL).
76. Roberts, *Poetry and the Cult*, 164.

> troops deploy and pass on in long lines. Loud sounds of rejoicing rise from diverse roads leading from different places; natives of Picenum and the people of Etruria come; the fierce Samnite and the Campanian dweller in lofty Capua meet together, and men of Nola too are there, everyone in happy mood with wife and dear children and eager to get quickly on the way.[77]

The crowd grew so large that an above ground church needed to be constructed to house the masses that gathered here to honor the martyr and worship their god through him. Even with such a large church, Prudentius notes that there was scarcely room for the masses. By the time that Prudentius wrote this poem, near the end of the fourth century or very early in the fifth, already there were large gatherings at the graves of the martyrs. What we saw here, and had previously seen with Paulinus's description of the crowds coming from Rome for Felix's birthday, were great numbers of foreigners. The presence of these foreigners was a new phenomenon.

The important dead created their own gravitational pull that drew in the closest bodies, but also now had the power to influence those from further and further away, including those who orbited their own shrines in distant lands. These pilgrims brought their own approach to worshiping the saint from their homeland; these were practices which were influenced by both the popular practices of the general population as well as instructions about worship by the episcopate.

Conclusion

Through our discussion of pilgrims and pilgrim narratives, I have shown how itinerant groups of Christians would become one of the unifying forces of Christianity around the turn of the fifth century. Pilgrims entered into a new social group, one that was not defined by wealth, gender, age, social status, or geographic location. Pilgrims were liminal to traditional group identities; they traveled to locations that were not only by law peripheral to urban centers, but also located great distances from the pilgrim's point of origin. The very nature of the feasts associated with the martyr shrine only further cemented the degree to which pilgrims would stand outside of social stratification. Martyr feasts were known for their inclusiveness, dissolving social barriers.

The earliest evidence for Christian sacred travel reveals that the first pilgrims' primary desire was to visit locations associated with biblical stories. However, the 60 years or so that separate the travels of the Bor-

---

77. Prudentius, *Pe.* 11.199–209 (Thomson LCL).

deaux Pilgrim from the pilgrimage of Egeria were marked by significant developments of the martyr cult in the fourth century; whereas the Bordeaux Pilgrim expressed no interest in the burials of the martyrs, Egeria was captivated by visiting their various tombs and recounting these visits for her readers. Egeria's interest in visiting the sites of the mortal remains of the martyrs and other important dead could not have been coincidental to the rise in the use of the martyrs as a means of creating a common Christian social identity that surrounded those remains. Yet, despite Egeria's initial interest in the martyr's tombs being a product of episcopal agendas, her devotion to them was personal and individual. She and the other pilgrims that she discussed meeting and sharing stories with, through their liminal role, traveled from one shrine to another. At each shrine they were influenced by different circumstances, and were perhaps party to (yet separate from) various local disputes surrounding the proper usage of martyrs. These they then carried with them to the next location, where the situation was repeated, again and again. Through their anti-structural status, they also served to create a universal Christianity that smoothed over local differences, especially surrounding the martyr cult.

When Prudentius visited the shrine of Hippolytus, he was foreign to the context of the Damasian inscription in both time and city of origin. His understanding, or reception, of the shrine and practices associated with Hippolytus were far different from those that Damasus intended when he had the inscription placed at Hippolytus's tomb. The struggle for dominance and power that plagued Damasus was no longer an issue at the time of Prudentius, but the repercussions of that struggle were still on display. Prudentius then urged the Spanish Church to whom he was writing to commemorate the feast day of Hippolytus on their calendar. Prudentius seems to have been writing out of personal piety, not propaganda. Yet, this piety helped spread the Damasian image of a unified church well beyond the Roman walls. His community of pilgrims through their own piety managed to create uniformity through the veneration of martyr festivals that could only have been the envy of Damasus, who too sought to create a unified church at the shrines of the martyrs.

Conclusion

> It is in response to the dread of oblivion that graveyards are created and gravestones inscribed. Who can honestly say he or she has never wondered whether anyone will visit his or her grave?[1]

I began this book by discussing Mark Taylor's *Grave Matters*, a work that considers the significance of graves, and especially those of the important dead, in our own society. More than half of the work consists of photographs of the final resting places of his important dead – philosophers and artists that he claimed as his own. The photographs allow the reader to become an armchair pilgrim to the sites of Taylor's saints. He was not bound to those whose graves he presents by bonds of blood, but rather through intellectual and aesthetic commonalities. Taylor's book, unintentionally I assume, neatly encompasses the shifting attitudes toward the remembrance of the important dead that took place in the early centuries of the Common Era, beginning with the shift from exclusively familial care of the dead to a more communal structure found within *collegia*, and ending with pilgrimage as a means of unifying a larger family. For Taylor, that larger family is his readers; in my work it is the Catholic Church.

Like Taylor, both Constantine and Damasus were the direct heirs of pre-Christian Roman practices associated with the dead. Voluntary organizations sought to supplement the family's traditional role in collectively commemorating the dead, as well as celebrating the important dead. The Christian community also began to complement that familial role through the burial of those members of their community whose family could not afford to properly bury them. Burial by the Christian community may not have been universal, as those families who could afford it still sought to set themselves apart from the collective group, yet there was a commonality of remembrance for the dead of the Christian community, the new family in Christ. Likewise the important dead of that family, the martyrs, were celebrated and the days of their death (seen as their birth by that community) were collectively remembered,

---

1. Mark C. Taylor, *Grave Matters* (London: Realtion, 2002), 36.

especially by the local community of which they had been a part. This was an extension of the previous traditional festivals held in honor of the dead in the Mediterranean world, mixed to some degree with the traditional cultic activities associated with the gods (e.g., supplication and offerings which outstripped typical mortuary practices). The graves of the important dead were the locations where a local collective memory was created, reinforced, and perpetuated.

Constantine used his building endeavors to position himself as the patron of the Church. The basilicas that he constructed for the church were not random buildings erected wherever it was convenient. They were intentionally built on locations that already had meaning within the Christian community, where Christians already visited, dined at, and sought aid from the divine through physical association with the graves of the important dead. The basilicas were erected over the graves of the important dead, the locations of collective memory. Through his construction of structures that traditionally had been associated with imperial power, Constantine could cement the association of his own authority with that of the Church. Finally, through his own chosen place of interment he identified himself as important as the apostles themselves, but consequently also equated the power of the apostles with that of the emperor. In the course of moving the bodies of Luke, Andrew, and Timothy, Constantine both granted martyrs to Constantinople and initiated the movement of relics (in this case whole corpses) to locations with which they had no connection in their lifetimes.

Slightly later, in Rome, Damasus was struggling to solidify his power as bishop. After a bloody and contentious fight to gain the episcopal seat he was ingenious in his usage of the cultural memory associated with the martyrs of Rome as a means of solidifying his place as the head of the Roman Church. Damasus, through his usage of ornate epitaphs, presented an image of a united church, easing the tensions of decades of infighting between Christians while he continued to purge the last vestiges of the schismatics from his city. He intentionally brought the schismatic Hippolytus back into the embrace of the church through a reversal of Hippolytus's disgust of Callistus and his successors. The only place where this change of heart is recorded is on the epitaph that Damasus penned for his tomb. The image at the seat of Christian cultural memory was unambiguously one of concord. The other ubiquitous feature of these inscriptions was the inclusion of the role of Damasus himself in their placement. Damasus also sought to enhance the prestige of Rome by claiming martyrs as her own, even against other cities that might have had a stronger claim. Damasus places the Roman stamp upon Peter and Paul (who also were once on less than friendly terms, but were now unified in Rome), claiming them successfully forever for

Rome. Through his intentional incorporation of some figures over others, and emphasis of unity over discord, Damasus crafted an image of the past which only served to solidify his position in his present.

Constantine and Damasus used the martyr cult to consolidate their power very effectively; this laid the foundation for others to build upon, and for those others to add their own innovations. Ambrose of Milan quickly incorporated the Constantinian basilica structure in his city, and was also eager to incorporate martyr remains into those structures. He may well have received relics from Constantinople, which he then integrated into his "Roman" basilica. Even with the presence of these remains, there was a feeling that Milan was secondary to other locations, as Milan had no local martyrs for veneration. Luckily Ambrose soon discovered the remains of the long-forgotten martyrs Protasius and Gervais. After quickly translating their bodies into his own basilica, Ambrose sowed the seed of his new martyrs to other bishops and congregations, who likewise at first had no relics for the consecration of their own buildings. Ambrose's unprecedented generosity in this regard had the direct consequence that his own fame, and that of his city, would be connected with that of the martyrs' remains wherever those seeds took root and bloomed. This was exactly the opposite of the practices of his contemporaries in Rome, who jealously guarded the physical remains of their martyrs. The dispersal of the relics from Milan also continued the dissolution of the barriers of the local martyr cults. Ambrose's generosity created martyrs who were embraced outside of Milan, which had previously only been the purview of biblical heroes, not local martyrs.

Through his control of the newly minted cult of Protasius and Gervais, as well as the others that he discovered, Ambrose was unique in his ability to determine what practices should and could be performed around their shrine. Unlike other cult centers associated with martyrs, there were *no* pre-existing practices in Milan that Ambrose had to suppress *vis-à-vis* the martyr cult. Ambrose could control the cult from its inception, giving him considerable influence over its development. To this end, Ambrose sought to limit what he felt were pagan practices associated with veneration paid to the graves, primarily feasting and drinking. The problem of drunkenness at the martyr festivals was prevalent throughout Europe, North Africa and the East, and would be for decades more, if not even longer. While Ambrose, Augustine, Shenoute, and many other Christian critics were censorious of the feast day practices associated with martyr festivals, Paulinus of Nola was explicitly tolerant. For Paulinus, allowing some degree of acceptance of the practices of his countrymen to continue within the embrace of the Church was preferable to the alienation of those same countrymen though prohibition. That is to say, he allowed some indulgence in wine and feasting, rather than alienate those who would otherwise not have attended the saint's day festivities. While this was Paulinus's explanation for his tolerance, one has to wonder if he would have been as tolerant if there had been any contenders for control of his congregation, much less had there been issues of doctrinal purity at stake. Unlike peaceful circumstances found in Nola, Ambrose struggled with Arians in Milan, and Augustine likewise contended with Donatists in North Africa. It cannot be coincidence that those who sought to control the martyr cult were explicitly engaged in problems with schismatics.

Augustine, early in his life, was at best ambivalent toward that martyr cult. He did not necessarily denigrate or prohibit it, but he did seek to downplay its importance. One reason for this was that his Donatist neighbors had long ago referred to themselves as the "Church of the Martyrs" and vigorously promoted the cult of the local martyrs. However, once he received the relics of Stephen and incorporated them into his church, Augustine began to affectionately promote the martyr cult. Like Damasus, he did not promote every martyr equally. There were many North African martyrs that Augustine could have chosen to emphasize. He could have promoted them in the way that Ambrose promoted the martyrs that he discovered; which, for Augustine, would have increased the prestige of Hippo. Augustine did not follow the lead of Ambrose. Instead, when Augustine talked of those Christians who had died for their faith in North Africa, he was expounding on why the martyrs of the Donatists should not be considered real martyrs. Those figures Augustine sought to promote were universal martyrs, those who transcended the local cult: Stephen, Protasius and Gervais, Peter and Paul. These figures united Christendom rather than dividing it into a collection of local churches which honored local martyrs. However, he was unable to vanquish the appeal for the local martyr, which we saw in his lamentation that many of his congregation attended festivals for the important local dead, while the church was nearly empty for the feast for Peter and Paul.

While the tombs of the dead were sites of cultural memory in non-Christian gentile practice, their acceptance in no way meant that the direction Christians took those practices was warmly accepted by everyone. There was a traditional aversion to corpses, and the emperor Julian "the Apostate" pushed back against the development of the Christian cult when he felt that it infringed on the sensibilities of his subjects, or the functioning of Roman cult sites. Some Christians were also critical of the martyr cult in the fourth century, feeling that the excesses of the all-night vigils soiled the whole endeavor. Others saw the martyr cult as a tool of their opponents in their struggle for control, and because of its association with their opponents they condemned it. Athanasius of

Alexandria was in that latter category: he argued against any need for place-based sanctity, and he was critical of what he claimed to have been a Meletian practice of placing martyr remains on stretchers – remains which could then be moved from location to location. His opponents embraced the martyr cult. Consequently, Athanasius rejected it, even projecting that refutation into the mouth of Anthony.

As the fourth century drew to a close, the newly emergent group of Christian pilgrims began to focus more and more attention on visiting the shrines of the martyrs. Much as the martyr shrines transcended time, linking the past of Christianity with its future, so too did the pilgrims transcend space. Monuments existed in the present, yet always pointed back to the past, and predicted a future where they would be viewed again. As monuments transcended time, pilgrims transcended place and status. Pilgrims operated in a special liminality, where they were in a location yet not of that location, thereby surpassing geographic boundaries. They existed in a world where their status before they became pilgrims was superseded by their status as pilgrims.

Pilgrims initially focused on the Holy Land, to walk where Jesus walked, to see his places of birth, ministry, and death. Yet during the late fourth century, the locations of the remains of the dead became increasingly important in pilgrimage accounts. Bishops sought to promote their own local cults, drawing pilgrims to experience the physicality of those locations. Some pilgrims would travel seeking healing, while others simply desired to venerate the remains. As pilgrimage networks developed, perhaps most importantly through the hospitality of Paula in the Holy Land, pilgrims shared with each other the locations that they had visited. When a location became more popular, more pilgrims visited it. They would then return home and tell tales about their experiences, thereby promoting the cults that had the greatest effect on them. Pilgrims did not have to travel great distances to continue this dissolution of the local nature of the martyr cult, nor did they always have to travel east. When Prudentius visited Rome, he in turn became an advocate for the inclusion of the feast day of Hippolytus into the ecclesiastical calendar of his readers. In part due to Prudentius's promotion of its martyrs Rome became a tremendously important pilgrimage location. Yet Romans were not content to remain at home and only venerate their martyrs, they traveled in great numbers to Nola to honor Felix under the tutelage of Paulinus.

Pilgrimage created a network of Christian collective memory. Bishops and emperors had attempted to craft and control the cultural memory of their communities through their use of the remains of the important dead. Frequently, those same actors sought to fight schisms within their community or present an image of the unified church through the choice of martyr or the epitaphs erected. Others sought to project the prestige of their city through the dispersal to other cities of the relics that they controlled. All of these practices clearly influenced the promotion of the cult of the saints, and directed it as it moved from a familial practice of the commemoration of the dead, to the local family in Christ commemorating their local heroes, the martyrs. However, it was only with the advent of trans-local pilgrimages that a uniform Christian collective memory could be produced surrounding the martyr's grave.

The meaning associated with the graves of the saints could never be determined unidirectionally. Their meaning, and the power to influence perception of those graves, was the product of a dialogue. Had there not been a popular cultural emphasis on the importance of proper burial, the Christian community may not have embraced it as one of their primary blessings in the third century. Christian leaders from Constantine to Shenoute sought to mold and craft the meaning of Christianity, and one of the battlegrounds for that was the shrine of the important dead. Yet, if these locations carried no importance of their own it would have been inconceivable that these Christian leaders would either have effected any change, or have even tried to influence the population through the martyrs' graves. No matter how hard the Christian leaders sought to influence their populations with the message associated with the martyr's remains, they ultimately were not in control of the dissemination of that message. It was the pilgrims, influenced to be sure by their leaders, who played a pivotal role in the reception of the message, and shared that message as they saw fit, promoting that which they felt was important, and ignoring that which they did not.

In this book, I have attempted to explain the uses of the locations of the remains of the martyrs as a means of projecting cultural memory. The observant reader will have noticed that rarely did I explicitly describe that cultural memory, other than to say that there was some association with the suffering of the martyr, and the importance of steadfast faith even to death. Cultural memory was created and projected at each of the martyr shrines, unique to the martyr venerated and the community which venerated that particular martyr. It has been my intention here to examine *how* those remains were used, what the struggles were that were fought over the dead, and ultimately how those struggles were resolved. This work has laid a foundation for further study into particular martyr veneration through, perhaps, a hermeneutics of power and influence. The structure established here will assist those further endeavors, as there remains significant work that can be done on the specific cults. One of these areas would be the initial translation of relics from Constantinople to Milan, the translation that initiated Ambrose's own endeavors. A more detailed discussion of the construction of sacred space, or the usage of ritual surrounding the martyrs' graves, would also be fruitful. Finally, little work has been done on the hesitancy for the martyrs and holy men themselves to be commemorated. Ignatius, Anthony, and Hilarion explicitly wanted to avoid such a fate for their corpses, and their wishes were summarily ignored.

Through my discussion of the martyr cult in the West, and presenting it roughly chronologically, I have filled a void in scholarship on the subject on the rise of the martyr cult in late antique Christianity. Too often issues of the early fifth century are conflated and presented alongside items from the early fourth with no discussion of the evolution of the martyr cult that transpired in the intervening decades. Aside from the theoretical substructure and the chronological format of the work I have put forward a number of original conclusions about material that has been examined previously. These include the discussion on Constantine's originality, not as regards the martyr cult as a whole, but in his movement of the bodies of the apostles (or desire for them to be moved) to a location that was neither associated with their lives nor with their death. Also, while it has been observed elsewhere that Constantine raised himself to be the equal to the apostles through their inclusion in his mausoleum, no-one has noted that this also raised the apostles to the level of the emperor. Shenoute is frequently considered to have been an opponent of the martyr cult as a whole. During my analysis of his works, I have demonstrated that he was critical of its misuse, but did not oppose it outright. Finally, the most important contribution that this work makes to scholarship on the rise of the martyr cult is its emphasis on the role that pilgrims, and pilgrimage, played in its development, and the way that pilgrims subverted the local bishops while unifying the practices associated with the martyr cult.

Mark Taylor's book comes after nearly two thousand years of the elevation of the status of the graves of the important dead. The cult of the saints ascended into prominence only after the early fifth century. Even if the dissemination of relics is a thing of the past, we continue to be captivated and drawn to the presence of the final resting places of our important dead. That is the draw of Taylor's book: we have become pilgrims, creating and subverting a unifying meaning through the dominion of the dead.

Bibliography

Abbreviations

ANF – Ante-Nicene Fathers
CIL – Corpus Inscriptionum Latinarum
CSEL – Corpus Scriptorum Ecclesiasticorum Latinorum
CCL – Corpus Christianorum, Series Latina
PL – Patrologia Latina (Migne)
PG – Patrologia Graeca (Migne)
LCL – Loeb Classical Library
NPNF – *Nicence and Post-Nicene Fathers*

Primary Literature

Throughout the process of researching and writing I have relied on various translations of ancient texts. In general I have opted to use these professional translations rather than my own. As there is little philological work in this book I have not necessarily avoided older translations, unless there was a clear reason to have done so. At various points I have translated excerpts myself, as documented in footnotes. Generally, due to the readily available nature of Migne's Patrologia Latina (PL), I have opted to draw my primary sources from there rather than the Corpus Scriptorum Ecclesiasticorum Latinorum (CSEL). However, when I have had access to a Loeb edition for a text I have chosen that over either of the former.

Ambrose. *Epistulae (Ep.)* PL 16. Translated by H. de Romestin, E. de Romestin and H.T.F. Duckwork in *NPNF*^{2} 10. Edited by Philip Schaff and Henry Wace. Edinburgh: T. & T. Clark, 1893.

Ammianus Marcellinus. *Rerum Gestarum Libri XXXI (Res. Gestae)*. Translated by (1) J. C. Rolfe. 3 vols. LCL 300, 315, 331. Cambridge, MA: Harvard University Press, 1939–1950; (2) Walter Hamilton, *The Later Roman Empire (A.D. 354–378)*. Harmondsworth, UK: Penguin Books, 1986.

Aristides. *Apologia (Apol)* Translated by D. M. Kay (from Greek) and J. Rendel Harris (from Syriac) in *ANF* 9. Edited by Allan Menzies. Edinburgh: T. & T. Clark, 1896.

Athanasius of Alexandria. *Vita Antonii (v. Anton.)* PG 26.837.

—*Epistularum festivalium (Ep. Fest.)* PG 26.1367, 1379, 1389, 1432 ff. Translated by Wilhelm Riedel and W. E. Crum, *The Canons of Athanasius of Alexandria: The Arabic and Coptic Versions*. London: Williams and Norgate, 1904.

Augustine. *City of God (Civ.)* Books 8–11 translated by David Wiesen. LCL 413. Cambridge, MA: Harvard University Press, 1968.

—*Confessions (Conf.)* PL 32.

—*Contra Faustum Manichaeum* (*Faust.*) PL 42. Translated by Richard Stothert in *NPNF*[1] 4. Edited by Philip Schaff. Edinburgh: T. & T. Clark, 1887.
—*Contra Gaudentium Donatistarum Episcopum* (*Gaud.*) PL 43.
—*De Cura pro Mortuis Gerenda* (*Cur.*) PL 40. Translated by H. Browne in *NPNF*[1] 3. Edited by Philip Schaff. Edinburgh: T. & T. Clark, 1887.
—*De moribus ecclesiae catholicae* (*Mor. Eccl.*) PL 32.
—*De Opere Monachorum* (*Mon.*) PL 40.
—*Epistulae* (*Ep.*) PL 33. Translated by (1) J. G. Cunningham in *NPNF*[1] 1. Edited by Philip Schaff. Edinburgh: T. & T. Clark, 1886; (2) Sister Wilfrid Parsons, *St. Augustine, Letters*, vol. 2 *(83–130)*. New York: Fathers of the Church, 1953.
—*Sermones* (*Serm.*) PL 38, 39. Extracts in the present work from translation by Edmund Hill and John E. Rotelle, *Sermons 306–340A On the Saints. The Complete Works of Saint Augustine* III/9. New York: New City Press, 1994.
Basil. *De vita ac miraculis Theclae* (*v. Thecl.*) PG 85.477.
—*Epistulae*. Translated by Roy Joseph Deferrari, *St. Basil: The Letters*. 4 vols. LCL 190, 215, 243, 270. Cambridge, MA: Harvard University Press, 1926–34.
—*Homilia in XL Mayrtyres* (*Mart.*) PG 31.508–40.
Bordeaux Pilgrim. *Itinerarium Burdigalense* PL 8.783.
Cicero. *De Legibus* (*De Leg.*) Translated by Clinton W. Keyes. LCL 213. Cambridge, MA: Harvard University Press, 1928.
—*Epistula Nonius* (*Nonius*) Cic. Fragm. ap. Non. 32, 18; LCL 462.
—*Philippics* (*Phil.*) Translated by Gesine Manuwald, *Marcus Tullius Cicero: Orationes Philippicae III-IX*. Berlin: Walter de Gruyter, 2007.
—*Tusculan Disputations*. LCL 141. Cambridge, MA: Harvard University Press, 1927.
Collectio Avellana (*Avel.*) CSEL 35.1, 2, 18–22.
Commodianus. *Instructions* (*Inst.*) CCSL 128. Turnhout: Brepols, 1960.
Constantine. *First Sirmondian Constitution*. Edited and translated by Clyde Pharr, *The Theodosian Code and Novels and the Sirmondian Constitution*. Princeton, NJ: Princeton University Press, 1952.
—*Oratio Constantini* PG 20.905. Translated by Mark Edwards in *Constantine and Christendom; The Oration to the Saints; The Greek and Latin Accounts of the Discovery of the Cross; The edict of Constantine to Pope Sylvester*. Liverpool: Liverpool University Press, 2003
Cyprian. *Epistulae* (*Ep.*) PL 3, 4.
Damasus. *Inscriptions*. Collected in Damasus and Maximilian Ihm, *Damasi Epigrammata. Accedunt pseudodamasiana aliaque ad Damasiana inlustranda idonea. Recensuit et adnotavit Maximilianus Ihm. Adjecta est tabula.* Lipsiae: B. G. Teubner, 1895.
Egeria. *Itinerarium Egeriae*. Translated by George E. Gingras, *Egeria: Diary of a Pilgrimage*. New York: Newman, 1970.
Epiphanius of Salamis. *Panarion*. Books 2 and 3 translated by Frank Williams, *The Panarion of Epiphanius of Salamis: Books II and III: De Fide*. Leiden: Brill, 1994
Eunapius of Sardis. *Lives of the Philosophers and Sophists* (*VS*). Translated by Wilmer Cave France Wright. LCL 134. Cambridge, MA: Harvard University Press, 1961.
Eusebius.*Historia Ecclesiastica* (*H.e.*) PG 20.45.
—*De vita Constantini* (*v. C.*) PG 20.905.
—*Martyrdom of Ignatius* (*M. Ign.*) PG 5.987B–988A. Translated by Alexander Roberts, James Donaldson, and Arthur C. Coxe in *ANF* 1. Edinburgh: T. & T. Clark, 1885.
Gaudentius of Brescia. *Sermones* (*Serm.*) PL 20.
Gregory of Nazianzus. *First Oration against Julian* (*Oratio*) PG 35.
Gregory of Nyssa. *Epistulae* (*Ep.*) PG 46.
Herodian. *History of the Empire* (*His. Emp.*) 2 vols. LCL 454–5. Cambridge, MA: Harvard University Press, 1969–70.
Hippolytus. *Apostolic Tradition*. Translated by Paul F. Bradshaw, Maxwell E. Johnson, and L. Edward Phillips, *The Apostolic Tradition: A Commentary*. Minneapolis, MN: Fortress Press, 2002.

—*Commentarium in Danielem* (*Com. Dan.*) PG 10.637, 669.
—*Philosophoumena* or *Refutatio ominum haeresium* (*Haer.*) PG 16.3017. Translated by F. Legge, *Philosophumena; or The Refutation of All Heresies*. London: Society for Promoting Christian Knowledge, 1921.
Ignatius. *Epistola ad Romanos* (*Ep. ad Rom.*) PG 5.692
Jerome. *Commentarium in Ezechielem* (*Ezech.*) PL 25. 1994. Translated in Michael Roberts, *Poetry and the Cult of the Martyrs: The Liber Peristephanon of Prudentius*, 158–9. Urbana: University of Michigan Press.
—*Contra Vigilant* (*Vigil.*) PL 23. Translated in *NPNF*[2] 6. Edited by Philip Schaff and Henry Wace. Edinburgh: T. & T. Clark, 1893.
—*Epistulae* (*Ep.*) PL 23.
—*vita Hilarionis eremitae* (*vit. Hil.*) PL 23.
John Chrysostom. *De Coemeterieo et de Cruce* (*Coemet.*) PG 49.393.
—*Homily on Martyrs* (*Hom. Mart.*) PG 50.661–6. Translated by Wendy Meyer and Paul Allen in *John Chrysostom*. New York: Routledge, 2000.
—*Laudation Martyrium Aegyptiorum* (*Pan. Aeg.*) PG 50.693.
Julian. *Contra Galileos* (*Gal.*) Translated by Wilmer Cave France Wright, LCL 157. Cambridge, MA: Harvard University Press, 1923.
—*Letters* (*Ep.*). Translated by Wilmer Cave France Wright, LCL 157. Cambridge, MA: Harvard University Press, 1923.
—*Misopogon* (*Mis.*) Translated by Wilmer Cave France Wright, LCL 29. Cambridge, MA: Harvard University Press, 1913.
Justinian. *Digest.*
Lactantius. *De Mortibus Persecutorum* (*Mort.*) CSEL 27.
—*Divine Institutes* (*Div. Inst.*) PL 6. Translated by William Fletcher in *ANF* 7. Edinburgh: T. & T. Clark, 1886.
Liber Pontificalis (*Lib. Pont.*) PL 127–8.
Lucian of Samosata. *On Funerals.*
Marcellinus and Faustinus. *Libellus Precum ad Imperatores* (*Lib. Pre.*) PL 13.098.
Marcus Diaconus. *Vita Porphyrii Gazensis*. Translated in G. F. Hill, *Mark the Deacon: Life of Porphyry, Bishop of Gaza*. Oxford: Clarendon Press, 1913.
Martyrologium Hieronymianum Cambrense. Edited by Hippolyte Delehaye. Bruxelles: Société des Bollandistes, 1913.
Optatus. *Contra Parmenianum Donatistam*. PL 11.916b. Translated by Mark Edwards, *Optatus: Against the Donatists*. Liverpool: Liverpool University Press, 1997.
Origen. *Contra Celsum*. PG 11.641. Translated by Henry Chadwick, *Origen: Contra Celsum*. Cambridge: Cambridge University Press, 1965.
—*Homiliae in Jeremiam* (*Hom. Jer.*) PG 13.256.
Ovid. *Fasti*. Translated by James G. Frazer, revised G. P. Goold. LCL 253. Cambridge, MA: Harvard University Press, 1987.
Passion of Perpetua and Felicitas (*M. Perp. et Fel.*).
Paulinus of Milan. *Vita Ambrosii* (*Vit. Ambr.*) PL 14.27A ff. Translated by John A. Lacy in *Early Christian Biographies*. Edited by Roy J. Deferrari. New York: Catholic University of America Press, 1952.
Paulinus of Nola. *Carmen* (*Carm.*) PL 61. 1975. Translated by P. G. Walsh as *The Poems of St. Paulinus of Nola*. New York: Paulist Press, 1975.
—*Epistulae* (*Ep.*) PL 61. Translated by P. G. Walsh, *Letters of St. Paulinus of Nola*. 2 vols. New York: Newman Press, 1967.
Philo of Alexandria. *De Specialibus Legibus* (*Spec.*) Translated by F. H. Colson. LCL 320, 341. Cambridge, MA: Harvard University Press, 1937–39.
—*In Flaccum* (*In Flacc.*). Translated by F. H. Colson. LCL 363. Cambridge, MA: Harvard University Press, 1941.
Prudentius. *Liber Peristephanon* (*Pe.*) Translated by J. Thomson. LCL 398. Cambridge, MA: Harvard University Press, 1953.

Rufinus of Aquileia. *Church History (Hist.)* Translated by Philip R. Amidon, *The Church History of Rufinus of Aquileia, Books 10 and 11*, Oxford: Oxford University Press, 1997.
Shenoute. *Since it Behooves Christians.* In *Œuvres de Schenoudi. Texte copte et traduction française.* Edited by E. Amélineau. Paris: E. Leroux, 1907.
—*Those Who Work Evil.* In *Œuvres de Schenoudi. Texte copte et traduction française.* Edited by E. Amélineau. Paris: E. Leroux, 1907.
Siculus Flaccus. *De Condicionibus Agrorum (De. Cond. Ag.).* Edited by Carl Thulin. Los Altos, CA: Packard Humanities Institute, 1991.
Socrates Scholasticus. *Historia Ecclesiastica (HE).* PL 69. 1989. Translated by E. Walford, revised by A.C. Zenos, in $NPNF^2$ 2. Edited by Philip Schaff and Henry Wace. Edinburgh: T. &T. Clark, 1886.
Sozomen. *Historia Ecclesiastica (HE).* PG 67.844.
Sulpicius Severus. *De vita beati Martini Liber unus (Mart.)* CSEL 1. Translated by Alexander Roberts in $NPNF^2$ 11. Edited by Philip Schaff and Henry Wace. Edinburgh: T. & T. Clark, 1894.
Tertullian. *Ad Scapulum* Edited by F. Oehler in vol. 1 of *Corporis haereseologici*. Bertolini: Asher et Socios, 1856.
—*Apologia (Apol.)* Translated by T. R. Glover in *Tertullian: Apology. De Spectaculis.* LCL 250. Cambridge, MA: Harvard University Press.
—*De Anima (An.)* CSEL 20.
—*De Baptisma (Bapt.)* CSEL 20.
—*De Corona (Cor.)* PL 2.
—*De Resurrectione Carnis (Res. De.)* PL 2.
Varro. *Terenti Varronis de lingua latina libri (De Ling. Lat.)* Edited by L. Spengel and A. Spengel. Berlin: Weidmann, 1885.
Victricius of Rouen. *De Laude Sanctorum* PL 20. Translated in Gillian Clark, "Victricius of Rouen: Praising the Saints," *Journal of Early Christian Studies* 7 (1999): 356–99.

Secondary Literature

Alchermes, Joseph Donella. "Cura Pro Mortuis and Cultus Martyrum: Commemoration in Rome from the Second through the Sixth Century," PhD thesis, New York University, 1989.
Alcock, Susan. *Archaeologies of the Greek Past: Landscape, Monuments, and Memories (W. B. Stanford Memorial Lectures).* Cambridge: Cambridge University Press, 2002.
Alikin, Valeriy A. *The Earliest History of the Christian Gathering: Origin, Development and Content of the Christian Gathering in the First to Third Centuries.* Leiden: Brill, 2010. http://dx.doi.org/10.1163/ej.9789004183094.i-342.
Armstrong, Gregory. "Constantine's Churches," *Gesta* 6 (1967): 1–9. http://dx.doi.org/10.2307/766661.
Ascough, Richard S. *Paul's Macedonian Associations: The Social Context of Philippians & 1 Thessalonians.* Tübingen: J. C. B. Mohr, 2003.
Assmann, Jan. "Collective Memory and Cultural Identity," *New German Critique* 65 (1995): 125–33. Translated by John Czaplicka.
Bal, Mieke. *Looking In: The Art of Viewing.* Amsterdam: Gordon and Breach, 2001.
Bardill, Jonathan. *Constantine, Divine Emperor of the Christian Golden Age.* Cambridge: Cambridge University Press, 2011.
Barrier, Jeremy W. *The Acts of Paul and Thecla: A Critical Introduction and Commentary.* Tübingen: Mohr Siebeck, 2009.
Barth, Frederik. *Ethnic Groups and Boundaries: The Social Organization of Culture Difference.* Long Grove, IL: Waveland Press, 1998.
Baruffa, Antonio. *The Catacombs of St. Callixtus: History, Archaeology, Faith.* Vatican City: Libreria Editrice Vaticana, 1993.

Bassett, Steven, ed. *Death in Towns: Urban Responses to the Dying and the Dead, 100–1600*. Leicester, UK: Leicester University Press, 1995.
Bell, Catherine. *Ritual Theory, Ritual Practice*. New York: Oxford University Press, 1992.
Benjamin, Walter. "The Work of Art in the Age of Mechanical Reproduction," [1936] 217–52 in *Illuminations: Essays and Reflections*. Edited by Hannah Arendt. Translated by Harry Zohn. New York: Schocken, 1968.
—"The Storyteller: Reflections on the Works of Nikolai Leskov," [1936] 83–110 in *Illuminations: Essays and Reflections*. Edited by Hannah Arendt. Translated by Harry Zohn. New York: Schocken, 1968.
Bitton-Ashkelony, Brouria. *Encountering the Sacred: The Debate on Christian Pilgrimage in Late Antiquity*. Berkeley: University of California Press, 2005. http://dx.doi.org/10.1525/california/9780520241916.001.0001.
Bockmuehl, Markus. "Peter's Death in Rome? Back to Front and Upside Down," *Scottish Journal of Theology* 60 (2007): 1–23.
Bodel, John. "Dealing with the Dead: Undertakers, Executioners and Potter's Field in Ancient Rome," 128–51 in *Death and Disease in the Ancient City*. Edited by Valerie M. Hope and Eireann Marshall. London: Routledge, 2000.
—"From Columbaria to Catacombs: Collective Burial in Pagan and Christian Rome," 177–242 in *Commemorating the Dead: Texts and Artifacts in Context: Studies of Roman, Jewish, and Christian Burials*. Edited by Laurie Brink and Deborah A. Green. New York: Walter de Gruyter, 2008.
Bowersock, G. W. *Martyrdom and Rome*. Cambridge: Cambridge University Press, 1995. http://dx.doi.org/10.1017/CBO9780511518546.
Boyarin, Daniel. *Dying for God: Martyrdom and the Making of Christianity and Judaism*. Stanford, CA: Stanford University Press, 1999.
Bradbury, Scott. *Severus of Minorca*. New York: Oxford University Press, 1996.
Bradshaw, Paul F., Maxwell E. Johnson and L. Edward Phillips. *The Apostolic Tradition: A Commentary*. Minneapolis, MN: Fortress Press, 2002.
Brakke, David "'Outside the Places, Within the Truth': Athanasius of Alexandria and the Localization of the Holy," 445–81 in *Pilgrimage and Holy Space in Late Antique Egypt*. Edited by David Frankfurter, 445–81. Leiden: Brill, 1998.
Brent, Allen *Hippolytus and the Roman Church in the Third Century: Communities in Tension Before the Emergence of a Monarch-Bishop*. Supplements to Vigiliae Christianae 31. Leiden: E. J. Brill, 1995.
—"Was Hippolytus a Schismatic?" *Vigiliae Christianae* 49 (1995): 215–44. http://dx.doi.org/10.1163/157007295X00022.
Brettman, Estelle S. *Vaults of Memory: Jewish and Christian Imagery in the Catacombs of Rome, An Exhibition*. Boston: International Catacomb Society, 1985.
Brown, Peter. "The Rise and Function of the Holy Man in Late Antiquity," *Journal of Roman Studies* 61 (1971): 80–101. http://dx.doi.org/10.2307/300008.
—*The Making of Late Antiquity*. Cambridge, MA: Harvard University Press, 1978.
—*The Cult of the Saints: Its Rise and Function in Latin Christianity*. Chicago: University of Chicago Press, 1981. http://dx.doi.org/10.7208/chicago/9780226076386.001.0001.
—*Society and the Holy in Late Antiquity*. Berkeley: University of California Press, 1982.
—*Augustine of Hippo: A Biography*. 2nd ed. Berkeley: University of California Press, 2000.
—"Enjoying the Saints in Late Antiquity," *Early Medieval Europe* 9 (2000): 1–24. http://dx.doi.org/10.1111/1468-0254.00057.
Burgess, R. W. "The Passio S. Artemii, Philostorgius, and the Dates of the Invention and Translations of the Relics of Sts. Andrew and Luke," *Analecta Bollandiana* 121 (2003): 5–36.
Burke, Peter. *The Art of Conversation*. Ithaca, NY: Cornell University Press, 1993.
Bynum, Caroline Walker. *Resurrection of the Body in Western Christianity, 200–1336*. New York: Columbia University Press, 1995.

Carroll, Maureen. *Spirits of the Dead: Roman Funerary Commemoration in Western Europe.* New York: Oxford University Press, 2006.

Castelli, Elizabeth. *Martyrdom and Memory: Early Christian Culture Making.* New York: Columbia University Press, 2004.

Champlin, Edward. *Final Judgments: Duty and Emotion in Roman Wills, 200 B.C. – A.D. 250.* Berkeley: University of California Press, 1991.

Clark, Gillian. "Translating Relics: Victricius of Rouen and Fourth-century Debate," *Early Medieval Europe* 10 (2001): 161–76.

Cobb, L. Stephanie. *Dying to Be Men: Gender and Language in Early Christian Martyr Texts.* New York: Columbia University Press, 2008.

Comings, Jill Burnett. *Aspects of the Liturgical Year in Cappadocia (325–430).* New York: Peter Lang, 2005.

Connerton, Paul. *How Societies Remember.* Cambridge: Cambridge University Press, 1989. http://dx.doi.org/10.1017/CBO9780511628061.

Conybeare, Catherine. *Paulinus Noster: Self and Symbols in the Letters of Paulinus of Nola.* New York: Oxford University Press, 2000.

Cooper, Kate. "The Martyr, the Matrona, and the Bishop: The Matron Lucina and the Politics of the Martyr Cult in Fifth- and Sixth-Century Rome," *Early Medieval Europe* 8 (1999): 297–317. http://dx.doi.org/10.1111/1468-0254.00050.

Courtonne, Yves. *Un Temoin du IVe Siecle oriental: Saint Basile en son temps d'apres as correspondance.* Paris: Les Belles Lettres, 1973.

Crossan, John Dominic. *The Historical Jesus: The Life of a Mediterranean Jewish Peasant.* New York: Harper One, 1991.

Cumont, Franz. *After Life in Roman Paganism.* New Haven, CT: Yale University Press, 1922.

Curran, John R. *Pagan City and Christian Capital: Rome in the Fourth Century.* New York: Oxford University Press, 2000.

Davies, Penelope J. E. "The Politics of Perpetuation: Trajan's Column and the Art of Commemoration," *American Journal of Archaeology* 101 (1997): 41–65. http://dx.doi.org/10.2307/506249.

—*Death and the Emperor: Roman Imperial Funerary Monuments from Augustus to Marcus Aurelius.* Austin: University of Texas Press.

Davis, Stephen J. *The Cult of Saint Thecla: A Tradition of Women's Piety in Late Antiquity.* Oxford: Oxford University Press, 2001.

Decret, François. *Early Christianity in North Africa.* Translated by Edward Smither. Eugene, OR: Cascade, 2009 [1996].

Delehaye, Hippolyte. *Les origines du culte des martyrs.* Bruxelles: Bureaux de la Société des Bollandistes, 1912.

DeMaris, Richard E. *The New Testament in its Ritual World.* Cambridge: Cambridge University Press, 1981.

Denzey, Nicola. *The Bone Gatherers: The Lost Worlds of Early Christian Women.* Boston: Beacon, 2007.

Derrida, Jacques. *Archive Fever: A Freudian Impression.* Translated by Eric Prenowitz. Chicago: University of Chicago Press, 1995.

Dill, Samuel. *Roman Society from Nero to Marcus Aurelius.* London: Macmillan, 1905.

Dixon, Suzanne. *Reading Roman Women: Sources, Genres and Real Life.* London: Duckworth, 2001.

Doig, Allan. *Liturgy and Architecture from the Early Church to the Middle Ages.* Aldershot, UK: Ashgate, 2008.

Dore, Isaak. "Foucault on Power," *UMKC Law Review* 78 (2009–10): 737–48.

Downey, G. *A History of Antioch in Syria.* Princeton, NJ: Princeton University Press, 1961.

Drake, H. A. "Suggestions of Date in Constantine's Oration to the Saints," *American Journal of Philology* 106 (1985): 335–49. http://dx.doi.org/10.2307/295033.

—*Constantine and the Bishops: The Politics of Intolerance.* Baltimore, MD: Johns Hopkins Press, 2000.

Drijvers, Jan Willem. *Cyril of Jerusalem: Bishop and City*. Leiden: Brill, 2004.
Dreyfus, Hubert C. and Paul Rabinow. *Michel Foucault: Beyond Structuralism and Hermeneutics*. 2nd ed. Chicago: University of Chicago Press, 1983.
Duchesne, Louis. *Etude Sur le Liber Pontificalis*. Paris: E. Thorin, 1887.
Durkheim, Émile. *The Elementary Forms of Religious Life*. Translated by Karen E. Fields. New York: Free Press, 1995 [1912].
Dyson, Stephen L. *Community and Society in Roman Italy*. Baltimore, MD: Johns Hopkins University Press, 2000.
Eade, John and Michael J. Sallnow. "Introduction," 1–29 in *Contesting the Sacred: The Anthropology of Christian Pilgrimage*. Edited by John Eade and Michael J. Sallnow. Chicago: University of Illinois Press, 2000.
Eastman, David L. *Paul the Martyr: The Cult of the Apostle in the Latin West*. Atlanta, GA: Society of Biblical Literature, 2011.
Edwards, Catharine. *Death in Ancient Rome*. New Haven, CT: Yale University Press, 2007.
Elsner, Jaś and Ian Rutherford. "Introduction," 1–38 in *Pilgrimage in Graeco-Roman and Early Christian Antiquity: Seeing the Gods*. Edited by Jaś Elsner and Ian Rutherford. New York: Oxford University Press, 2005.
Finney, Paul Corby. "Early Christian Architecture: The Beginnings (A Review Article)," *Harvard Theological Review* 81 (1988): 319–39.
Foucault, Michel. *The History of Sexuality*. Vol. 1: *An Introduction*. Translated by Robert Hurley. New York: Vintage 1990 [1978].
—*Power/Knowledge: Selected Interviews and Other Writings, 1972–1977*. Edited by Colin Gordon. New York: Pantheon Books, 1980.
—"Afterword: The Subject and Power," 255–84 in *Michel Foucault: Beyond Structuralism and Hermeneutics*. By H. C. Dreyfus and Paul Rabinow. 2nd ed. Chicago: University of Chicago Press, 1983.
—*The History of Sexuality*. Vol. 3: *The Care of the Self*. Translated by Robert Hurley. New York: Vintage, 1988 [1984].
Frankfurter, David. "Beyond Magic and Superstition," 255–84 in *Late Ancient Christianity*. Vol. 2 of *A People's History of Christianity*. Edited by Virginia Burrus. Minneapolis, MN: Fortress Press, 2005.
—*Pilgrimage and Holy Space in Late Antique Egypt*. Illustrated ed. Leiden: Brill, 1998.
—*Religion in Roman Egypt: Assimilation and Resistance*. Princeton, NJ: Princeton University Press, 2000.
—"Where the Spirits Dwell: Possession, Christianization, and Saints' Shrines in Late Antiquity," *Harvard Theological Review* 103 (2010): 27–46. http://dx.doi.org/10.1017/S0017816009990290.
Frend, William H. C. *The Donatist Church: A Movement of Protest in Roman North Africa*. Oxford: Clarendon Press, 1952.
—*Martyrdom and Persecution in the Early Church*. Oxford: Oxford University Press, 1965.
Gallagher, Michael. "Foucault, Power and Participation," *International Journal of Children's Rights* 16 (2008): 395–406. http://dx.doi.org/10.1163/157181808X311222.
Gingras, George E. *Egeria: Diary of a Pilgrimage*. New York: Newman, 1970.
Goehring, James E. *Ascetics, Society, and the Desert: Studies in Early Egyptian Monasticism*. Harrisburg, PA: Trinity, 1999.
Goldschmidt, R. C. *Paulinus' Churches at Nola*. Amsterdam: Noord-Hollandsche Uitg. Maatschappij, 1940.
Gordon, Colin. "Introduction," xi–xli in *Power*. Vol. 3 of *The Essential Works of Foucault 1954–1984*, by Michel Foucault. Edited by James D. Faubion. New York: New Press, 1994.
Grabar, Andre. "From Martyrium to the Church: Christian Architecture, East and West," *Archaeology* 2 (1949): 95–104.
Grig, Lucy. *Making Martyrs in Late Antiquity*. London: Duckworth, 2004.

—"Portraits, Pontiffs, and the Christianization of Fourth Century Rome," *Papers of the British School at Rome* 72 (2004): 203–30. http://dx.doi.org/10.1017/S0068246200002725.

Halbwachs, Maurice. *On Collective Memory*. Edited and translated by Lewis A. Coser. Chicago: University of Chicago Press, 1992.

Handley, Mark. *Death, Society and Culture: Inscriptions and Epitaphs in Gaul and Spain, AD 300-750*. London: British Archaeological Reports, 2003.

Harland, Philip. *Associations, Synagogues, and Congregations: Claiming a Place in Ancient Mediterranean Society*. Minneapolis, MN: Fortress Press, 2003.

Hirschfield, Amy K. "An Overview of the Intellectual History of Catacomb Archaeology," 11–38 in *Commemorating the Dead: Texts and Artifacts in Context: Studies of Roman, Jewish, and Christian Burials*. Edited by Laurie Brink and Deborah A. Green. New York: Walter de Gruyter, 2008.

Hobsbawm, Eric and Terence Ranger, eds. *The Invention of Tradition*. Cambridge: Cambridge University Press, 1983.

Holum, Kenneth G. "Hadrian and Saint Helena: Imperial Travel and the Origins of Christian Pilgrimage," 66–81 in *The Blessings of Pilgrimage*. Edited by Robert Ousterhout. Chicago: University of Illinois Press, 1990.

Hope, Valerie. "Inscription and Sculpture: the Construction of Identity in the Military Tombstones of Roman Mainz," 155–86 in *The Epigraphy of Death: Studies in the History and Society of Greece and Rome*. Edited by Graham J. Oliver, Liverpool: Liverpool University Press, 2000.

—"Fighting for Identity: The Funerary Commemoration of Italian Gladiators," *Bulletin of the Institute of Classical Studies* 44, Supplement 73 (2000): 93–113.

—"Trophies and Tombstones: Commemorating the Roman Soldier," *World Archaeology* 35 (2003): 79–97. http://dx.doi.org/10.1080/0043824032000078090.

—*Death in Ancient Rome: A Sourcebook*. New York: Routledge, 2007. http://dx.doi.org/10.4324/9780203392485.

—*Roman Death: Dying and the Dead in Ancient Rome*. London: Continuum, 2009.

—"Remembering to Mourn: Personal Mementos of the Dead in Ancient Rome," 176–95 in *Memory and Mourning: Studies on Roman Death*. Edited by Valerie M. Hope and Janet Huskinson. Oxford: Oxbow Press, 2011.

Hope, Valerie M. and Eireann Marshall. *Death and Disease in the Ancient City*. New York: Routledge, 2000.

Hunt, Edward David. *Holy Land Pilgrimage in the Later Roman Empire: AD 312–460*. New York: Oxford University Press, 1984.

—"Were there Christian Pilgrims before Constantine?," 25–40 in *Pilgrimage Explored*. Edited by J. Stopford. Woodbridge, UK: York Medieval Press, 1999.

Jaeger, Mary. *Livy's Written Rome*. Ann Arbor: University of Michigan Press, 1997.

Jenott, Lance and Elaine Pagels. "Anthony's Letters and the Nag Hammadi Codex I: Sources of Religious Conflict in Fourth-Century Egypt," *Journal of Early Christian Studies* 18 (2010): 557–89.

Johnson, Mark J. "Pagan-Christian Burial Practices of the Fourth Century: Shared Tombs?" *Journal of Early Christian Studies* 5 (1997): 37–59. http://dx.doi.org/10.1353/earl.1997.0029.

—*The Roman Imperial Mausoleum in Late Antiquity*. Cambridge: Cambridge University Press, 2009.

Juschka, Darlene M. "Whose Turn is it to Cook? Communitas and Pilgrimage Questioned," *Mosaic* 36 (2003): 189–204.

Kaufman, Peter Iver. "Augustine, Martyrs and Misery," *Church History* 63 (1994): 1–14 http://dx.doi.org/10.2307/3167829.

Kelly, J. N. D. *Jerome: His Life, Writings, and Controversies*. New York: Harper & Row, 1975.

Kennedy, Charles A. "The Cult of the Dead in Corinth," 227–36 in *Love and Death in the Ancient Near East*. Edited by John H. Marks and Robert M. Goods. New York: Four Quarters, 1987.

Kilde, Halgren. *Sacred Power Sacred Space: An Introduction to Christian Architecture and Worship*. New York: Oxford University Press, 2008. http://dx.doi.org/10.1093/acprof:oso/9780195314694.001.0001.

Kines, Ian "Dialogues with Death," 83–91 in *The Archaeology of Death*. Edited by Robert Chapman, Ian Kines and Klavs Randsborg. Cambridge: Cambridge University Press, 1981.

Kloppenburg, John S. "Collegia and *Thiasoi*: Issues in Function, Taxonomy and Membership," 16–30 in *Voluntary Associations in the Graeco-Roman World*. Edited by John S. Kloppenburg and Stephen Wilson. New York: Routledge, 1996.

Kloppenburg, John S. and Stephen Wilson, eds. *Voluntary Associations in the Graeco-Roman World*. New York: Routledge, 1996.

Kraemer, Ross S. "Jewish Tuna and Christian Fish: Identifying Religious Affiliation in Epigraphic Sources," *Harvard Theological Review* 84 (1991): 141–62. http://dx.doi.org/10.1017/S0017816000008130.

Krautheimer, Richard. "The Constantinian Basilica," *Dumbarton Oaks Papers* 21 (1967): 115–40. http://dx.doi.org/10.2307/1291261.

—*Studies in Early Christian, Medieval, and Renaissance Art*. New York: New York University Press, 1969.

—*Corpus Basilicarum Christianarum Romae*. 5 vols. Vatican City / New York: Pontifico Instituto de archeologia Christiana / Institute of Fine Arts, 1937–77.

—*Three Christian Capitals: Topography and Politics*. Berkeley: University of California Press, 1983.

—*Early Christian and Byzantine Architecture* 4th ed. London: Penguin Books, 1986.

Lafferty, Maura. K. "Translating Faith from Greek to Latin: Romanitas and Christianitas in Late Fourth-Century Rome and Milan," *Journal of Early Christian Studies* 11 (2003): 21–62. http://dx.doi.org/10.1353/earl.2003.0010.

Lancel, Serge. *Saint Augustine*. London: SCM Press, 2010.

LeGoff, Jaques. *History and Memory*. Translated by Steven Rendall and Elizabeth Claman. New York: Columbia University Press, 1992.

Limberis, Vasiliki M. *Architects of Piety: The Cappadocian Fathers and the Cult of the Martyrs*. Oxford: Oxford University Press, 2011. http://dx.doi.org/10.1093/acprof:oso/9780199730889.001.0001.

Lincoln, Bruce. *Discourse and the Construction of Society: Comparative Studies of Myth, Ritual, and Classification*. New York: Oxford, 1989.

Littlechilds, Rebecca Leigh. "The Epitaphs of Damasus and the Transferable Value of Persecution for the Christian Community at Rome in the Fourth-Century AD," MA thesis, University of Victoria, 2009.

Liu, Jinyu. *Collegia Centonariorum: The Guilds of Textile Dealers in the Roman West*. Leiden: Brill, 2009. http://dx.doi.org/10.1163/ej.9789004177741.i-428.

Lokin, Jan H. A. "The Work of Penelope: The Composition and Decomposition of Roman Law," 17–34 in *Antiquity Renewed: Late Classical and Early Modern Themes*. Edited by Z. R. W. M. von Martels and Victor Michael Schmidt. Leuven: Peeters, 2003.

MacDonald, Mary N. "Introduction: Place and the Study of Religions," 1–20 in *Experiences of Place*, edited by Mary N. Macdonald. Cambridge, MA: Harvard University Press, 2003.

Mackie, Gillian. *Early Christian Chapels in the West: Decoration, Function and Patronage*. Toronto: University of Toronto Press, 2003.

MacMullen, Ramsay. *Enemies of the Roman Order: Treason, Unrest, and Alienation in the Empire*. Cambridge, MA: Harvard University Press, 1966. http://dx.doi.org/10.4159/harvard.9780674864962.

—*Roman Social Relations, 50 B.C. to A.D. 284*. New Haven, CT: Yale University Press, 1974. http://dx.doi.org/10.4159/harvard.9780674864962.

—"The Epigraphic Habit in the Roman Empire," *American Journal of Philology* 103 (1982): 233–46. http://dx.doi.org/10.2307/294470.

—"Christian Ancestor Worship in Rome," *Journal of Biblical Literature* 129 (2010): 597–613.
Mango, Cyril. "Constantine's Mausoleum and the Translation of Relics," *Byzantinische Zeitschrift* 83 (1990): 51–62. http://dx.doi.org/10.1515/byzs.1990.83.1.51.
Markus, R. A. *The End of Ancient Christianity*. Cambridge: Cambridge University Press, 1990.
—"How on Earth Could Places Become Holy?" *Journal of Early Christian Studies* 2 (1994): 257–71. http://dx.doi.org/10.1353/earl.0.0110.
McLynn, Neil B. *Ambrose of Milan: Church and Court in a Christian Capital*. Berkeley: University of California Press, 1994.
Meeks, Wayne A. *The First Urban Christians: The Social World of the Apostle Paul*. 2nd ed. New Haven, CT: Yale University Press, 2003.
Miles, Richard. "Introduction: Constructing Identities in Late Antiquity," 1–15 in *Constructing Identities in Late Antiquity*. Edited by Richard Miles. New York: Routledge, 1999. http://dx.doi.org/10.4324/9780203260357.
Misztal, Barbara *Theories of Social Remembering*. Maidenhead, UK: Open University Press / McGraw-Hill Education, 2003.
Mitford, Jessica. *The American Way of Death Revisited*. New York: Vintage, 2000.
Morris, Ian. *Death-Ritual and Social Structure in Classical Antiquity*. Cambridge: Cambridge University Press, 1992. http://dx.doi.org/10.1017/CBO9780511611728.
Moss, Candida. *Ancient Christian Martyrdom: Diverse Practices, Theologies, and Traditions*. New Haven, CT: Yale University Press, 2012.
—*The Myth of Persecution: How Early Christians Invented a Story of Martyrdom*. New York: HarperOne, 2013.
Nielsen, Thomas, Lars Bjertrup, Mogens Herman Hansen, Lene Rubinstein and Torben Vestergaard. "Athenian Grave Monuments and Social Class," *Greek, Roman and Byzantine Studies* 30 (1989): 411–20.
Noy, David. "'Half-Burnt on an Emergency Pyre': Roman Cremations Which Went Wrong," *Greece and Rome* (Second Series) 47 (2000): 186–96.
Odahl, Charles Matson. *Constantine and the Christian Empire*. London: Routledge, 2004. http://dx.doi.org/10.4324/9780203552698.
Ogilvie, M. R. *The Romans and Their Gods in the Age Of Augustus* New York: W. W. Norton, 1970.
Osiek, Carolyn. "Roman and Christian Burial Practices and the Patronage of Women," 243–70 in *Commemorating the Dead: Texts and Artifacts in Context: Studies of Roman, Jewish, and Christian Burials*. Edited by Laurie Brink and Deborah A. Green. New York: Walter de Gruyter, 2008.
Oliver, Graham. "Athenian Funerary Monuments: Style, Grandeur and Construction," 59–80 in *Epigraphy of Death: Studies in the History and Society of Greece and Rome*. Edited by Graham J. Oliver. Liverpool: Liverpool University Press, 2000.
Patterson, John. "Patronage, Collegia and Burial in Imperial Rome," 15–27 in *Death in Towns: Urban Responses to the Dying and the Dead, 100–1600*. Edited by Steven Bassett. Leicester: Leicester University Press, 1995.
Perkins, Judith. *The Suffering Self: Pain and Narrative Representation in the Early Christian Era*. London: Routledge, 1995. http://dx.doi.org/10.4324/9780203210062.
Perry, Jonathan Scott. *The Roman Collegia: The Modern Evolution of an Ancient Concept*. Leiden: Brill, 1999.
Petersen, Lauren Hackworth. "The Baker, His Tomb, His Wife, and Her Breadbasket: The Monument of Eurysaces in Rome," *Art Bulletin* 85 (2003): 230–57. http://dx.doi.org/10.2307/3177343.
Price, Simon. "From Noble Funerals to Divine Cult: The Consecration of Roman Emperors," 56–105 in *Rituals of Royalty: Power and Ceremonial in Traditional Societies*. Edited by D. Cannadine and S. Price,. Cambridge: Cambridge University Press, 1987.
Rebillard, Éric. *The Care of the Dead in Late Antiquity*. Cornell Studies in Classical Philology 59. Ithaca, NY: Cornell University Press, 2009.

Roberts, Michael. *Poetry and the Cult of the Martyrs: The* Liber Peristephanon *of Prudentius*. Urbana: University of Michigan Press, 1993.
Ross, Jill. "Dynamic Writing and Martyrs' Bodies in Prudentius' Peristephanon," *Journal of Early Christian Studies* 3 (1995): 325–53. http://dx.doi.org/10.1353/earl.0.0072.
Rossi, Giovanni Battista de. *La Roma Sotterranea Cristiana*. Rome: Cromo-litografia Pontificia, 1864.
Rubenstein, Richard E. *When Jesus Became God: The Struggle to Define Christianity During the Last Days of Rome*. San Diego: Harcourt, 1999.
Rutgers, Leonard V. "Radiocarbon Dates from the Jewish Catacombs of Rome," *Radiocarbon* 44 (2002): 541–7.
Saghy, Marianne. "*Scinditur in Partes Populus*: Pope Damasus and the Martyrs of Rome," *Early Medieval Europe* 9 (2000): 227–83.
Savage, Kirk. "The Politics of Memory: Black Emancipation and the Civil War Monument," 127–49 in *Commemorations: The Politics of National Identity*. Edited by John R. Gillis. Princeton, NJ: Princeton University Press, 1994.
Sawyer, John F. A. "Hebrew Words for the Resurrection of the Dead," *Vetus Testamentum* 23 (1973): 218–34. http://dx.doi.org/10.2307/1517093.
Schacter, Daniel L. *The Seven Sins of Memory: How the Mind Forgets and Remembers*. New York: Houghton Mifflin, 2002.
Schroeder, Caroline T. *Monastic Bodies: Discipline and Salvation in Shenoute of Atripe*. Illustrated ed. Philadephia: University of Pennsylvania Press, 2007. http://dx.doi.org/10.9783/9780812203387.
Schwartz, Barry. "Memory as a Cultural System: Abraham Lincoln in World War II," *American Sociological Review* 61 (1996): 908–27. http://dx.doi.org/10.2307/2096461.
—*Abraham Lincoln and the Forge of National Memory*. Chicago: University of Chicago Press, 2000.
Schweitzer, Albert. *The Quest of the Historical Jesus*. Translated by W. Montgomery, J. R. Coates, Susan Cupitt and John Bowden. Minneapolis, MN: Fortress Press, 2001 [1996].
Smith, David I. *Learning from the Stranger: Christian Faith and Cultural Diversity*. Grand Rapids: Wm. B. Eerdmans, 2009.
Smith, Jonathan Z. *Map is not Territory: Studies in the History of Religions*. Chicago: University of Chicago Press, 1993.
Smither, Edward L. "Persuasion or Coercion: Augustine on the State's Role in Dealing with Other Religions and Heresies," Faculty Publications and Presentations 14, Liberty Baptist Theological Seminary and Graduate School, 2006. Available at: http://digitalcommons.liberty.edu/cgi/viewcontent.cgi?article=1013&context=lts_fac_pubs
Snyder, Graydon F. *Ante Pacem: Archaeological Evidence of Church Life Before Constantine*. Revised ed. Macon, GA: Mercer University Press, 2003.
Stead, G. Christopher. "Rhetorical Method in Athanasius," *Vigiliae Christianae* 30 (1976): 121–37. http://dx.doi.org/10.1163/157007276X00113.
Taylor, Joan E. *Christians and the Holy Places: The Myth of Jewish-Christian Origins*. Illustrated ed. New York: Oxford University Press, 1993.
Taylor, Mark C. *Grave Matters*. London: Realtion, 2002.
Tilley, Maureen A. *Donatist Martyr Stories: The Church in Conflict in Roman North Africa*. Liverpool: Liverpool University Press, 1996. http://dx.doi.org/10.3828/978-0-85323-931-4.
Tite, Philip L. "Voluntary Martyrdom and Gnosticism," *Journal of Early Christian Studies* 23 (2015): 27–54. http://dx.doi.org/10.1353/earl.2015.0013.
Torres, Juana. "Emperor Julian and the Veneration of Relics," *Antiquité Tardive* 17 (2009): 205–14. http://dx.doi.org/10.1353/earl.0.0050.
Toynbee, J. M. C. *Death and Burial in the Roman World*. Baltimore, MD: Johns Hopkins University Press, 1996 [1972].
Trout, Dennis E. "Christianizing the Nolan Countryside: Animal Sacrifice at the Tomb of

St. Felix," *Journal of Early Christian Studies* 3 (1995): 281–98. http://dx.doi.org/10.1353/earl.0.0050.

—*Damasus of Rome: The Epigraphic Poetry. Introduction, Texts, Translations, and Commentary* (Oxford: Oxford University Press, 2015).

—*Paulinus of Nola: Life, Letters, and Poems*. Berkeley: University of California Press, 1999.

—"Damasus and the Invention of Early Christian Rome," *Journal of Medieval and Early Modern Studies* 33 (2003): 517–36. http://dx.doi.org/10.1215/10829636-33-3-517.

Turner, Victor. *Process, Performance and Pilgrimage: A Comparative Symbology*. New Delhi: Naurang Rai, 1979.

Van der Horst, Pieter W. *Ancient Jewish Epitaphs: An Introductory Survey of a Millennium of Jewish Funerary Epigraphy (300 BCE – 700 CE)*. Kampen: Kos Pharos, 1991.

Van Dyke, Ruth and Susan Alcock, eds., *Archaeologies of Memory*. Malden, MA: Wiley-Blackwell, 2002.

Veilleux, Armand. "Preface: Shenoute or the Pitfalls of Monasticism," in *The Life of Shenoute by Besa*. Translated by David N. Bell, v–xv. Kalamazoo, MI: Cistercian Publications, 1994.

Volp, Ulrich. *Tod und Ritual in den christlichen Gemeinden der Antike*. Supplements to Vigiliae Christianae 65 Leiden: Brill, 2002.

Ward-Perkins, J. B. "Memoria, Martyr's Tomb and Martyr's Church," *Journal of Theological Studies* 17 (1966): 20–37. http://dx.doi.org/10.1093/jts/XVII.1.20.

White, Cynthia. *The Emergence of Christianity: Classical Traditions in Contemporary Perspective*. Westport, CT: Greenwood Press, 2007.

Wilken, Robert Louis. *The Land Called Holy: Palestine in Christian History and Thought*. New Haven, CT: Yale University Press, 1994.

Williams, Daniel H. *Ambrose of Milan and the End of the Arian-Nicene Conflicts*. Oxford: Clarendon Press, 1995. http://dx.doi.org/10.1093/acprof:oso/9780198264644.001.0001.

Williams, R. D. "Changing Attitudes to Virgil: A Study in the History of Taste from Dryden to Tennyson," 119–38 in *Virgil*. Edited by D. R. Dudley, London: Routledge and Kegan Paul, 1969.

Williams, Rowan. "Arius and the Meletian Schism," *Journal of Theological Studies* 37 (1987): 35–52.

Williams, Wes. *Pilgrimage and Narrative in the French Renaissance: The Undiscovered Country*. New York: Oxford University Press, 1998. http://dx.doi.org/10.1093/acprof:oso/9780198159407.001.0001.

Woods, David. "The Date of the Translation of the Relics of SS. Luke and Andrew to Constantinople," *Vigiliae Christianae* 45 (1991): 286–92. http://dx.doi.org/10.1163/157007291X00116.

Wortley, John. "The Origins of Christian Veneration of Body-Parts," *Revue de l'histoire des religions* 1 (2006): 5–28.

Yasin, Ann Marie. "Commemorating the Dead – Constructing the Community: Church Space, Funerary Monuments and Saints' Cults in Late Antiquity," PhD thesis, University of Chicago, 2000.

—"Funerary Monuments and Collective Identity: From Roman Family to Christian Community," *Art Bulletin* 87 (2005): 433–57. http://dx.doi.org/10.1080/00043079.2005.10786254.

—*Saints and Church Spaces in the Late Antique Mediterranean: Architecture, Cult, and Community*. Cambridge: Cambridge University Press, 2009.

Young, James Edward. *Texture of Memory: Holocaust Memorials and Meaning*. New Haven, CT: Yale University Press, 1993.

—*At Memory's Edge: After-Images of the Holocaust in Contemporary Art and Architecture*. New Haven, CT: Yale University Press, 2000.

Zerubavel, Eviatar. *Time Maps: Collective Memory and the Social Shape of the Past*. Chicago: University of Chicago Press, 2003. http://dx.doi.org/10.7208/chicago/9780226924908.001.0001.

Index

Abraham, tomb of 158
Acacius, tomb of 66
ad sanctos burial 1, 12, 14, 37, 48, 60, 90, 91, 100–1, 108, 112
Ad Scapulum (Tertullian) 41
Adam (biblical figure) 158
afterlife, Roman view of 21–3, 35
   see also resurrection of the dead
Agnes of Rome (martyr) 63
Agricola (martyr) 93, 114
Alchermes, Joseph Donella 47
Alcock, Susan 58, 100
Alexandria 41, 131, 135, 140, 141, 144–5, 158
   see also Athanasius; North Africa
Alikin, Valeriy 37, 46
Allen, Paul 146
altars:
   concept rejected 147
   martyrs not worshipped at 102, 107
   pilgrimage and 152, 169
   relics at 91, 93, 97, 98, 111–12, 114
      authenticity and 116–17
      of Job 160
   shrines with destroyed 131
   spiritual 46, 75
Amantius (priest) 68
Ambrose of Milan 17, 56, 76, 82, 84, 85, 98, 110, 116, 122, 127, 152, 177
   control over practices 94, 105–6, 118, 123, 151, 174, 175
   criticized by Shenoute 121
   "discovery" of relics 47, 51, 72, 90–3, 95, 98 123, 159
   translation of relics 88, 89, 90, 96–7, 98–9, 110, 114, 124, 160, 161, 163, 174
Ammianus Marcellinus 4, 63, 68
ancestors:
   ancestral souls 22
   Christian family tombs 37
   important dead as 35
   saints as 76, 80–1
Ancona 163–4
Andrew (apostle) 63–4, 78, 89, 94, 96–7, 114, 173
Anthony of the Desert 122, 136–7, 138, 139, 141, 142, 144, 176, 178
Antinous (deified) 33
Antioch 41, 45–6, 86, 130–1
Apologia (Aristides) 43, 45
Apologia (Tertullian) 41, 43–4
apostles 29, 61, 77–81, 93, 113, 114, 129, 147, 148
   Constantine and 58, 61–7, 80, 173, 178
      Basilica Apostolorum 63, 77, 81, 94
   Ambrose and 89, 97
   pilgrimage ande160
   relics rejected 126, 142
Apostolic Tradition (attrib. Hippolytus) 41, 44
apotheosis 23, 30, 65, 80
Appian Way 61, 62, 77, 113, 147, 162
Aquileia 93
Aquitaine 84, 98
Arcadius (bishop) 87
archaeological evidence 5–6, 13, 14, 77, 147
archetype, martyr as 54
archives 7–8
   graves and tombs as 8, 54, 72, 150
Arians 4, 47, 90, 92, 95, 124, 135, 141, 175
   Meletians and 137, 139
   recanted 68
Arius *see* Arians
arkeion 8
   see also archives
Aristides 43, 45
Armstrong, Gregory 60, 61, 62

Asaph 157
asceticism 54, 136
  see also Anthony of the Desert; monks
Ascholius of Thessalonica 87
Ascough, Richard S. 32, 36
ashes, as relics 22, 75, 85, 88–9, 110, 112, 113, 114, 131, 132, 152, 160
Asia Minor 53, 64
Assmann, Jan 10–11
Athanasius 5, 17, 86–7, 92, 116, 122, 131, 132, 135–140, 141, 155, 158, 175–6
  Vita Antonii 122, 135, 136–7, 141, 144, 176
Augustine of Hippo 17, 37, 56, 82, 84, 91, 100–9, 115, 118, 119, 122, 124, 127, 135, 141, 142, 155, 174
  advising Paulinus 112, 147
  Donatists and 6–7, 54, 92, 103, 104, 108, 175
  letter from Maximus of Madaura 134
  mother of 150–1
  sermon on relics of Stephen 151, 163–4,
  translation of relics and 95, 98
Augustus (emperor) 30, 65
Aurelius of Carthage 105
Avitus of Braga 106

Babylas (bishop) 86, 130–1
Bal, Mieke 57
baptism 50, 51, 103
Bardill, Jonathan 63, 65
Barochas (Christian) 133
Barrier, Jeremy 161
Barth, Frederik 33
Baruffa, Antonio 75
Basil of Caesarea 87–9, 127, 149, 152, 161–2
basilicas 14, 28, 37, 38, 97–8, 116:
  at Aquileia 93
  Basilica Apostolorum (Constantinople) 63, 65–6, 78, 80, 81, 94, 178
  Basilica of Julius 68
  Basilica of Sicininus 4, 68
  burials and 14, 28, 37, 38
  Constantine and 16, 56, 58–65, 66, 71, 80, 81, 98, 173, 174
  Damasus and 76, 81, 173–4
  at Fundi 97, 111, 112–13
  at Hippo 107
  Lateran 60
  at Jerusalem 156
  at Nola 111–12
  at Milan 89–91, 93, 94, 98, 99
  at Primuliacum 84–5
  at tomb of Hippolytus 169
  wealth of the Church and 97
Bell, Catherine 55
Benjamin, Walter 1, 150
Besa 123
  see also Shenoute
Bethlehem 151, 157, 159
Bible:
  biblical sites 146, 155, 156–7, 162, 170
  Peter and Paul in 79
  tombs of biblical figures 131, 138, 157, 158, 159, 160, 178
  see also apostles; Stephen; pilgrimage
birthdays:
  anniversaries of deaths as 34, 35, 51
  Felix of Nola and 84, 109–10, 113, 115, 125, 170
  Virgil's 30
bishops *see* episcopate (bishops)
Bitton-Ashkelony, Brouria 149, 152, 162
Bockmuehl, Markus 77–8
Bodel, John 23, 24, 42–3, 44
Bonn 47
Bordeaux Pilgrim 151, 156–7, 160, 161, 165, 171
Bowersock, G.W. 45
Boyarin, Daniel 28, 45, 93
Bradbury, Scott 106
Bradshaw, Paul F. 41, 44
Brakke, David 135, 138
Brent, Allen 73–4
Brettman, Estelle S. 7
Brown, Peter 15–16, 19, 49, 53, 56, 71, 97, 99, 100, 103, 134, 150, 156
Burgess, R.W., 64
burial 3–4, 9, 13–14, 19, 21, 24, 26–9, 33–4, 47–8, 51, 129
  at altars 111, 112, 114
  cost 31

of emperors 30
identity in the Roman Empire and 12
of important Christians 45–8, 83, 87
    ad sanctos 1, 12, 14, 37, 48, 60,
        90, 91, 100–1, 108, 112
memory and 5, 15, 25–6
origins of Christian 36–9, 42–3, 80,
    127, 172, 177
pollution and 23–4
of the poor 43–5
reinterment 62, 86, 88, 90, 93, 96,
    120–1, 124, 139, 140
in secret location 137–8, 139–40, 141
see also basilicas; catacombs;
    cemeteries; *collegia*; exhumation;
    funerals; inscriptions; relics;
    tombs
Burke, Peter 9
Bynum, Caroline Walker 27, 122

Caesarea 87–8, 162
Calahorra 167
Caleb (biblical figure) 158
Caligula (emperor) 30
Callistus (bishop of Rome) 28, 39–40,
    41, 74, 75, 173
    see also catacombs
Cappadocia 149
    see also Caesarea
Caria (Anatolia) 131
Carmen (Paulinus of Nola) 63, 64, 78,
    96, 113, 114, 115
Carroll, Maureen 26, 27, 28, 32, 35, 36,
    37, 39, 41, 69
Cassian 166
Castelli, Elizabeth 11, 15, 46
catacombs 5, 7–8, 27–9, 36, 38, 40–2,
    76, 85
    Constantine's basilica and 61
    martyrs in 47, 49, 62, 69, 71, 74–5,
        77, 78–9, 85, 133
    see also cemeteries
cemeteries 8, 36, 38–44, 53, 59–60, 144,
    172
    see also burial; catacombs; *collegia*;
        relics; tombs
Champlin, Edward 22
chapels 47, 63, 112
    Sacrament Chapel 28

charity 41, 130
    burial of the poor as 43, 45
Christianization:
    Julian and 128
    of space 156
Chrysostom, John 41, 42, 89, 146
Church History (Eusebius) *see Historia*
    Ecclesiastica (Eusebius)
Church History (Rufinus) *see Historia*
    Ecclesiastica (Rufinus)
Church History (Socrates Scholasticus)
    see Historia Ecclesiastica (Socrates
    Scholasticus)
Church History (Sozomen) *see Historia*
    Ecclesiastica (Sozomen)
Church of the Nativity 157
Cicero 19, 23–4, 30, 87
Circumcellions 6, 54, 104
    see also Donatists
citizenship, Roman 24, 77
City of God (Augustine) 91, 101, 102,
    106–7, 163
Clark, Gillian 89, 96, 106
Clarus (saint) 111
Cobb, Stephanie L. 46
Codex Theodosianus 126
coffins:
    Constantine's 66
    Saint Peter's 61–2, 66
    transporting Babylas 130
Collectio Avellana 67–8
collective memory 8, 10–11, 13, 15, 20,
    57, 58, 100, 173, 176–7
collegia 27, 32–4, 42, 43, 44, 172
    Christianity as 36–8
columbaria 26–7, 34, 38, 42–4
Comings, Jill Burnett 87
Commentarium in Danielem
    (Hippolytus) 41, 161
Commentarium in Ezechielem (Jerome)
    29
communal burial 26–7, 32, 44
congregations 4, 46, 59, 83, 123–4, 174
    Ambrose's 90, 91, 92, 93, 94, 127
    Athanasius's 140
    Augustine's 100, 103, 107, 108, 109,
        127, 151, 163, 175
    Basil's 87, 88, 127
    Gregory of Nyssa's 127

healings and 163
Paulinus's 110, 113, 116, 125, 127, 175
Connerton, Paul 67
consecration, and relics 90–1, 94, 97–8, 110, 113, 114, 174
Constantina (Constantine's daughter) 63
Constantine (emperor) 53, 96, 172–3, 177
   martyrs and 2, 16, 48, 55–6, 56–7, 58–9, 67, 80, 82, 92, 95, 123, 174
   seeking healing 152, 162–3, 164
   monument projects 13, 16, 29, 56, 57, 59–63, 67, 71, 79, 80, 154, 155, 173
      his tomb 16, 63–6, 80–1, 173, 178
   view of Rome 78, 98
Constantinople 64, 96, 154
   relics in 16, 63, 65, 78, 80, 81, 86, 98, 144, 173
      of the Forty Martyrs in 88–9
      moved to Milan 89, 94, 174, 177
Constantius I (emperor) 66, 67–8, 88
Constantius II (emperor) 126
Constantius Gallus (Caesar) 86, 130
Contra Celsum (Origen) 148
Contra Faustum Manichaeum (Augustine) 102
Contra Galileos (Julian) 129, 132
Contra Gaudentium (Augustine) 6
Contra Parmenianum Donatistam (Optatus) 86
Contra Vigilant (Jerome) 142–3, 147
Conybeare, Catherine 110
Cooper, Kate 63, 128
Cornelius (deacon)133
Courtonne, Yves 162
cremation 26, 30, 34
   of emperor's effigy 23
   see also ashes, as relics; *columbaria*
Crossan, John Dominic 10
crypts *see* catacombs
cultural memory 7, 10, 11, 13, 67, 99–100, 108, 113
   contact relics and 136
   remains and 2, 3, 5, 17, 26, 49, 56, 57, 83, 95, 107, 126, 140, 141, 145, 175, 177
      nineteenth-century Christians 40

   pilgrimage and 150, 152, 153, 154, 175
   inscriptions and 70–1, 74, 76, 81, 173
   martyrdom and 15
Cumont, Franz 21–2
Cunningham, J. G. 134
Curran, John R. 60, 68, 79
Cyprian 38, 46
Cyril of Jerusalem 155
Czaplicka, John 10

Damasus (bishop of Rome) 15, 16, 55–6, 67–8, 82, 83, 84, 91, 92, 95, 98, 99, 104, 116, 123, 136, 171, 172, 175
   use of thugs 4, 68, 135–6
   inscriptions 5, 13, 14, 29, 57, 68–73, 74–80, 93, 110, 111, 162, 165, 167, 173–4
      on Hippolytus 10, 73–4, 167, 168, 171
Daphne (suburb of Antioch) 86, 130
David (king) 157
Davies, Penelope J.E. 20, 21, 25, 29–30, 65
Davis, Stephen J. 161
De Anima (Tertullian) 41
De Baptisma (Tertullian) 161
De Coemeterieo et de Cruce (John Chrysostum) 41
De Condicionibus Agrorum (Siculus Flaccus) 24
De Corona (Tertullian) 34, 51
De Cura pro Mortuis Gerenda (Augustine) 100–1, 112, 147
De Mortibus Persecutorum (Lactantius) 53
De Opere Monachorum (Augustine) 104
De Laude Sanctorum (Victricius of Rouen) 96
De Moribus Ecclesiae Catholicae (Augustine) 105
De Legibus (Cicero) 23
De Resurrectione Carnis (Tertullian) 147
De Specialibus Legibus (Philo) 156
De vita ac miraculis Theclae (Basil) 152
De vita beati Martini Liber unus (Sulpicius Severus) 116
De vita Constantini (Eusebius) 53, 64, 152, 163

De Rossi, Giovanni Battista 40
Decian persecutions 137, 139
Decret, François 155
Delehaye, Hippolyte 45, 99
Delphi 129
DeMaris, Richard E. 51
demons:
 exorcism 92, 140, 158
 martyr veneration as worshiping 118
 temptations and 136
Denzey, Nicola 63, 78, 128
Derrida, Jacques 8
descendants *see* ancestors
Diana (goddess) 33
Digest (Justinian) 19
Dill, Samuel 30, 33
Diocletian persecution 47, 53, 137, 139
Dionysius (archbishop) 88
divination *see* necromancy
Divine Institutes (Lactantius) 43

divinization *see* apotheosis
Dixon, Suzanne 4, 12
Doig, Allan 94
Domitii (Italy) 30
Donatists 4, 6–7, 54, 84, 86, 92, 103–4, 108, 109, 124–5, 132, 175
 see also schismatics
Dore, Isaak 9, 94
Downey, G. 130
Drake, H.A. 4, 7, 58–59, 60, 64, 82–3
Dreyfus, H.C. 8
Drijvers, Jan Willem 155
Duchesne, Louis 61
Durkheim, Émile 24
Dyson, Stephen L., 24

Eade, John 153
Easter 137, 143, 163–4
Eastman, David L. 61, 62, 77
Edessa 161
edicts, imperial 53–4, 96, 126
 Edict of Milan 4, 53, 71
Edwards, Catharine 25
Egeria (pilgrim) 151, 157–61, 165, 171
Egypt:
 bodies kept in homes 87, 136, 141
 martyrs in temples 134
 persecutions in 53

 remains moved in 85–6, 89, 122, 132, 139, 141
 see also Alexandria; Anthony; Athanasius; North Africa; Shenoute
Elisha 158
Elsner, Jas 153, 154
Elysium Fields 21
Emesa 131
emperors:
 apotheosis and 23, 30, 65, 80
 monuments of deceased 29–30
 graves of 20, 25, 66
 sacrifice to 53, 107
 status compared with saints 48, 65, 80, 173, 178
 see also edicts, imperial; *individual emperors*
epigraphy *see* epitaphs
Epiphanius 137, 139
episcopate (bishops) 4, 11, 44, 38, 39, 58
 basilicas and 71, 97
 care of the dead and 40–1, 44
 co-episcopate in Rome 74
 control over practices 5, 6, 83, 84, 93, 123, 127, 141
 development of martyr cult and 2, 5, 16–17, 49, 82, 96, 97, 99–100, 108, 116, 136, 140, 162, 170, 174
 pilgrimage and 149, 150, 153, 162, 171, 176, 178
 independence from 10, 139
 see also individual bishops
Epistulae (Ambrose) 85, 89, 91, 94, 163
Epistulae (Athanasius) 86, 135, 137, 140
Epistulae (Augustine) 104–5, 134
Epistulae (Basil) 87–8
Epistulae (Cyprian) 38, 46
Epistulae (Gregory of Nyssa) 149
Epistola ad Romanos (Ignatius) 45
Epistulae (Jerome) 53, 142, 151, 152, 157–9
Epistulae (Julian) 130
Epistulae (Paulinus of Nola) 78, 97, 110–13, 148
Epistula Nonius (Cicero) 30
epitaphs (epigraphy) 3, 7, 13, 25, 29, 34, 35, 36, 57, 69–70, 72, 73, 74, 79, 81, 173, 177

see also Damasus; inscriptions
Esquiline Hill 23
Eternal City 62, 69, 74, 79, 96
Etruria 170
Eucharist 46, 86, 119, 121
Eunapius of Sardis 129, 134
Euphemia (martyr) 114
Eurysaces, monument to 21
Eusebia (keeper of relics) 88
Eusebius 39, 41–2, 45, 53–4, 58, 64, 77, 146, 152, 155, 163, 165
Eustochium (daughter of Paula) 157
Evodius of Uzalis 106
executions 13, 51, 81, 132
   executioners 23, 24
   bones of executed criminals 134
exhumation 91–2, 95, 120–1, 140
   of Caligula's remains 30
   of Peter's remains 61–2
   to carry remains around 87, 122, 127, 138–40
Exodus 146
exorcism 92, 140, 158
   see also demons
Ezekiel (prophet) 157

Fasti (Ovid) 21, 22
Faustinus 4, 68
Faustus 102
feast days 17, 107, 109, 113, 115, 125, 171, 174–6
Felix II (antipope) 67–8
Felix of Nola 84, 90, 92, 99, 109–10, 112–16, 124–5, 162, 170, 176
Festal Epistles see Epistles (Athanasius)
festivals:
   martyrs' 51, 103, 108, 109–10, 113, 149, 162, 167, 175
   new Christian community and 169, 171, 173
   problem behavior at 103, 105–6, 114–15, 118, 119, 124–5, 135, 143, 173–4
   Parentalis 22
   placing of relics 88
   see also funerals
Filocalus, Furius Dionysius 72
Finney, Paul Corby 60
First Oration against Julian (Gregory of Nazianzus) 132
Forty Martyrs 85, 88–9, 152
Forum Cornelii 166
Foucault, Michel 8–9, 50, 94, 144
Frankfurter, David 117–18, 121
Frend, William H.C. 6, 45, 103, 132
Fundi 97, 111, 112–13
funerals:
   baptism as 51
   funerary meals 22, 27, 34
   to held at night 130
   see also collegia; memorial meals
funerary societies *see collegia*

Galerius (emperor) 53
Gallagher, Michael 9
Gaudentius of Brescia 88–9, 95, 152, 161
Gaza 133–4
Geertz, Clifford 13
gender 153, 170
Gervais (martyr) 47, 85, 90, 92–3, 95, 97, 99, 107, 163, 174, 175
Ghirza (tomb type) 27
Gingras, George 159
Goehring, James E. 54
Goldschmidt, R.C. 112
Golgotha 156
Gordon, Colin 9
Gospel of John 136
Gospel of Luke 146
Grabar, Andre 48
Gratian (emperor) 126
graves *see* burial
gravestones 1, 71, 172
   see also cemeteries
graveyards *see* cemeteries
Gregory of Nazianzus 92, 132
Gregory of Nyssa 127, 148–9, 161–2
Grig, Lucy 46, 69, 78

hagiographies 15, 46, 50–1, 52, 132, 165–6
Halbwachs, Maurice 10
Handley, Mark 69
Harland, Philip 32
heaven (Christian afterlife) 31, 36, 53, 75, 77
Hebron 158

Helen (Constantine's mother) 156–7
"heresy" 4, 6, 83, 84, 103, 104
　see also Arians; schismatics
Hermes (martyr) 77
Herodian (historian) 23
Heroopolis (Egypt) 160
Hesychius 140
Hezekiah (king) 157
Hilarion 140, 178
Hippolytus 10, 39–41, 44, 69, 73–4, 81, 87, 134, 161, 165, 166, 167–9, 171, 173, 176
Hirschfeld, Amy 40
Historia Ecclesiastica (Eusebius) 91
Historia ecclesiastica (Rufinus) 130–1, 158
Historia Ecclesiastica (Socrates Scholasticus) 65-6
Historia Ecclesiastica (Sozomen) 66, 86, 88, 131, 132
　see also Sozomen
History of the Empire (Herodian) 23
Hobsbawm, Eric 11
Holocaust memorials 12–13
Holum, Kenneth G. 157
Homilia in XL Martyres (Basil) 89
Homiliae in Jeremiam (Origen) 41
Homily on Martyrs (John Chrysostom) 146
Hope, Valerie M. 3, 12, 20, 25, 26, 35

iconography 19, 36, 49
idolatry:
　compared with martyr veneration as 102, 143, 144
　sacrifices to idols 34, 38
　see also apotheosis; pagans; polytheism
Ignatius 45, 92, 178
impurity *see* pollution, corpses and
In Flaccum (Philo) 33
inscriptions 35
　cultural memory and 70–1, 74, 76, 81, 173
　Damasus and 5, 13, 14, 29, 57, 68–73, 74–80, 93, 110, 111, 162, 165, 167, 173–4
　　on Hippolytus 10, 73–4, 167, 168, 171

Primitivos, and 147
　see also epitaphs
Instructions (Commodianus) 38
interment *see* burial
Isaac (patriarch) 158
Isaiah (prophet) 157
isapostolos, Constantine as 64
　see also Apostles
Itinerarium Burdigalense see Bordeaux Pilgrim
Itinerarium Egeriae (Egeria) 159–61

Jacob (patriarch) 158
Jaeger, Mary 25
Jenott, Lance 139
Jerome 28–9, 53, 56, 75, 85, 119, 122, 140, 142–3, 147, 151, 152, 157–9
Jerusalem 27, 89, 106, 112, 120, 146, 147, 148–9, 151, 152, 154, 155 156–7, 159, 162
Jesse 157
Jews and Judaism:
　burial practices 34, 36, 45, 49, 93
　　Jewish catacombs 27–8
　compared with Arians 95
　rejection of witchcraft 129
　sacred space and 147
　　pilgrimage and 146, 156
　see also Holocaust memorials
Jewish-Christians 148
Job (biblical figure) 160
John the Baptist 89, 114, 131, 152, 158–9, 162
Johnson, Mark J. 28, 36, 42, 64
Joseph (patriarch) 157
Josephus 146, 156
Judaism *see* Jews and Judaism
Julian ("the Apostate") 86, 126–33, 134, 144, 158, 175
Juschka, Darlene M. 153
Justina (empress) 90, 95
Justinian (emperor) 19

Kaufman, Peter Iver 107
Kelly, J.N.D. 29
Kennedy, Charles A. 34
Kilde, Halgren 60
Kines, Ian 50
Kloppenburg, John S. 32

koimeterion 39–42
  see also cemeteries
Kraemer, Ross S. 35, 36, 49
Krautheimer, Richard 60–1, 89–90

Lactantius 43, 53
Lafferty, Maura K. 70, 73, 76, 98
Lancel, Serge 100
Lanuvium 33
lapsi 6, 38, 137, 139
Lateran Basilica 60, 61
Law of the Twelve Tables 23–4
Lawrence (martyr) 56, 63
Lazarus (biblical figure) 158
Legge, F. 40
LeGoff, Jaques 57
libation to the dead 22, 115
Libellus Precum as Imperatores (Marcellinus and Faustinus) 4, 68, 71–2
Liber Peristephanon (Prudentius) 29, 72, 99, 165, 166, 167, 168–70
Liber Pontificalis 61, 62, 63, 67–8, 71, 72, 77
Liberius (bishop of Rome) 67–8
Licinius (emperor) 53
Life of Ambrose (Paulinus) 91–2, 93, 95
Life of Anthony (Athanasius) *see Vita Antonii*
Life of Martin (Sulpicius Severus) 85, 116
Life of Porphyry of Gaza (Marcus Diaconus) 133
Limberis, Vasiliki M. 45
Limbo 21
Lincoln, Bruce 11
Littlechilds, Rebecca Leigh 79
Liu, Jinyu 32
Lives of the Philosophers and Sophists (Eunapius of Sardis) 129, 134
Livy 25–6
Lodi 90
Lucian of Samosata 87, 106
Luciferians 4, 68
Lucilla (Christian) 86, 132
Lucina (matron) 28, 62–3
Lucinis 68
Luke (biblical figure) 16, 63–4, 96, 97, 114, 173

Gospel of 146

MacDonald, Mary N. 48
Macedonius (bishop) 65–6
Mackie, Gillian 47, 90, 126
MacMullen, Ramsay 32, 34, 37–8, 60
Majuma 140
manes 22
Mango, Cyril 63–4, 98, 99, 126
Manicheans 102
Marcellus (author) 4, 68
Marcianus (author) 19
Marcus Diaconus 133
Markus, R.A. 2, 54, 56, 137, 155, 156
Martialis (bishop) 38
Martin of Tours 85, 111, 116–17
martyrdom 7, 13, 14, 15, 45–6, 54, 71, 87
  self-induced 6, 104
  women made male by 128
Martyrdom of Ignatius (Eusebius) 45, 92
martyria 42, 47–8, 88, 91, 160–1
Martyrologium Hieronymianum Cambrense 89, 94
mausolea 37
  see also basilicas; monuments; tombs
Mausoleum of Augustus 30
Maxentius (emperor) 53, 60
Maximinus (emperor) 53
Maximus (emperor) 96
Maximus of Madaura 134
McLynn, Neil B. 90, 91, 94
Meeks, Wayne A. 32, 34, 37
Meletians 6, 87, 92, 132, 135, 137–9, 140–1, 176
Melito of Sardis 146
Melitus 137
  see also Meletians
memorial meals 27, 28, 31, 34, 58–9, 102–3
  see also collegia; funerals
memorialization 11, 12–13, 20, 23, 26, 32, 34, 69, 70
memorials (structures) 12–13, 21, 25–6, 43, 51, 56, 81, 83, 99, 100, 105, 117,
  chapels 47
  see also festivals
mensae 47
Metellan islands 43

Milan 47, 84–5, 88, 89–95, 96, 97, 98, 99, 105, 106, 124, 126, 145, 150–1, 159, 174, 175, 177
see also Ambrose of Milan
Miles, Richard 1, 8
Miletus 131
miracles and relics 84, 91, 92, 95, 100, 106, 108, 122–3, 132, 151, 163
Misopogon (Julian) 128, 131, 134
Misztal, Barbara 10
Mitford, Jessica 83
monasticism 88, 131, 136–7, 140, 157
monks 54, 160
nuns 88
see also Anthony of the Desert
monuments 3, 8, 10, 11, 12, 13, 20–1, 23–30, 31, 43, 49, 58, 167, 176
see also memorialization; memorials (structures)
Morris, Ian 12, 13
Moses 160
Moss, Candida 45, 46, 128
Mount Nebo 160
mummification 87, 141
museums 2, 13, 57
mythology 77, 168

Nabor 90–1
Nazarius (martyr) 93, 97, 114
necromancy 117–18, 129, 140
charms 107
Nero (emperor) 30, 45
Nicene Council 4, 68
Nicomedia 53
Nielsen, Thomas 31
Nola 84–5, 96, 98–9, 109, 110, 111–12, 114–16, 124–5, 162, 170, 175, 176
see also Paulinus of Nola
North Africa 4, 6, 14, 83–4, 91, 105–6, 117, 125, 132, 149, 151, 155, 174–5
see also Egypt
Novatian schism 73
see also Hippolytus
Noy, David 30
Nyssa 145
see also Gregory of Nyssa

Obadiah 158
Odahl, Charles Matson 63

Ogilvie, M.R. 22
Oliver, Graham J. 32
On Funerals (Lucian of Samosata) 87
On the Care of the Dead see De Cura pro Mortuis gerenda
Opinions (Paulus) 23
Optatus 86
oracles 86, 129, 130
Oratio Constantini (Constantine) 58–9
Origen 39, 41, 148
Orosius 106
"orthodoxy" 4, 15, 107, 136
see also heresy
Osiek, Carolyn 41
Ostian Way 62
Ovid 21, 2

pagans 15, 36, 42, 63, 70, 86, 105, 107, 131, 134
see also apotheosis; idolatry; necromancy; polytheism
Pagels, Elaine 139
Palestine 17, 53, 148, 149
see also Bethlehem; Jerusalem; pilgrimage
Palladia (pilgrim) 163–4
Panarion (Epiphanius of Salamis) 137, 139
Parentalis (festival) 22
Passion of Perpetua and Felicitas 46, 128
Passover 146
patriarchs, Biblical 138, 158
patronage 41, 45, 99, 101, 156
Ambrose as patron of relics 96
Constantine as patron of saints 58, 67, 80, 173
of saints 115
Patterson, John 33
Paul (biblical figure) 34, 35, 166–7, 175
contact relic 142
remains of 56, 57, 61–3, 69, 76–7, 78–9, 98, 113, 147, 148, 152, 156, 162
Rome and 81, 173–4
triclia for 147
see also Pauline communities
Paul (pilgrim) 151, 163–4
Paula (pilgrim) 151, 157–9, 161–2, 176

Pauline communities 4, 32, 36, 37
Paulinus of Milan 91–3, 94, 95
Paulinus of Nola 14, 17, 56, 63–4, 78, 82, 84–5, 95–6, 97–9, 109–16, 122, 123, 124–5, 127, 137, 142, 147, 148, 151, 158, 162, 164, 165, 170, 174–5, 176
Paulus (author) 23
Pelagianism 106
Perkins, Judith 3, 50
Peristephanon Liber see Prudentius.
Perpetua (martyr) 128
Perry, Jonathan Scott 34
Peter (biblical figure) 56–7, 61–3, 69, 76, 77, 78, 79, 98, 113, 147, 156, 162, 166–7, 173, 175
  Constantine and 80
  Rome as inheritor 81
  triclia for 147
Peter the Exorcist 63
Petersen, Lauren Hackworth 21
Petra 27
Pharisees 147
Philippics (Cicero) 19,
Philo 33, 156
Philosophumena (Hippolytus) 39–40
pilgrimage 2, 5, 14, 15, 84, 91, 97, 110, 113, 125, 131, 149–52, 170–1, 176–7
  catacombs and 29, 47, 75, 76
  family graves and 20, 21, 31
  healing and 162–4
  Jewish 146
  narratives of 156–62, 165, 167, 169
  medals for 78
  origins of Christian 148
  space accessible for 48, 62, 63
  as unifier 2, 10, 152–6, 172
  Virgil's tomb and 30
Pliny the Younger 30
pollution, corpses and 24, 16, 23, 115, 129, 130, 133
polytheism 17, 154
  see also paganism
pomerium 25
pope, as problematic term 69
  see also individual bishops of Rome
Potestas, Allia 25
prayer 36, 55, 101–2, 108, 114, 111, 116–17, 119, 120, 128, 131, 134, 136, 163, 166, 169
preaesentia of relics 150, 156
preservation of martyr's corpse 122
Price, Simon 23, 65
priests:
  Christian 112, 119, 121, 123
  pagan 129, 130
  see also episcopate
Primitivos, inscription by 147
Primuliacum 84–5
Proculus (martyr) 114
prohibitions:
  on burying non-Christians with Christians 28, 36
  on burying a corpse in a city 23–4, 133–4
  of practices at martyr shrines 105, 106, 150–1, 174–5
  on disturbing a corpse 61–2
  on venerating a martyr 17, 42, 125
Protasius (saint) 47, 85, 90, 92–3, 95, 97–9, 107, 163, 174–5
protomartyr *see* Stephen (biblical figure)
Prudentius 72, 73, 98, 134, 151–2, 162, 164–70, 171, 176
Psalms 117, 119, 130
Pulcheria (empress) 88
purification 23, 119, 120
  see also pollution (impurity), corpses and
putrification 122

Rabinow, Paul 8
Rachel's tomb 158
radiocarbon dating 27–8
Ranger, Terence 11
Rebillard, Éric 28, 36, 38, 40, 41, 42
recantation 68, 168
relics 2, 76–7, 78, 85–6, 90–3, 95–9, 103–4, 107, 108–10, 111, 113, 116, 131
  of ascetics 54, 136, 137
  criticism 102, 118, 121, 122, 144, 155
    by Julian 128
  miracles and 84, 106, 123
  translation of 5, 16, 29, 49, 67, 86, 126–7, 142, 156, 158, 163, 173, 174, 175, 177, 178
    Constantine's tomb and 63, 66

distribution of 85, 87–90, 94, 124, 125, 138–9
pilgrims and 149, 150, 152, 153, 154, 161
see also ashes, as relics; basilicas; burial; exhumation; mummification; tombs
Republic, Roman 21–2, 50
Rerum Gestarum (Ammianus) 4, 68
resurrection of the dead 35–6
see also afterlife, Roman view of
reverence 44, 55, 95, 101–2, 119, 122, 129, 134, 138, 142
rite 31, 156
Roan 98
Roberts, Michael 99, 165, 168, 169
Rome, city of:
history tied to Christianity 14, 15, 68–9, 70, 79, 81
deaths in 23, 43
martyr cult in 56–7, 67, 68, 72–3, 76–8, 84, 91, 96, 98, 113, 148, 156, 162, 167, 173–4, 176
new remains banned from 126
monuments in 29–30, 80
building by Constantine 60–3, 154
Christian burial 36
see also Appian Way; catacombs; Damasus
Romulus 57, 81
Rome as "Romulus's city" 64, 78
Ross, Jill 165–6
Rubenstein, Richard E. 136
Rufinus of Aquileia, 130–1, 158
Rutgers, Leonard V. 28
Rutherford, Ian 153–4

Sabbas the Goth (martyr) 87
sacred, the 96, 136, 159
Saghy, Marianne 2, 15, 56, 57, 68, 69, 70, 71
Sallnow, Michael 153
Salona 47
salvation 112, 147
Samaria 118, 158
Satan 136
see also demons
Saturinus (martyr) 77
Savage, Kirk 12, 58

schismatics 4, 71–2, 73–4, 81, 82, 83, 132, 137, 167–8, 173, 175, 177
see also Circumcellians; Donatists; "heresy"; Meletians
Schroeder, Caroline T. 9, 119
Schwartz, Barry, 10, 12, 13
Schweitzer, Albert, 82
scripture *see* Bible
Seleucia 152
sepulchers *see* tombs
Sermones (Augustine of Hippo) 91, 95, 103, 104, 107–8, 109, 151, 163–4
On Obedience (Augustine) 103
Sermones (Gaudentius of Brescia) 88, 89, 152
Severus 85, 95, 97, 99, 110–12, 116–17, 142
sheepskin, Anthony's 136, 137, 142
Shenoute 9, 85, 117–23, 125, 127, 139, 141, 162, 174, 177, 178
Siculus Flaccus 24
Silvanus, Cult of 32
Simplicianus (bishop) 95
Since It Behooves Christians (Shenoute) 85, 117, 118–19, 120
Sirmondian Constitutions 61
Sixtus (bishop of Rome) 75, 76
Smith, David I. 22
Smith, Jonathan Z. 69
Snyder, Graydon 27, 40, 47–8, 49, 147
Socrates Scholasticus 65–6
Solomon (king) 157
soul 21–3, 35, 46, 75, 90, 111
Sozomen 66, 86, 88, 130, 131, 132, 137, 139, 154
Spain 106, 164
statue of Jesus 132
Stead, G. Christopher 139
stelai 26
Stephen (biblical figure) 16, 95, 103, 106, 107–8, 109, 124, 151, 163–4, 175
stretchers, martyrs carried on 85, 87, 122, 132, 138, 140–1, 176
Sulpicius Severus *see* Severus
Sylvester (bishop of Rome) 61

taboo and corpses; *see* prohibition
talismans, relics as 84, 99

Tarsus 152
Taylor, Joan 148
Taylor, Mark C. 1–2, 172
temples:
   basilicas as 59, 63
   Jerusalem Temple 119, 120, 146–7
   to martys 86
   pagan 53, 86, 130–1, 134
Terenti Varronis de lingua latina libri (Varro) 25–6
Tertullian 33, 34, 39, 41, 43–4, 51, 53, 147
Testamentum Domini 44
   see also Apostolic Tradition
Thecla (biblical figure) 152, 161
Theodosius (emperor) 96, 126
theology:
   burial practices and 35, 36
   efficacy of martyrs and 101, 120, 142–3
Therasia 111
Thomas (biblical figure) 89, 94, 114, 160–1
Those Who Work Evil (Shenoute) 85, 117–18, 120–22
Thyrsus (martyr) 88
Tilley, Maureen 4, 6, 132
Timothy (biblical figure) 63, 64, 78, 173
Tite, Philip L. 54
tombs 5, 10, 16, 30, 40–1, 55, 126–7
   Christian memory and 19, 83, 175
   in catacombs 75, 76, 78
   church building and 93
   of Biblical figures 138, 147, 156–7, 157, 158–9, 160, 162
   of the emperor 66, 72
   of martyrs 44, 53, 56, 57, 60–2, 83, 111–12, 113, 119–20, 121, 122, 136, 145, 160, 161, 167, 175–6
     criticism of 128–9, 130–1, 134, 142, 144
     problem behavior at 102, 104, 105–6, 108, 114–5, 120–1, 123
     efficacy of 100
     mistaken identity 116–17, 118
     pilgrimage and 149–50, 151, 152, 153, 156, 162, 165, 171
   Roman 20–1, 25, 26–7, 31
   see also basilicas; burial; catacombs; cemeteries; inscriptions; relics
Tomius Coelius 147
Torres, Juana 128
Toynbee, J. M. C. 21, 22, 23, 24, 27
Trajan's Column 30
tribunal, Christian 60
triclia 147
Trout, Dennis 14, 13, 57, 70, 79, 115, 142
Turner, Victor 152–3, 163, 169
Tusculan Disputations (Cicero) 87

unburied corpses 23
uncleanliness *see* pollution
undertakers 23, 24
underworld 35
   see also afterlife
unmarked graves 47, 51, 92
Ursinus (deacon) 4, 68

Valentinian II (emperor) 90, 96, 126
Valerian (emperor) 42, 167
Van der Horst, Pieter W. 36
Van Dyke, Ruth 100
Varro, Marcus Terentius 25–6
Veilleux, Armand 122–3
veneration:
   of the dead 2, 38, 48
   of Virgil's tomb 30
   see also relics
Via Appia *see* Appian Way
Via Ardeatina 76
Via Tiburtina 73
Victor (bishop of Rome) 40
Victricius of Rouen 89, 95–6, 98
vigils 17, 83, 103, 104, 108, 114, 118, 119, 124, 135, 142, 175
Vigilantius 142–3, 144, 147
Virgil 21, 30, 57, 69
   Virgilian prose 14, 70, 81
visions, religious 88, 93, 120–1, 129, 163–4
Vita Ambrosii (Paulinus) 91–2, 93, 95
Vita Antonii (Athanasius) 122, 135, 136–7, 141, 144, 176
Vita Constantini (Eusebius) 53–4, 64, 152, 163
vita Hilarionis eremitae (Jerome) 140
Vita Porphyrii Gazensis (Marcus

Diaconus) 133
Vitalis (martyr) 93, 114
Volp, Ulrich 45

Ward-Perkins, J.B. 48, 60
White, Cynthia 74
Wilken, Robert Louis 156
Williams, Daniel H. 89, 90
Williams, R.D. 30, 137
Williams, Rowan 139
Williams, Wes 148
Wilson, Stephen 32
witchcraft *see* necromancy
Woods, David 64
worship:
    of emperors 23
    of martyrs and saints 17, 86–7, 101–2, 123, 152, 166, 170
        criticized 118, 134, 141–2
        by Meletians 138, 139
    sacred sites and 159
    see also relics; veneration
Wortley, John 87–8, 140–1

Yasin, Ann Marie 14, 31, 37, 38, 56
Young, James Edward 12–13

Zephyrinus (bishop of Rome) 39–40, 41
Zerubavel, Eviatar 13

www.ingramcontent.com/pod-product-compliance
Lightning Source LLC
Chambersburg PA
CBHW071843230426
43671CB00012B/2056